FROMMER'S

COMPREHENSIVE TRAVEL GUIDE

TAMPA & ST. PETERSBURG '91-'92

by Patricia Tunison Preston
and John Preston

PRENTICE
HALL
PRESS

NEW YORK • LONDON • TORONTO • SYDNEY • TOKYO • SINGAPORE

FROMMER BOOKS

Published by Prentice Hall Press
A division of Simon & Schuster Inc.
15 Columbus Circle
New York, NY 10023

ISBN 0-13-337874-8
ISSN 1047-7896

Design by Robert Bull Design
Maps by Geografix Inc.

Manufactured in the United States of America

Frommer's Tampa and St. Petersburg '91–'92

Editor-in-Chief: Marilyn Wood
Senior Editors: Judith de Rubini, Pamela Marshall, Amit Shah
Editors: Alice Fellows, Paige Hughes
Assistant Editors: Suzanne Arkin, Ellen Zucker

CONTENTS

LIST OF MAPS

TAMPA/ST. PETERSBURG

TAMPA/ST. PETERSBURG WALKING TOURS

ABOUT THIS FROMMER GUIDE

What Is a Frommer's City Guide? It's a comprehensive, easy-to-use guide to the best travel values in all price ranges—from very expensive to budget. The one guidebook to take along with you on any trip.

WHAT THE SYMBOLS MEAN

 FROMMER'S FAVORITES—hotels, restaurants, attractions, and entertainments you should not miss

 SUPER-SPECIAL VALUES—really exceptional values

 FROMMER'S SMART TRAVELER TIPS—hints on how to secure the best value for your money

IN HOTEL AND OTHER LISTINGS

The following symbols refer to the standard amenities available in all rooms:

A/C air conditioning   TEL telephone   TV television
MINIBAR refrigerator stocked with beverages and snacks

The following abbreviations are used for credit cards:

AE American Express	DISC Discover	EU Eurocard
CB Carte Blanche	ER enRoute	MC MasterCard
DC Diners Club		V VISA

TRIP PLANNING WITH THIS GUIDE

Use the following features:

Calendar of Events . . . to plan for or to avoid

What's Special About Checklist . . . a summary of the cities' highlights—which lets you check off those that appeal most to you

Easy-to-Read Maps . . . showing walking tours; city sights; hotel and restaurant locations—all referring to or keyed to the text

Fast Facts . . . all the essentials at a glance: climate, consulates, currency, emergencies, information, safety, tipping, and more

OTHER SPECIAL FROMMER FEATURES

Cool for Kids—hotels, restaurants, and attractions
Did You Know . . . ?—offbeat, fun facts

INTRODUCING TAMPA AND ST. PETERSBURG

Tampa and St. Petersburg, two totally different cities joined by Tampa Bay, comprise one of the fastest-growing metropolitan areas in the United States. Each has its own distinctive history and layout, but together they are synonymous with sunshine and the good life. Rimmed by the Gulf of Mexico on Florida's west coast, these two cities are in the center of the state, within easy reach of other Florida destinations—just over 80 miles from Orlando and less than 270 from Miami.

Tampa, once considered little more than a landing port for shipments of bananas from Colombia, or a cigar-making enclave, has been born again as a city in the last decade. The downtown area, once dingy, is glowing with new skyscrapers, financial centers, high-tech industries, and entertainment facilities.

St. Petersburg, on the other hand, was known for years primarily as a winter haven for seniors, but in the past decade, the city has been rejuvenated with new industries, an influx of younger citizens, and exciting downtown developments.

With a year-round warm climate and miles of sandy beaches, it's not surprising that tourism is the number-one industry for both cities. More than three million visitors, about one-third from overseas, flock to the Tampa Bay area annually.

Just 15 miles apart, these two cities are served by Tampa International Airport, one of the best in the nation and often touted as an attraction in itself. Tampa and St. Petersburg are connected by three bridges that span Tampa Bay: the Courtney Campbell, the Howard Frankland, and the Gandy.

1. HISTORY OF THE TAMPA BAY AREA

EARLY HISTORY

The Tampa Bay area was first inhabited by large settlements of Native Americans, particularly the Tocobaga and Timucuan tribes.

The first Europeans arrived in the 16th century. From 1521 to 1539, Spanish adventurers and explorers Juan Ponce de León, Pánfilo de Narváez, and Hernando de Soto explored the area. While searching for gold, de Soto discovered five mineral springs near a large Tocobaga village in what is now Safety Harbor, north of St. Petersburg and west of Tampa. He named the large body of water near the village (Tampa Bay) "La Bahía del Espíritu Santo" or "Bay of the Holy Spirit" since the Native Americans believed the springs had healing qualities—a legend that persists today.

The first use of the name Tampa is usually attributed to a shipwrecked Spaniard named Fountaneda, who spent time living among the natives in the late 1570s. He referred to the area by the Native American name: "Tanpa," variously defined to mean "a town near the bay" or "sticks of fire." Early cartographers apparently changed the spelling to Tampa.

Almost two hundred years later, in 1757, a Spanish expedition led by Don Francisco María Celi charted the first detailed map of Tampa Bay and the surrounding waterways. At about the same time, pirates are said to have been active along the Florida coastline and Caribbean waters.

In 1763, the region came under British rule when the Spanish traded Florida for Havana. Within a decade, Lord Hillsborough, a British colonial secretary of state, lent his name to the river, the bay; eventually the county on the east side of Tampa Bay would also bear his name.

FLORIDA — THE TWENTY-SEVENTH STATE

In the early 1820s, Florida became a territory of the U.S., and Gen. Andrew Jackson took charge as the region's first governor. In 1824 after the first American settlers had arrived in the Tampa Bay area, Col. George Brooke built a U.S. Army post, known as Fort Brooke, at the mouth of the Hillsborough River (today the site of downtown Tampa). Ten years later the County of Hillsborough was established by the Territorial Legislature.

On the west side of Tampa Bay, in an area that is now Safety Harbor, Dr. Odet Phillipe, a former surgeon in the French Navy under Napoléon, established a plantation in 1842. With citrus stock brought from the Bahamas, Phillipe cultivated Florida's first grapefruit grove. Florida became the 27th state of the Union in 1845.

In 1848, U.S. Army Lt. Col. Robert E. Lee surveyed the area for possible coastal defense installations. He recommended Mullet Key, a site later used as a military post in both the Civil and Spanish-American wars. In that same year, a 90-mph gale ripped across the area, with waters rising from the Gulf to Tampa Bay. All islands and keys were inundated and John's Pass (the narrow strip of water between the southern tip of Sand Key Island and the northern end of Treasure Island) was created.

Meanwhile, a thriving settlement had grown up around the site of Fort Brooke, an important center for trade and transportation. In 1855, this settlement was incorporated as the town of Tampa.

Twenty years later, Gen. John Williams, son of the first mayor of Detroit, headed for Florida. Ordered by his doctor to find a milder climate to cure his asthma, Williams bought 1,600 acres west of Tampa Bay and the already-thriving Tampa. After failing as a farmer because his northern methods were unsuited for the semitropical region, Williams set out to build a new city—what would become St. Petersburg.

RAILROADS, CIGARS, AND HOTELS

In 1884, Tampa became even more accessible for travel and trade when railroad tycoon Henry B. Plant brought his narrow-gauge South Florida Railroad to Tampa. The following year, 1885, Tampa residents organized a board of trade (predecessor of today's chamber of commerce). That same year, a prominent physician, Dr. W. C. Van Biber of Baltimore, drew international attention to the area west of Tampa Bay (where Williams was building his city) when he presented a paper, "Where Should a Health City Be Built," to a meeting of the American Medical Society in New Orleans. This spot, he declared, had all the elements to be regarded as the "healthiest place on earth."

Shortly thereafter, in 1886, recognition of a different sort came to the area. Vincente Martínez Ybor, an immigrant from Cuba via Key West, established Tampa's first cigar factory in what eventually became known as Ybor City, and Tampa became the "cigar capital of the world."

John Williams was well into his task of building a city when, in 1887–88, Russian immigrant Peter Demens (Petrovich A. Demenshev) and three partners extended their Orange Belt Railroad from Sanford, northeast of Orlando, to the west of Tampa Bay area. Popular legend has it that, when the railroad was complete, Williams and Demens drew lots to determine which of them would get to name their new community. Demens won, and christened the new city St. Petersburg, after his hometown in Russia. As a consolation, Williams erected the city's first commercial building—the 40-room Detroit Hotel, naming it for his hometown.

In Tampa, Henry B. Plant opened the Tampa Bay Hotel, a fashionable winter resort for the rich and famous, in 1891. Touted at the time as "the world's most elegant hotel," it had over 500 rooms filled with antiques and art from around the world, with a striking Moorish facade topped by 13 silver minarets. Plant followed this achievement by spreading his influence to the other side of Tampa Bay during 1893–96, when he took over the Orange Belt Railroad and built the huge Belleview Hotel (later to become the Belleview Biltmore) north of St. Petersburg, overlooking Clearwater Harbor.

In 1897–98, the U.S. became involved in the Spanish-American War, and Tampa became a staging point for 30,000 troops. One of the officers based here was Teddy Roosevelt, who set up his headquarters at the commandeered Tampa Bay Hotel. He trained his Rough Riders on the hotel's grounds. On the St. Pete side, Fort DeSoto was built on Mullet Key to protect Tampa Bay during the war—but the war ended before construction was finished and the fort's cannons were never fired.

THE TWENTIETH CENTURY

By 1903, St. Petersburg became an incorporated city, and in 1907 Noel Mitchell, a St. Pete real estate salesman, ordered 50 orange benches for people who wished to rest and enjoy the sun on the city's streets. Other businesses followed suit, but the many benches they installed differed in size and color. Eventually, Mitchell sponsored an ordinance that standardized the color of all city benches, thus beginning the era of St. Petersburg's green benches (a city trademark that lasted until 1969).

Another colorful bit of St. Pete history began in 1910, when the *St. Petersburg Independent,* a newspaper founded four years earlier, made its famous "sunshine offer"—a pledge to distribute free newspapers on any day when the sun didn't shine. This inspired the nickname "Sunshine City" for St. Pete. A year later, in 1911, Tampa and St. Petersburg were separated into two different counties when Pinellas County was created out of the western portion of Hillsborough County.

The area won a place in the history of aviation in 1914 when the first commercial airline service in the U.S. was inaugurated between St. Pete and Tampa by pioneer aviator Tony Jannus. The fare was $400, a small fortune at the time, for a 23-minute flight.

As the 1920s roared in, a building boom exploded in the region, with St. Petersburg adding 12 major hotels, including the posh Don CeSar, still in operation today. In Tampa, the Davis Islands were created by dredging Hillsborough Bay, and became one of Tampa's most attractive residential sections. In 1924, the first bridge (the $3 million George Gandy Bridge) opened between Tampa and St. Petersburg.

The Depression and the onset of the World War II era hit Tampa Bay in the thirties and forties. Many major St. Petersburg–area hotels, such as the Don CeSar, the Vinoy, and the Belleview Biltmore, were taken over by the military for use as hospitals during World War II. The legendary Tampa Bay Hotel was annexed permanently by the University of Tampa. MacDill Air Force Base was established on Hillsborough Bay. Also at this time, the Courtney Campbell Bridge, linking upper Hillsborough and Pinellas counties, opened.

In the fifties and sixties the Tampa Bay area began to perk up again. The first Sunshine Skyway bridge, then the longest open-water crossing in the United States, was built in 1954, linking St. Petersburg with the Bradenton/Sarasota area; the area's first television station, WSUN, began broadcasting; St. Pete unveiled a new Museum of Fine Arts and the Bayfront Center; and Tampa became the site of Busch Gardens. The population of both cities began to soar, and the Howard Frankland Bridge, the third of the overwater links between them, opened.

The last two decades have been equally positive for the Tampa Bay area, starting in 1971 with the opening of the state-of-the-art Tampa International Airport, increasing tourist access. Downtown St. Petersburg launched the Bayfront Center, an entertainment and sports complex, plus the Dalí Museum, a new Pier, and has revitalized the waterfront as well. Downtown Tampa blossomed, too, with dozens of new skyscrapers and a Performing Arts Center; and Harbour Island was developed as a new recreational and residential focal point for the city.

In the past year, as the 1990s take hold, expansion has continued, with the opening of the Florida Suncoast Dome in St. Petersburg and a brand-new riverside convention center in Tampa. Future developments in St. Petersburg include a new nine-block, $200 million waterfront shopping district, and the extensive $88 million dollar restoration of the landmark Vinoy Hotel by the Stouffer Corporation, slated for a 1992 reopening. Across the bay, Tampa is the future site for the $84 million waterfront Florida Aquarium, a new four-story marine-science center, set to debut in 1993 and touted as the largest facility of its kind in the world.

2. RECOMMENDED BOOKS

Campbell, A. Stuart. *The Cigar Industry of Tampa*. Gainesville: University of Florida Press, 1939.

Dunn, Hampton. *Yesterday's Clearwater*. Miami: E.A. Seaman, 1973.

———. *Yesterday's St. Petersburg*. Miami: E. A. Seaman, 1973.

———. *Yesterday's Tampa.* Miami: E. A. Seaman, 1977.

Fuller, Walter P. *This Was Florida's Boom.* St. Petersburg: Times Publishing Company, 1954.

Grismer, Carl. *The Story of St. Petersburg.* St. Petersburg: P. K. Smith and Co., 1948.

———. *Tampa: History of the City of Tampa and Region of Florida.* Ed. D. B. McKay. St. Petersburg: St. Petersburg Printing Co., 1950.

Lewis, Gordon. *Florida Fishing: Fresh and Saltwater.* St. Petersburg: Great Outdoors, 1957.

Marth, Del, and Martha Marth. *Florida Almanac.* St. Petersburg: A. S. Barnes, 1980.

Neill, Wilfred. *The Story of Florida's Seminole Indians.* St. Petersburg: Great Outdoors Publishing, 1964.

Roosevelt, Theodore. *The Rough Riders.* New York: Charles Scribner and Sons, 1906.

Schell, Rolfe F. *De Soto Didn't Land at Tampa.* Ft. Myers Beach, Island Press, 1974.

Young, June Hurley. *The Don CeSar Story.* St. Petersburg: Partnership Press, 1983.

———. *Florida's Pinellas Peninsula.* St. Petersburg: Byron Kennedy & Son, 1983.

CHAPTER 2

PLANNING A TRIP TO TAMPA AND ST. PETERSBURG

This chapter is devoted to the where, when, and how of your trip—the advance-planning issues required to get it together and take it on the road. This chapter will also resolve other important questions, such as when to go and where to obtain more information about the destination.

To get the most for your money, consider traveling to the St. Petersburg/Tampa area in the off-season, i.e., the months of May and June, September through November, and, to a lesser extent, July and August.

1. INFORMATION

While you are planning your trip, you can obtain helpful brochures and information by contacting tourist offices in advance. For the St. Petersburg area:

- Pinellas Suncoast Tourist Development Council, 4625 East Bay Drive, Suite 109, Clearwater, FL 34624-9973 (tel. 813/530-6452, fax 813/530-6132)
- Pinellas Suncoast Canadian Office, 232B Gerrard Street E., Toronto, Ontario, Canada M5A 2E8 (tel. 416/927-1505, fax 416/927-7809)
- Pinellas Suncoast U.K. Office, 182/184 Addington Road, 1st floor, Selsdon, Surrey CR2 8LB, England (tel. 081/651-4742, fax 081/651-5702)

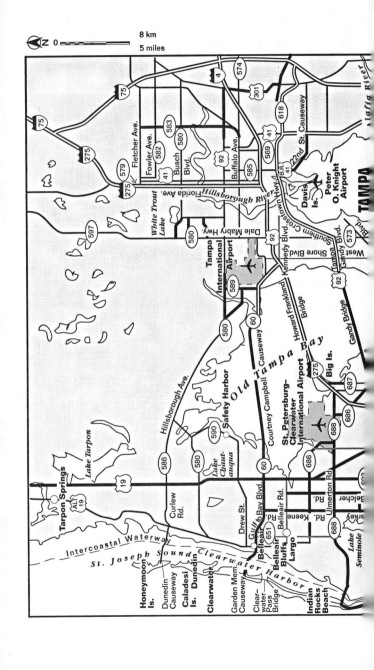

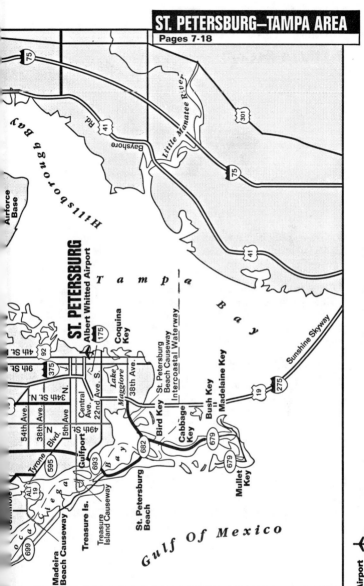

Airforce
Base

Hillsborough Bay

Little Manatee River

Bayshore Rd.

T a m p a   B a y

ST. PETERSBURG

Albert Whitted Airport

Coquina Key

Lake Maggiore

38th Ave. S.

St. Petersburg Beach Causeway

Intercoastal Waterway

Bird Key

Bush Key

Madelaine Key

Sunshine Skyway

Central Ave.

22nd Ave. S.

4th Ave. N.

54th Ave. N.

38th Ave. N.

5th Ave. N.

Tyrone Blvd.

49th St.

Gulfport

Treasure Is.

Treasure Island Causeway

St. Petersburg Beach

Cabbage Key

Mullet Key

V e g a   B a y

Madeira Beach Causeway

G u l f   O f   M e x i c o

Airport

- Pinellas Suncoast Central Europe Office, Alt-Erlenbach 25, 6000 Frankfurt am Main 56, Vorwahl von Frankfurt 4509, West Germany (tel. 06101/44052, fax 06101/4524)

For the Tampa area:

- Tampa/Hillsborough Convention and Visitors Association, 111 Madison St., Suite 1010, Tampa, FL 33602-4706 (tel. 813/223-1111 or toll free 800/44-TAMPA; fax 813/229-6616)

2. WHEN TO GO

THE CLIMATE

The Tampa/St. Petersburg area has a warm and wonderful tropical climate year round, just perfect for vacationing. St. Petersburg boasts an average of 361 days of sunshine each year, with an average temperature of 73.6°F, while Tampa's average temperature is 72.8°F. The annual average water temperature along the beaches is 75°F.

There can be extremes, with high humidity and heavy thunderstorms, particularly during the summer months. In January and early February, temperatures can dip to freezing levels at night, but this rarely happens more than once every few years.

AVERAGE TAMPA TEMPERATURES AND RAINFALL

	Jan	Feb	Mar	Apr	May	June	July	Aug	Sept	Oct	Nov	Dec
Avg. High (°F)	71.0	72.0	76.0	82.0	87.0	90.0	90.0	90.0	89.0	84.0	77.0	72.0
Avg. Low (°F)	50.0	50.0	56.0	61.0	67.0	72.0	74.0	74.0	73.0	65.0	56.0	51.0
Avg. Rain (in.)	2.0	3.0	3.0	2.0	3.0	5.0	7.0	8.0	6.0	2.0	2.0	2.0

AVERAGE ST. PETERSBURG TEMPERATURES AND RAINFALL

	Jan	Feb	Mar	Apr	May	June	July	Aug	Sept	Oct	Nov	Dec
Avg. High (°F)	70.0	71.0	76.2	81.9	87.1	89.5	90.0	90.3	88.9	83.7	76.9	71.6
Avg. Low (°F)	49.5	50.4	56.1	61.1	67.2	72.3	74.2	74.2	72.8	65.1	56.4	50.9
Avg. Rain (in.)	2.2	2.8	2.1	2.3	3.1	6.9	7.7	8.0	6.6	2.6	1.6	2.1

TAMPA AND ST. PETERSBURG CALENDAR OF EVENTS

JANUARY *average high temp: 71°, rainy days: 6*

☐ **Hall of Fame Bowl,** Tampa. Two of the nation's top college teams meet at Tampa Stadium in this highly rated annual bowl game. Jan. 1.

☐ **Feast of the Epiphany,** Tarpon Springs. Day-long celebration of Greek Orthodox traditions that includes a dive for the cross, releasing a white dove of peace, ethnic foods, music, and dancing in this Greek enclave 35 miles north of St. Petersburg. Jan. 6.

✪ *SUPER BOWL XXV* *1991 is Super Bowl Year for Tampa! This is a milestone—the 25th anniversary of this National Football League event. A city-wide "Super Celebration" is planned to mark the occasion, including Tampa's biggest annual party, the Gasparilla Parade.*
    Where: Tampa Stadium. **When:** January 27, 1991. **How:** To order tickets, contact the Tampa Stadium, 4201 N. Dale Mabry Hwy., Tampa, FL 33603 (tel. 813/872-7977)

✪ *GASPARILLA PIRATE INVASION AND PARADE* *In a spirit akin to that of Mardi Gras, Tampa's leading business executives don the garb of legendary buccaneer José Gaspar and his band of pirates, and sail into the harbor on a triple-masted galleon. This signals the start of a month-long program of parades, concerts, fiestas, races, and art festivals.*
    Where: Harbour Island, Bayshore Boulevard, and downtown Tampa. **When:** Late Jan or early Feb. **How:** For complete details, contact Ye Mystic Krewe of Gasparilla, P.O. Box 1415, Tampa, FL 33601 (tel. 813/228-7338).

FEBRUARY *average high temp: 72°, rainy days: 7*

☐ **GTE Suncoast Classic,** Tampa. The greatest players on the Senior PGA tour tee off in this $350,000 tournament at Tampa Palms Golf and Country Club. 1st week in Feb.

✪ *FLORIDA STATE FAIR* *Just about anything that grows in Florida—from champion livestock to fine foods and wines—is on display at this gathering, along with craft demonstrations, circus acts, carnival rides, horse shows, rodeos, alligator wrestling, pig racing, fireworks, stock car races, and entertainment by top stars of the country and western genre.*
    Where: Florida State Fairgrounds, 4800 U.S. Hwy. 301, Tampa. **When:** 2nd week of Feb. **How:** Tickets available at

the gate, $4 for adults, $2 for children 6-11. Contact the Florida State Fair Authority, P.O. Box 11766, Tampa, FL 33680 (tel. 813/621-7821).

MARCH *average high temp:* 76°, *rainy days:* 7

☐ **St. Petersburg International Folk Fair,** St. Petersburg. A three-day festival, held since 1975, featuring the cultural customs of more than 40 countries. 1st weekend in Mar.

○ *FLORIDA STRAWBERRY FESTIVAL AND PARADE* This is not only a feast of luscious berries (on shortcake, in milkshakes, etc.), but also an array of rides, amusements, and top-name country music entertainment. It's held 25 miles east of Tampa at Plant City, known as the "winter strawberry capital of the world."
Where: Florida Strawberry Festival Fairgrounds, Fla. Rte. 574, off exit 10 or 11 of I-4, Plant City. **When:** First 11 days of Mar. **How:** Tickets at the gate, $4, children under 10 free if accompanied by an adult. Contact the Florida Strawberry Festival, P.O. Drawer 1869, Plant City, FL 34289-1869 (tel. 813/752-9194).

○ *ST. PETERSBURG FESTIVAL OF THE STATES* St. Pete plays host to award-winning high school bands from around the country, with more than 100 events, from parades and pageantry to a windsurfing competition, fishing tournament, regatta, air show, jazz fest, and antique-car rally.
Where: Downtown St. Petersburg. **When:** End of Mar and 1st week of Apr for 17 days. **How:** Most events are outdoors and free. Contact Suncoasters of St. Petersburg, P.O. Box 1731, St. Petersburg, FL 33731 (tel. 813/898-3654).

☐ **Winter Equestrian Festival/American Invitational,** Tampa. Top riders and jumping horses of the world at the Florida State Fairgrounds. Last 2 weeks in Mar.
☐ **Spring Arts and Crafts Festival,** Tampa. Artists from around the country display jewelry, pottery, paintings, and more at Ybor Square. Last weekend in Mar.

APRIL *average high temp:* 82°, *rainy days:* 5

☐ **Artworks!** St. Petersburg. Festival of sights, sounds, and images, with live theater, art shows, antique auto shows, and outdoor concerts. Last week in Apr.
☐ **Fun 'n' Sun Festival,** Clearwater. Includes a band competition, parades, boat regatta, and sportsfest; a tradition since 1953. Last week in Apr.
☐ **St. Anthony's Tampa Bay Triathlon,** St. Petersburg. Florida's largest swim-bike-run meet. Last weekend in Apr.

MAY average high temp: 87°, rainy days: 6

☐ **Fiesta de la Riba,** St. Petersburg. Spanish-themed festival at the Dalí Museum, commemorating Salvador Dalí's birthday. May 5.

☐ **Shakespeare in the Park,** St. Petersburg. The American Stage company performs at Demens Landing on the waterfront. Throughout May.

JUNE average high temp: 90°, rainy days: 12

☐ **Annual Sandcastle Contest,** St. Petersburg Beach. Sand-sculpting and castle-building for prizes and fun. Last weekend in June.

JULY average high temp: 90°, rainy days: 16

☐ **Pirate Days & Invasion,** Treasure Island. A celebration of the island's colorful history, in conjunction with Independence Day weekend. First week in July.

☐ **Summer Arts and Crafts Festival,** Tampa. Artists from around the country display jewelry, pottery, paintings, and more at Ybor Square. 1 weekend in mid-July.

SEPTEMBER average high temp: 89°, rainy days: 13

☐ **GTE World Challenge,** Tampa. An exciting 1.92-mile, 12-turn race around the Florida State Fairgrounds, plus remote-control car races and exhibits of exotic, classic, and vintage cars. Last weekend in Sept.

OCTOBER average high temp: 84°, rainy days: 7

☐ **Fall Arts & Crafts Festival,** Tampa. Artists from around the country display jewelry, pottery, paintings, and more at Ybor Square. First weekend in Oct.

☐ **Brandon Balloon Festival,** Tampa. Dozens of hot-air balloons lift off at sunrise from the Florida State Fairgrounds—plus concerts, cookoffs, exhibits, and more. 1 weekend in mid-Oct.

☐ **Guavaween,** Tampa. This is Ybor City's version of a Halloween parade, with costumes, music, food, and a giant street party. Last weekend in Oct.

✪ *JOHN'S PASS SEAFOOD FESTIVAL   One of the most popular seafood festivals on Florida's west coast. Music, arts and crafts, and enormous quantities of fresh fish are the star attractions at this rustic waterfront village west of St. Petersburg.*

*   **Where:** John's Pass Village and boardwalk, Madeira Beach. **When:** Last weekend of October. **How:** Most events are free. Contact Gulf Beaches Chamber of*

Commerce, 501 150th Ave., Madeira Beach, FL 33108 (tel. 813/392-7373).

○ **GTE ST. PETERSBURG GRAND PRIX** *The streets of downtown St. Petersburg are transformed into a 2.1-mile high-speed course for this annual Sports Car Club of America event, attracting top international drivers.*

   Where: Downtown St. Petersburg. **When:** Last weekend of October. **How:** For advance program and other information, contact the St. Petersburg Area Chamber of Commerce, 100 2nd St. N., St. Petersburg, FL 33731 (tel. 813/821-4069).

NOVEMBER *average high temp: 77°, rainy days: 6*

☐ **Kahlua Cup International Yacht Races,** Clearwater. Annual event that draws craft from around the world. 2nd weekend in Nov.

☐ **Florida Classic Football Game,** Tampa. Bethune-Cookman College vs. Florida A&M—one of the longest-running college football rivalries, which fills Tampa Stadium. Last Sat in Nov.

☐ **Festival of Lights & Ybor City Gallery Walk,** Tampa. Streets of Ybor City are lined with candles as local artists open their studios and galleries to the public. Last Sat in Nov.

DECEMBER *average high temp: 72°, rainy days: 6*

☐ **Winter Arts & Crafts Festival,** Tampa. Artists from around the country display jewelry, pottery, paintings, and more at Ybor Square. 1st weekend in Dec.

☐ **Michelob AGA Championship,** Tampa. This marks the final contest of the American Grand Prix Association Series, the premier show-jumping circuit in the country. Dec. date varies.

☐ **Christmas Boat-A-Cade,** Madeira Beach. A holiday highlight for 25 years, with lighted and decorated boats parading at night in Boca Ciega Bay. Last weekend before Dec 25.

☐ **Christmas in the Park,** St. Petersburg. A holiday celebration based at Straub Park on the waterfront, near the Pier. Throughout Dec.

☐ **The Holidays in Tampa.** Celebrations and seasonal activities ranging from *Nutcracker* ballets and concerts to festivals of trees and lights, Victorian Christmas strolls, a jingle bell fun run, and an arts-and-crafts show. Throughout Dec.

3. WHAT TO PACK

The Tampa–St. Petersburg life-style is informal and relaxed and so is the dress. Casual and comfortable clothing is acceptable almost everywhere.

For men, ties and jackets are usually not required, but it's wise to pack at least one of each if you plan to patronize some of the finer restaurants or cultural events. For women, a couple of dressy outfits might also come in handy for special outings, but on the whole, slacks and shorts are recommended. Be sure to bring along a light linen jacket, blazer, or sweater for the ubiquitous air conditioning. If you are traveling in the summer months, when the probability of a quick thunder shower is high, pack a collapsible umbrella or a light raincoat or shell.

With sunshine guaranteed just about every day of the year, this area is a natural for outdoor sports, so be sure to bring along whatever gear you enjoy using, from running shoes to golf clubs and tennis rackets. Take several pairs of comfortable shoes or sneakers for walking along the beaches or bayfronts. If you'll be fishing or boating, a light windbreaker always comes in handy. And, above all, don't forget your bathing suit, suntan lotion, and sunglasses. They are all indispensable.

4. GETTING THERE

BY AIR

AIRLINES

One of the most accessible destinations in the U.S., the Tampa/St. Petersburg area is served by more than two dozen major scheduled airlines with nonstop or single-plane service from over 65 cities. Both scheduled and charter services also operate from major gateways in Canada and Europe.

Scheduled airlines flying into Tampa International Airport include: Air Canada (tel. 800/422-6232), Air Jamaica (tel. 800/523-5585), American (tel. 800/433-7300), Bahamasair (tel. 800/222-4262), British Airways (tel. 800/247-9297), Cayman Airways (tel. 800/422-9626), Comair (tel. 800/354-9822), Continental (tel. 800/525-0280), Delta (tel. 800/221-1212), Eastern (tel. 800/327-8376), Mexicana (tel. 800/531-7921), Midway (tel. 800/621-5700), Midwest Express (tel. 800/452-2022), Northwest (tel. 800/225-2525), Pan American (tel. 800/221-1111), Trans World (tel. 800/438-2929), United (tel. 800/241-6522), and USAir (tel. 800/428-4322).

The following are among the charter carriers flying into Tampa International from domestic and foreign gateways: American Trans Air, Canadian Airlines International, Condor, Martinair Holland, and Odyssey International.

In addition, a large charter program operates from Canada into St. Petersburg–Clearwater International Airport. Carriers providing these services include Canadian Airlines International, Canada 3000, Inter Canadian, and Odyssey International. Check with a travel agent for information about charter flights.

TYPICAL FARES

Because the St. Petersburg/Tampa area is one of the most popular destinations in the southeastern U.S., the airlines offer a wide choice of flights and have many seats to fill. For this reason, promotional fares are usually plentiful, particularly in the off-season when carriers seek to stimulate traffic. Generally speaking, except for holiday periods, fares are at their lowest from May through early December.

 **FROMMER'S SMART
TRAVELER—AIRFARES**

VALUE-CONSCIOUS TRAVELERS SHOULD TAKE
ADVANTAGE OF THE FOLLOWING:

1. Shop all the airlines that fly to Tampa International Airport and check if any charters go from your area into St. Petersburg–Clearwater International Airport.
2. Always ask for the lowest-priced fare, not just for a promotional fare.
3. Keep calling the airline of your choice—availability of reduced-priced seats changes daily. Airlines would rather sell a seat at a low price than have it fly empty. As the departure date nears, additional low-cost seats often become available.
4. Be flexible with your time and days of departure—getting the best price usually means flying midweek, and sometimes it requires departing at off-peak hours.
5. Avoid holidays and other high-traffic periods, such as Thanksgiving, Christmas, and Easter. Fares are at their highest during these times, and discount fares are often subject to "blackout" restrictions.

Of all the carriers with a heavy presence in the Tampa/St. Petersburg market, Continental or Eastern usually set the trend by offering slashed-rate fares in the slack seasons, and invariably the other airlines match them. From the Northeast, fares go as low as $79 to $89 one-way, based on a round-trip purchase; from the Midwest, $109 to $129; and from the West Coast, $129 to $149. Of course, these fares are highly restricted, subject to change without notice, and must be purchased in advance, but, if you are looking for a bargain, you can usually find one, unless you want to travel at Thanksgiving, Christmas, or from mid-February to mid-April.

If you are not lucky enough to qualify for a promotional fare, then it can cost you as much as $400 to $500 to fly round-trip between Tampa/St. Petersburg and most Eastern and Midwest destinations, or as high as $500 to $900 from most western cities. Two good rules to remember: plan in advance and shop around.

For more information, consult a travel agent or contact the airlines directly, by using toll-free numbers.

BY TRAIN

Amtrak offers daily service between East Coast cities and Tampa (with a bus connection to St. Petersburg) via its *Silver Star* and *Silver Meteor* trains. From New York, the trip takes approximately 26 hours, with intermediate stops at Philadelphia, Washington, D.C., Savannah, Jacksonville, and other East Coast points. From the Midwest, you can transfer to these trains at Philadelphia or Washington, and from the West Coast you can connect in a slightly more roundabout fashion via New Orleans or Jacksonville.

Individual ticket prices vary, but by using Amtrak's "All Aboard America" fares, you'll pay one flat fee for round-trip travel within one region or among the three regions of the United States. For example, you can travel between Florida and any East Coast city for between $179 and $189; or from the Midwest to the eastern corridor, for $229 to $269; or from the West Coast to the east for $259 to $309. These fares allow you to make up to three stops, if you wish. The lowest rates are available in the winter and spring, with a validity period of up to 180 days. If you are from Europe and plan to do a lot of traveling beyond Tampa/St. Petersburg, inquire from your travel agent about a USA Railpass, available only to overseas visitors.

If you prefer to bring your own car, reserve space on Amtrak's Auto Train, operating daily between Lorton, Virginia, about one hour south of Washington, D.C., and Sanford, Florida, an hour northeast of Orlando. You'll travel in comfort and style while your car (with baggage safely stored inside) is professionally handled and secured in enclosed car carriers. Your ticket also provides you with a seat for the overnight journey, and complimentary buffet dinner and breakfast. Depending on the date of travel, one-way fares range from $69 to $140 for adults; $34.50 to $70 for children aged 2 through 12, and $115 to $249 for your car.

For more information on all Amtrak services and rates, call toll free 800/872-7245 (800/USA-RAIL) or write Amtrak Distribution Center, P.O. Box 7717, Itasca, IL 60143.

BY BUS

Greyhound Trailways operates bus service from many U.S. cities to both Tampa and St. Petersburg. One of the best fare deals is the "Moneysaver," a ticket allowing travel between any two cities for $68 each way or $118 round-trip. A 30-day advance purchase is required.

For more extensive travel, look into the Ameripass. It allows unlimited travel for a flat fee: $189 for seven days, $249 for 15 days, $349 for 30 days, with extensions available at $10 per day.

BY CAR

Situated in the heart of central Florida's west coast, the Tampa/St. Petersburg area can be easily reached by car. In the winter season, you'll see thousands of license plates bearing the imprints of many U.S. states and Canadian provinces as well as the local Florida designations of Pinellas and Hillsborough counties.

The main arteries leading to the Tampa Bay area are I-75, I-275, I-4, U.S. 19, U.S. 19A, U.S. 41, U.S. 92, U.S. 301, and S.R. 60.

To help you plan, here are some approximate driving distances from selected cities (in miles):

Atlanta	470	Montréal	1,520
Boston	1,390	New Orleans	635
Chicago	1,230	New York City	1,150
Cleveland	1,120	Orlando	85
Detroit	1,230	Pittsburgh	1,040
Miami	275	Toronto	1,480

BY BOAT

Rimmed by the waters of the Gulf of Mexico and Tampa Bay, the Tampa/St. Petersburg region is a popular port of call for boaters. If you decide to navigate your own craft to this area, there are many marinas catering to visiting boaters. However, be forewarned that some marinas have waiting lists and limits on the length of stay, so be sure to make arrangements to dock in advance. Among the marinas that welcome short-term or out-of-state visitors are:

- St. Petersburg Municipal Marina, 300 2nd Ave. SE, St. Petersburg (tel. 813/893-7329)
- Harborage at Bayboro, 1415 2nd St. S., St. Petersburg (tel. 813/894-7497)
- Sailors Wharf, 1421 Bay St. SE, St. Petersburg (tel. 813/823-1155)
- Maximo Moorings, 4801 37th St. S., St. Petersburg (tel. 813/867-1102)
- Harbour Island Dock, The Waterwalk, Harbour Island, Tampa (tel. 813/229-5324)

FOR THE FOREIGN TRAVELER

Although American fads and fashions have spread across Europe and other parts of the world so that America may seem like familiar territory before your arrival, there are still many peculiarities and uniquely American situations that any foreign visitor will encounter. This chapter is meant to clue you in on what they are.

International visitors should also read the Introduction carefully.

1. PREPARING FOR YOUR TRIP

NECESSARY DOCUMENTS

Canadian nationals need only proof of Canadian residence to visit the United States. Citizens of Great Britain and Japan need only a current passport. Citizens of other countries, including Australia and New Zealand, usually need two documents: a valid **passport** with an expiration date at least six months later than the scheduled end of their visit to the United States and a **tourist visa** available at no charge from a U.S. embassy or consulate.

To get a tourist or business visa to enter the United States, contact the nearest American embassy or consulate in your country; if there is none, you will have to apply in person in a country where there *is* a U.S. embassy or consulate. Present your passport, a passport-size photo of yourself, and a completed application, which is available through the embassy or consulate.

You may be asked to provide information about how you plan to finance your trip or show a letter of invitation from a friend with whom you plan to stay. Those applying for a business visa may be asked to show evidence that they will not receive a salary in the United States.

Be sure to check the length of stay on your visa; usually it is six months. If you want to stay longer, you may file for an extension with the Immigration and Naturalization Service once you are in the country. If permission to stay is granted, a new visa is not required unless you leave the United States and want to reenter.

MEDICAL REQUIREMENTS

No inoculations are needed to enter the U.S. unless you are coming from, or have stopped over in, areas known to be suffering from epidemics, especially of cholera or yellow fever. Applicants for immigrants' visas (and only they) must undergo a screening test for AIDS under a law passed in 1987.

If you have a disease requiring treatment with medications containing narcotics or drugs, carry a valid, signed prescription from your physician to allay any suspicions that you are smuggling drugs. Ditto for syringes.

TRAVEL INSURANCE

All such insurance is voluntary in the U.S.; however, given the very high cost of medical care, I cannot too strongly advise every traveler to arrange for appropriate coverage before setting out. There are specialized insurance companies that will, for a relatively low premium, cover: loss or theft of your baggage; trip-cancellation costs; guarantee of bail in case you are sued; sickness or injury costs (medical, surgical, and hospital); costs of an accident, repatriation, or death. Such packages (for example, "Europe Assistance" in Europe) are sold by automobile clubs at attractive rates, as well as by insurance companies and travel agencies.

2. GETTING TO THE U.S.

Travelers from overseas can take advantage of the **APEX (Advance Purchase Excursion) fares** offered by all the major U.S. and European carriers. Aside from these, attractive values are offered by **Icelandair** on flights from Luxembourg to New York or Orlando; and by **Virgin Atlantic** from London to New York/Newark or Miami.

Some large airlines (for example, TWA, American Airlines, Northwest, United, and Delta) offer travelers on their transatlantic or transpacific flights special discount tickets under the name **Visit USA,** allowing travel between any U.S. destinations at minimum rates. They are not on sale in the U.S., and must therefore be purchased before you leave your foreign point of departure. This system is the best way of seeing the U.S. at low cost. You should obtain information well in advance from your travel agent or the office of the airline concerned, since the conditions attached to these discount tickets can be changed without advance notice.

For further information about travel to and around Tampa/St. Petersburg, see "Getting There" in Chapter 2, and "Getting Around" in Chapters 4 and 8.

3. ESSENTIAL INFORMATION

Accommodations   See Chapters 5 and 9.

Automobile Rentals   See "Getting Around" in Chapters 4 and 8.

Business Hours   See "Fast Facts" in Chapters 4 and 8.

Climate   See Chapter 2.

Currency and Exchange   The U.S. monetary system has a decimal base: one **dollar** ($1) = 100 **cents** (100¢).

The most common **bills** (all green) are the $1 ("a buck"), $5, $10, and $20 denominations. There are also $2 (seldom encountered), $50, and $100 bills (the two latter are not welcome when paying for small purchases).

There are six denominations of **coins**: 1¢ (one cent, or "penny"); 5¢ (five cents, or "nickel"); 10¢ (ten cents, or "dime"); 25¢ (twenty-five cents, or "quarter"); 50¢ (fifty cents, or "half dollar"); and the rare—and prized by collectors—$1 piece (both the older, large silver dollars and the newer, small Susan B. Anthony coin).

Traveler's checks denominated in *dollars* are accepted without demur at most hotels, motels, restaurants, and large stores. But as any experienced traveler knows, the best place to change traveler's checks is at a bank.

However, the method of payment most widely used is the **credit card:** VISA (BarclayCard in Britain), MasterCard (EuroCard in Europe, Access in Britain, Diamond in Japan), American Express, Diners Club, and Carte Blanche, in descending order of acceptance. You can save yourself trouble by using "plastic money," rather than cash or traveler's checks, in 95% of all hotels, motels, restaurants, and retail stores (except for those selling food or liquor). A credit card can serve as a deposit for renting a car, as proof of identity (often carrying more weight than a passport), or as a "cash card," enabling you to draw money from banks that accept them.

Note: The "foreign-exchange bureaus" so common in Europe are rare even at airports in the U.S., and nonexistent outside major cities. Try to avoid having to change foreign money, or traveler's checks denominated other than in U.S. dollars, at a small-town bank, or even a branch bank in a big city; in fact, leave any currency other than U.S. dollars at home—it may prove more nuisance to you than it's worth. If you do bring foreign currency to Tampa/St. Petersburg, there is a currency exchange desk at Tampa International Airport, on the Third Level, and most major banks exchange currency.

Customs and Immigration   Every adult visitor may bring in, free of duty: one liter of wine or hard liquor; 200 cigarettes or 100 cigars (but *no* cigars from Cuba) or three pounds of smoking tobacco;

$400 worth of gifts. These exemptions are offered to travelers who spend at least 72 hours in the U.S. and who have not claimed them within the preceding six months. It is altogether forbidden to bring into the country foodstuffs (particularly cheese, fruit, cooked meats, and canned goods) and plants (vegetables, seeds, tropical plants, etc.). Foreign tourists may bring in or take out up to $10,000 in U.S. or foreign currency with no formalities; larger sums must be declared to Customs on entering or leaving.

The visitor arriving by air, no matter what the port of entry— Tampa, New York, Boston, Miami, Honolulu, Los Angeles, or the rest—should cultivate patience and resignation before setting foot on U.S. soil. The U.S. Customs service is among the slowest and most suspicious on earth. On some days, especially summer weekends, you may wait two hours or more to have your passport stamped at major international airports. Add the time it takes to clear Customs and you will see that you should make very generous allowance for delay in planning connections between international and domestic flights— an average of two to three hours at least.

In contrast, for the traveler arriving by car or by rail from Canada, the border-crossing formalities have been streamlined to the vanishing point. And for the traveler by air from Canada, Bermuda, and some points in the Caribbean, you can sometimes go through Customs and Immigration at the point of *departure,* which is much quicker and less painful.

Electric Current   U.S. wall outlets give power at 110–115 volts, 60 cycles, compared to 220 volts, 50 cycles, in most of Europe. Besides a 110-volt converter, small appliances of non-American manufacture, such as hair dryers or shavers, will require a plug adapter with two flat, parallel pins.

Embassies and Consulates   All embassies are located in the national capital, Washington, D.C.; some consulates are located in major cities, and most nations have a mission to the United Nations in New York City.

Listed here are the embassies and consulates of the major English-speaking countries—Australia, Canada, Ireland, New Zealand, and the United Kingdom. If you are from another country, you can get the telephone number of your embassy by calling "information" in Washington, D.C. (tel. 202/555-1212).

Australia   The **embassy** is at 1601 Massachusetts Ave. NW, Washington, DC 20036 (tel. 202/797-3000). **Consulates** are located in the following cities: **Chicago**—Quaker Tower, 321 N. Clark St., Suite 2930, IL 60610 (tel. 312/645-9440); **Honolulu**— 1000 Bishop St., Penthouse, HI 96813 (tel. 808/524-5050); **Houston**—3 Post Oak Central A.H., 1990 Post Oak Rd., Suite 800, TX 77056 (tel. 713/629-9131 or 520-3179); **Los Angeles**—611 N. Larchmont Blvd., CA 90004 (tel. 213/469-4300); **New York**— International Building, 636 Fifth Ave., NY 10111 (tel. 212/245-4000); **San Francisco**—360 Post St., CA 94108 (tel. 415/362-6160).

Canada The **embassy** is at 501 Pennsylvania Ave. NW, Washington, DC 20001 (tel. 202/682-1740). **Consulates** are located in the following cities: **Atlanta**—One CNN Center, Suite 400 South Tower, GA 30303 (tel. 404/577-6810); **Boston**—3 Copley Pl., Suite 400, MA 02116 (tel. 617/536-1731); **Buffalo**—One Marine Midland Center, Suite 3550, NY 14203 (tel. 716/825-1345); **Chicago**—310 S. Michigan Ave., Suite 1200, IL 60604 (tel. 312/427-1031); **Cleveland**—Illuminating Bldg., 55 Public Square, OH 44113 (tel. 216/771-0150); **Dallas**—St. Paul Place, 750 N. St. Paul, Suite 1700, TX 75201 (tel. 214/922-9811); **Detroit**—660 Renaissance Center, Suite 1100, MI 48243 (tel. 313/567-2340); **Los Angeles**—300 S. Grand Ave., 10th floor, CA 90071 (tel. 213/687-7432); **Minneapolis**—701 Fourth Ave., South, MN 55415 (tel. 612/333-4641); **New York**—1251 Ave. of the Americas, NY 10020 (tel. 212/586-2400); **San Francisco**—One Maritime Plaza, Golden Gateway Center, CA 94111 (tel. 415/981-8541); **Seattle**—412 Plaza 600, Sixth and Stewart, WA 98101 (tel. 206/443-1777).

Ireland The **embassy** is at 2234 Massachusetts Ave. NW, Washington, DC 20008 (tel. 202/462-3939). **Consulates** are located in the following cities: **Boston**—Chase Bldg., 535 Boylston St., MA 02116 (tel. 617/267-9330); **Chicago**—400 N. Michigan Ave., IL 60611 (tel. 312/337-1868); **New York**—515 Madison Ave., NY 10022 (tel. 212/319-2555); **San Francisco**—655 Montgomery St., Suite 930, CA 94111 (tel. 415/392-4214).

New Zealand The **embassy** is at 37 Observatory Circle NW, Washington, DC 20008 (tel. 202/328-4800). A **consulate** is located in **Los Angeles**—Tishman Bldg., 10960 Wilshire Blvd., Westwood, Suite 1530, CA 90024 (tel. 213/477-8241).

United Kingdom The **embassy** is at 3100 Massachusetts Ave. NW, Washington, DC 20008 (tel. 202/462-1340). **Consulates** are located in **Atlanta**—245 Peachtree Center Ave., Suite 912, GA 30303 (tel. 404/524-5856); **Chicago**—33 N. Dearborn St., IL 60602 (tel. 312/346-1810); **Houston**—601 Jefferson, Suite 2250, TX 77002 (tel. 713/659-6270); **Los Angeles**—3701 Wilshire Blvd., Suite 312, CA 90010 (tel. 213/385-7381); **New York**—845 Third Ave., NY 10022 (tel. 212/752-8400).

Emergencies In all major cities you can call the police, an ambulance, or the fire brigade through the single emergency telephone number **911.** Another useful way of reporting an emergency is to call the telephone-company operator by dialing **0** (zero, *not* the letter "O"). Outside major cities, call the county sheriff or the fire brigade at the number you will find in the local telephone book.

If you encounter such travelers' problems as sickness, accident, or lost or stolen baggage, it will pay you to call **Travelers Aid,** an organization that specializes in helping distressed travelers, whether American or foreign. Check the local telephone book for the nearest office, or dial 0 and ask the telephone operator.

Holidays   On the following legal national holidays, banks, government offices, post offices, and many stores, restaurants, and museums are closed:

January 1 (New Year's Day)
Third Monday in January (Martin Luther King Day)
Third Monday in February (President's Day, Washington's Birthday)
Last Monday in May (Memorial Day)
July 4 (Independence Day)
First Monday in September (Labor Day)
Second Monday in October (Columbus Day)
November 11 (Veteran's Day/Armistice Day)
Last Thursday in November (Thanksgiving Day)
December 25 (Christmas Day)

The Tuesday following the first Monday in November is Election Day, and is a legal holiday in presidential-election years.

Information   See Chapter 2.

Legal Aid   The foreign tourist, unless positively identified as a member of the Mafia or of a drug ring, will probably never become involved with the American legal system. If you are pulled up for a minor infraction (for example, of the highway code, such as speeding), never attempt to pay the fine directly to a police officer; you may wind up arrested on the much more serious charge of attempted bribery. Pay fines by mail, or directly into the hands of the clerk of the court. If accused of a more serious offense, it is wise to say and do nothing before consulting a lawyer. Under U.S. law, an arrested person is allowed one telephone call to a party of his choice. Call your embassy or consulate.

Liquor Laws   See Chapter 4.

Mail   If you want your mail to follow you on your vacation, you need only fill out a change-of-address card at any post office. The post office will also hold your mail for up to one month. If you aren't sure of your address, your mail can be sent to you, in your name, **c/o General Delivery** at the main post office of the city or region where you expect to be. The addressee must pick it up in person, and produce proof of identity (driver's license, credit card, passport, etc.).

Generally to be found at intersections, mailboxes are blue with a red-and-white logo, and carry the inscription "U.S. MAIL." If your mail is addressed to a U.S. destination, don't forget to add the five-figure ZIP Code, after the two-letter abbreviation of the state to which the mail is addressed (FL for Florida).

Measurements and Sizes   While most of the rest of the world is on the metric system, for nonscientific purposes the United States still adheres to its own units of measurement. For tables to help you with conversions, both for standard measurements and clothing and shoe sizes, see the Appendix.

Medical Emergencies See "Emergencies," above.

Newspapers and Magazines See Chapters 4 and 8.

Post See "Mail."

Radio and Television Audiovisual media, with three coast-to-coast networks—ABC, CBS, and NBC—joined in recent years by the Public Broadcasting System (PBS) and the cable network CNN, play a major part in American life. In the big cities, televiewers have a choice of about a dozen channels (including the UHF channels), most of them transmitting 24 hours a day, without counting the pay-TV channels showing recent movies or sports events. In smaller communities the choice may be limited to four TV channels (there are 1,200 in the entire country), and a half dozen local radio stations (there are 6,500 in all), each broadcasting a particular kind of music—classical, country, jazz, pop, gospel—punctuated by news broadcasts and frequent commercials. For stations in Tampa/St. Petersburg, see Chapters 4 and 8.

Safety In general, the U.S. is safer than most other countries, particularly in rural areas, but there are "danger zones" in the big cities which should be approached only with extreme caution.

As a general rule, isolated areas such as gardens and parking lots should be avoided after dark. Elevators and public-transport systems in off-hours, particularly between 10pm and 6am, are also potential crime scenes. You should drive through decaying neighborhoods with your car doors locked and the windows closed. Never carry on your person valuables like jewelry or large sums of cash; traveler's checks are much safer.

Taxes In the U.S. there is no VAT (Value-Added Tax), or other indirect tax at a national level. Every state, and each city in it, is allowed to levy its own local tax on all purchases, including hotel and restaurant checks, airline tickets, etc. It is automatically added to the price of certain services such as public transportation, cab fares, phone calls, and gasoline. It varies from 4% to 10% depending on the state and city, so when you are making major purchases such as photographic equipment, clothing, or high-fidelity components, it can be a significant part of the cost.

The **sales tax rate** is 7% for St. Petersburg and 6% for Tampa.

Telephone, Telegraph, and Telex Pay phones are an integral part of the American landscape. You will find them everywhere: at street corners, in bars, restaurants, public buildings, stores, service stations, along highways, etc. Outside the metropolitan areas, public telephones are more difficult to find. Stores and gas stations are your best bet. In the Tampa/St. Petersburg Area, local calls cost 25¢.

For **long-distance or international calls,** stock up with a supply of quarters; the pay phone will instruct you when, and in what quantity, you should put them into the slot. For direct overseas calls, first dial 011, followed by the country code (Australia, 61; Republic of Ireland, 353; New Zealand, 64; United Kingdom, 44; and so on), and then by the city code (for example, 71 or 81 for London, 21 for Birmingham) and the number of the person you wish to call. For long-distance calls in Canada and the U.S., dial 1 followed by the area code and number you want.

Before calling from a hotel room, always ask the hotel phone operator if there are any telephone surcharges. These are best avoided by using a public phone, calling collect, or using a telephone charge card.

For **reversed-charge or collect calls,** and for **person-to-person calls,** dial 0 (zero, *not* the letter "O") followed by the area code and number you want; an operator will then come on the line, and you should specify that you are calling collect, or person-to-person, or both. If your operator-assisted call is international, ask for the overseas operator.

For local **directory assistance** ("information"), dial 411; for long-distance information dial 1, then the appropriate area code and 555-1212.

Like the telephone system, **telegraph** and **telex** services are provided by private corporations like ITT, MCI, and above all, Western Union. You can bring your telegram in to the nearest Western Union office (there are hundreds across the country), or dictate it over the phone (a toll-free call, 800/325-6000). You can also telegraph money, or have it telegraphed to you, very quickly over the Western Union system.

Telephone Directory   See "Yellow Pages," below.

Time   The U.S. is divided into six **time zones.** From east to west, these are: Eastern Standard Time (EST), Central Standard Time (CST), Mountain Standard Time (MST), Pacific Standard Time (PST), Alaska Standard Time (AST), and Hawaii Standard Time (HST). Always keep changing time zones in mind if you are traveling (or even telephoning) long distances in the U.S. For example, noon in New York City (EST) is 11am in Chicago (CST), 10am in Denver (MST), 9am in Los Angeles (PST), 8am in Anchorage (AST), and 7am in Honolulu (HST).

Daylight Saving Time is in effect from 1am on the first Sunday in April until 2am on the last Sunday in October except in Arizona, Hawaii, part of Indiana, and Puerto Rico.

Tipping   See "Fast Facts—St. Petersburg," in Chapter 4.

Toilets   Foreign visitors often complain that public toilets are hard to find in most U.S. cities. True, there are none on the streets, but the visitor can usually find one in a bar, restaurant, hotel, museum, department store, or service station—and it will probably be clean (although the last-mentioned sometimes leaves much to be desired). Note, however, a growing practice in some restaurants and bars of displaying a notice that "toilets are for the use of patrons only." You can ignore this sign, or better yet, avoid arguments by paying for a cup of coffee or soft drink which will qualify you as a patron. The cleanliness of toilets at railroad stations and bus depots may be more open to question, and some public places are equipped with pay toilets, which require you to insert one or two 10¢ coins (dimes) into a slot on the door before it will open.

Yellow Pages   There are two kinds of telephone directory available to you. The general directory is the "white pages," in which private and business subscribers are listed in alphabetical order. The inside front cover lists emergency numbers for police, fire, and ambulance, and other vital numbers (like the Coast Guard, poison control center, crime-victims hotline, etc.). The first few pages are devoted to community-service numbers, including a guide to long-distance and international calling, complete with country codes and area codes.

The second directory, the "yellow pages," lists all local services, businesses, and industries by type, with an index at the back. The listings cover not only such obvious items as automobile repairs by make of car, or drugstores (pharmacies), often by geographical location, but also restaurants by type of cuisine and geographical location, bookstores by special subject and/or language, places of worship by religious denomination, and other information that the tourist might otherwise not readily find. The yellow pages also include city plans or detailed area maps, often showing postal ZIP Codes and public transportation routes.

CHAPTER 4

GETTING TO KNOW ST. PETERSBURG

Sitting on a sheltered curve of land between Tampa Bay and the Gulf of Mexico, St. Petersburg blends the businesslike pulse of a city with the relaxed rhythm of a resort. Sleek new office towers rise beside historic Spanish-style landmarks, wide and busy thoroughfares edge shady palm-tree lined parks, and huge building cranes hover over the skyline as sailboats breeze by. Even the layout is diverse—the compact downtown business district hugs the bayfront, surrounded by huge residential areas reaching toward the beaches. Houses range from hacienda-style villas to contemporary sun-roofed cottages, clusters of condominiums, or endless rows of mobile homes.

St. Pete, as it is fondly known, is home to over 250,000 people, with more new residents settling in every day. Long favored by senior citizens because of its idyllic climate, it is now a mecca for people of all ages who seek economic opportunity and the good life under fair skies.

1. ORIENTATION

ARRIVING

BY AIR

Tampa International Airport, off Memorial Highway and Florida Route 60, Tampa (tel. 813/276-3400), approximately 16 miles northeast of downtown St. Petersburg, is the gateway for all scheduled domestic and international flights. Currently handling more than 10 million passengers a year, it has been voted the best airport in the U.S. in various passenger polls. Services include a small shopping mall, six restaurants, three lounges, an art gallery, duty-free shops, and a complete international arrivals/Customs facility. The 56 landing gates (Airside) are connected to the main terminal (Landside) and baggage-claim areas via high-speed "people movers" that shuttle

St. Petersburg–Clearwater International Airport, on Roosevelt Boulevard (Fla. Rte. 686), Clearwater (tel. 813/535-7600), approximately 10 miles north of St. Petersburg, is primarily a charter facility, serving over 150,000 international passengers annually. It has a new international arrivals facility for Customs, immigration, and agriculture inspections.

Albert Whitted Municipal Airport, 108 8th Ave. S., St. Petersburg (tel. 813/893-7654), located downtown on the bayfront, serves as a landing strip for private planes.

GETTING INTO TOWN   The Limo Inc., 11901 30th Court N., St. Petersburg (tel. 813/572-1111 or toll-free 800/282-6817) offers 24-hour door-to-door service between Tampa Airport or St. Petersburg–Clearwater Airport and any destination (hotel, condo, private home, mobile home park, or otherwise) via a fleet of air-conditioned vans. No reservations are required on arrival; just proceed to any Limo desk outside of each baggage-claim area. Departures to most destinations are every 20 minutes or less. For a return trip to the airport, reservations for pickup should be made at least six hours prior to flight departure and preferably a day in advance. Flat-rate fare one-way is $10.25 per person to any St. Pete or Gulf beach destination.

Yellow Cab Taxis (tel. 813/821-7777) line up outside the baggage-claim areas; no reservations are required. Average fare from Tampa Airport to St. Petersburg or any of the Gulf beaches is approximately $25 to $35 per taxi (one or more passengers). Travel time is a half hour to 45 minutes, depending on exact destination and traffic. Fare from St. Petersburg–Clearwater Airport is approximately $15 to $20, depending on the final destination; travel time can be 15 minutes to a half hour.

BY TRAIN

Amtrak trains from points north terminate at the **Tampa Amtrak Station,** 601 Nebraska Ave. N., Tampa (tel. 813/221-7600). However, if your destination is St. Petersburg, shuttle bus service meets all trains and transfers passengers to the St. Petersburg Amtrak Station, 33rd Street N. and 37 Avenue N., St. Petersburg (tel. 813/522-9475).

BY CAR

The St. Petersburg area is linked to the interstate system and is accessible from I-75, I-275, I-4, U.S. 19, and Florida Route 60.

BY BUS

Greyhound Trailways buses from destinations around the United States arrive at the carrier's downtown depot at 180 Ninth St. N., St. Petersburg (tel. 813/894-4128).

TOURIST INFORMATION

Once you have arrived, you'll find many local visitor information offices, such as the following:

- **St. Petersburg Chamber of Commerce,** 100 2nd Ave. N., St. Petersburg, FL 33701 (tel. 813/821-4069), open Mon–Fri 9am–5pm
- **Suncoast Welcome Center,** 2001 Ulmerton Rd. (at the juncture of I-275 and Rte. 688), Clearwater, FL 34622 (tel. 813/573-1449), open daily 9am–5pm.
- **The Pier Visitor Information Center,** 800 2nd Ave. N.E., St. Petersburg, FL 33701 (tel. 813/821-6164), open daily 10am–8pm
- **St. Petersburg Beach Chamber of Commerce,** 6990 Gulf Blvd., St. Petersburg Beach, FL 33706 (tel. 813/360-6957), open Mon–Fri 9am–5pm.
- **Treasure Island Chamber of Commerce,** 152 108th Ave., Treasure Island, FL 33706 (tel. 813/367-4529), open Mon–Fri 8am–4:30pm.
- **The Gulf Beaches on Sand Key Chamber of Commerce,** 501 150th Ave., Madeira Beach, FL 33708 (tel. 813/391-7373); also at 105 5th Ave., Indian Rocks Beach, FL 34635 (tel. 813/595-4575). Both offices open year round Mon–Fri 9am–5pm; mid-Jan to Apr only, Sat 9am–3pm.
- **The Greater Clearwater Chamber of Commerce,** 128 N. Osceola Ave. Clearwater, FL 34615 (tel. 813/461-0011), open Mon–Fri 8:30am–5pm.
- **Welcome Center** (on Courtney Campbell Causeway), 3350 Gulf-to-Bay Blvd., Clearwater, FL 34619 (tel. 813/726-1547), open daily 9am–5pm. Look for another Welcome Center on the beach at 40 Causeway Blvd., Clearwater Beach, FL 34630 (tel. 813/446-2424), open Mon–Fri 8:30am–12:30pm, 1:30–5pm.

CITY LAYOUT

St. Petersburg is laid out according to a grid system, with streets running north to south and avenues running east and west. Central Avenue, a wide four-lane thoroughfare that cuts across the city from Tampa Bay to Treasure Island on the Gulf of Mexico, is the dividing line for north and south addresses.

With the exception of Central Avenue, most streets and avenues downtown are one-way. As a rule, south of Central Avenue, even-numbered avenues go west and odd-numbered avenues go east; north of Central Avenue, even-numbered avenues go east and odd-numbered avenues go west. In the case of streets, most even-numbered streets go south and most odd-numbered streets go north. If it sounds confusing, it is—but if you spend a few hours walking, you'll catch on to the pattern pretty quickly.

The main exceptions are thoroughfares along the bayfront, such as Bayshore Drive and Beach Drive, where two-way traffic is permitted. These streets are curved or diagonal and not strictly part of the grid. The Pier, which extends out into the bay, is on a street that is an

- St. Petersburg is credited by the *Guinness Book of World Records* with having the longest run of consecutive sunny days—768 days from February 9, 1967 to March 17, 1969.

- St. Petersburg's *Evening Independent* (published from 1910 to 1986) was given away free on those days when the sun did not shine. In 76 years, it was given away free 295 times—an average of less than four times per year!

- St. Petersburg was the launching point for the world's first scheduled commercial flight in 1914. A Benoist airboat, piloted by Tony Jannus, inaugurated passenger service from St. Petersburg to Tampa, a 21-mile trip.

- The Belleview Biltmore Hotel in Belleair/Clearwater, north of St. Pete, is the world's largest occupied wooden structure.

- The St. Petersburg Shuffleboard Club, on 4th Avenue N., is the largest shuffleboard club in the world and is home to the National Shuffleboard Hall of Fame.

eastward extension of Second Avenue N., so that address is indicated by Second Avenue NE.

Two-way traffic is also permitted on boulevards, usually diagonal thoroughfares west or north of downtown, such as Tyrone Boulevard, Gandy Boulevard, and Roosevelt Boulevard.

Along the beach strip, west of St. Petersburg, Gulf Boulevard is the main two-way north-south thoroughfare, and most avenues, which cross in an east-west direction, have two-way traffic. Avenues are numbered in continuous fashion, starting with 1st Avenue at the southern tip of the Pass-A-Grille section of St. Petersburg Beach and extending north to 200th Avenue at the top of Indian Shores; at the Indian Rocks Beach city line, the numbers start again from 1st Avenue and go upward as Gulf Boulevard continues north through Belleair Beach.

To find an address, first determine if it is north or south; the rest is just a matter of following numbers. For instance, we know that 101 Second Avenue North is two avenues north of Central Avenue. The street number, 101, tells us it is in the 100 block, between First and Second Streets North, just as no. 305 on the same avenue would be between Third and Fourth Streets North.

On the beach strip, the addresses on Gulf Boulevard correspond to the numbering of avenues. For example, 5500 Gulf Boulevard is at 55th Avenue.

NEIGHBORHOODS IN BRIEF

The **bayfront** area, overlooking Tampa Bay, is the major focus of St. Petersburg's downtown district. Here you will find the Pier, all of the major museums, the Bayfront performing arts center, Al Lang Stadium, hotels, restaurants, and leading shops, as well as the city's playgrounds—Spa Beach, Demens Landing, Bayboro Harbor, and Straub Park. Walk inland along Central Avenue and you will see many of the city's old landmark buildings as you approach the new Suncoast Dome. This downtown core of the city is also

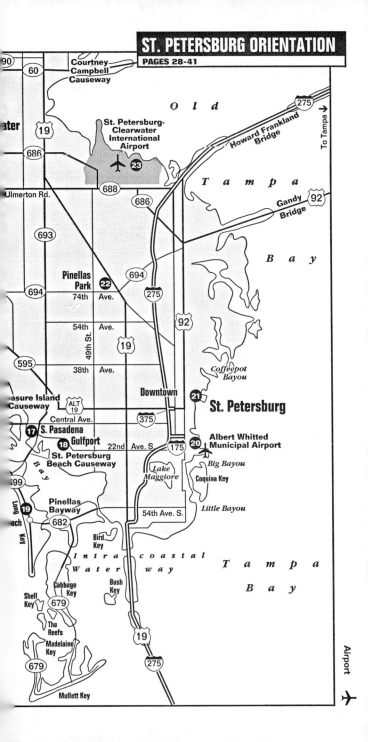

WHAT'S SPECIAL ABOUT ST. PETERSBURG

Beaches
- Pass-A-Grille, for its wide open vistas and quiet off-the-main-road location.
- Treasure Island, for its wide, sandy strand.

Natural Spectacles
- Sunsets from Fort DeSoto Park with views of both Tampa Bay and the Gulf of Mexico.
- Watching pelicans take to free flight after a restorative stay at the Suncoast Seabird Sanctuary, the largest wild bird hospital in the U.S.

Parks and Gardens
- Sand Key Park, with vistas of the Gulf of Mexico and Clearwater Pass.
- DeSoto Park, five islands off the coast with bird, plant, and animal sanctuaries.

Architectural Highlights/Buildings
- The Suncoast Dome, a slant-roofed stadium that is the first cable-supported dome of its kind in the U.S. and the largest of its type in the world.
- The Belleview Biltmore, the world's largest occupied wooden structure.

Museums
- Salvador Dalí Museum, housing the world's largest collection of works by the Surrealist Spanish artist.

Events/Festivals
- Festival of the States, a winter celebration with 17 days of parades, pageantry, and outdoor fun.
- John's Pass Seafood Festival. Tons of the "local catch" dominate this fun-filled weekend at one of the St. Pete area's top fishing spots.

For the Kids
- Boyd Hill Nature Park, for an up-close view of sea birds, reptiles, and other native species.
- Adventure at sea aboard Captain Memo's Pirate Cruise Ship.

Activities
- Swimming, sunning, shelling, or shore-walking along St. Petersburg's strip of sandy white beaches.
- Sailing aboard a ketch, sloop, yacht, or windjammer from St. Pete Beach or Clearwater Harbor.

Shopping
- The Gas Plant Antique Arcade, showcase for 100 area dealers.
- Evander Preston Contemporary Jewelry, for one-of-a-kind hand-hammered gold pieces.
- Wagon Wheel Flea Market, the area's largest open-air market.

home to leading churches, an open-air post office, and Mirror Lake, a sylvan setting just right for sitting on a bench and having a restful moment.

Fanning out from the bayfront, the city of St. Petersburg is composed of various residential clusters. Some radiate great success and others reflect a leaner life-style. Two of the more popular inland neighborhoods include **Pinellas Park** and **Seminole,** both of which have large stretches of small one-story houses, condominium dwellings, or mobile-home parks. One of the most exclusive neighborhoods is **Snell Isle,** a little over a mile north of the Pier. This section is composed of upscale waterfront homes overlooking Tampa Bay. Similarly, south of the Pier, the homes on **Tropical Shores** and **Coquina Key** also overlook Tampa Bay, while newer sections such as **Gulfport** and **Pasadena,** to the southwest of midtown, overlook Boca Ciega Bay.

Neighboring Beach Districts

Mention St. Pete and most people will say "beach." Among the many beach communities in the area, the 7½-mile stretch known as **St. Petersburg Beach** is the leader. Just west of mainland St. Petersburg, nestled between Boca Ciega Bay and the Gulf of Mexico, it is lined with motels, hotels, restaurants, and all types of shops and water-sports attractions. The lower tip, known as Pass-A-Grille, has some lovely old houses and has been attracting visitors for over 150 years. The beachfront is dominated by the "Pink Palace," the landmark Don CeSar Hotel, listed on the National Register of Historic Places.

Treasure Island, like its literary namesake, was once reputed to be the site of buried pirate treasure and a hideout for a band of buccaneers. It is located just north of St. Petersburg Beach and is 3½ miles in length. It has a wide sandy beach, lined with motels, restaurants, and other attractions.

The 12-mile-long **Sand Key Island** sits north of Treasure Island, extending from John's Pass to Sand Key Park. The most southerly of its communities is **Madeira Beach,** often called "Mad Beach" because it is busy and popular with all age groups. A center for deep-sea fishing, Madeira Beach offers many places to stay and eat overlooking either the Gulf or Boca Ciega Bay. It is also home to the *Europa Sun* cruise ship and the only McDonald's in the world on a floating dock.

North of Madeira is a cluster of beaches: **Redington Beach,** with a casual "old Florida" atmosphere and a row of small cottages tucked amid palms and pines; **North Redington Beach,** often called the "Million-Dollar Mile" because it is lined with high-priced condominiums and apartments; and **Redington Shores,** the site of the Redington Long Pier, extending over 1,000 feet into the Gulf of Mexico.

Next is **Indian Shores,** home of the Suncoast Seabird Sanctuary, a unique hospital for pelicans and other injured seabirds. To the north, there is **Indian Rocks Beach,** a narrow strip edged by the Intracoastal Waterway as well as the Gulf, and **Belleair Beach,** one of the most exclusive residential areas on the coast. This strip ends with **Sand Key Park,** a public beach and park nestled between the Gulf and Clearwater Harbor.

Clearwater Beach, with a wide sandy stretch of beachfront, lies on an island linked to downtown Clearwater by a causeway and to the north end of Sand Key Island by a bridge. The beach is popular with young and old alike, and the marina offers a wide array of fishing party boats, sight-seeing vessels, sailing rentals, and all sorts of water-sports activity. Clearwater Beach is about 20 miles northwest of St. Petersburg, and 20 miles west of Tampa.

MAPS

The St. Petersburg Chamber of Commerce is a good source for up-to-date maps of the downtown area. The chambers of commerce along the beach will likewise supply you with free maps of their particular areas. To buy a good map either in advance by mail or on the spot, the best source is Rand McNally Commercial Maps, 4278 28th St. North, St. Petersburg, FL 33714 (tel. 813/525-0879).

2. GETTING AROUND

BY PUBLIC TRANSPORTATION
BY BUS

Pinellas Suncoast Transit Authority/PSTA (tel. 530-9911) operates regular bus service in the downtown St. Petersburg area and throughout Pinellas County. The system is very popular with the locals who use it for transport to shopping malls or for commuting from residential areas. At least a half a dozen bus routes traverse part of the Central Avenue thoroughfare, and some go toward the beaches and connect with local beach transport. For more information check at the PSTA Information Booth at Williams Park, between 3rd and 4th Streets North. Buses run Monday to Saturday from 7am to 10pm, Sunday 8am to 5:30pm; fare is 60¢.

BATS City Transit, 6655 Gulf Blvd., St. Petersburg Beach (tel. 367-3086), offers bus service along the beach strip, from Pass-a-Grille northward along Gulf Boulevard and via the St. Petersburg Beach Causeway to the South Pasadena Shopping Center, where a connection can be made to the PSTA buses to downtown. Buses run hourly Monday through Saturday from 7am to 6pm and Sunday 7:45am to 6pm, but phone to check exact schedule. Fare is 85¢.

Treasure Island Dune Buggy, c/o City Hall, 120 108th Ave., Treasure Island (tel. 360-0811), is an hourly bus service along the Treasure Island strip, making stops at several hotels, motels, and shopping centers. It also connects with PSTA routes for service to downtown St. Pete and other parts of Pinellas County. Buses run Monday through Saturday from 8:15am to 5pm. Fare is $1.

BY MOTORIZED TROLLEY

The **Clearwater Beach Trolley** is operated by the PSTA (tel. 530-9911) in the Clearwater Beach area along Mandalay Avenue and S. Gulfview Boulevard. It runs continuously from Bay Esplanade/Resort, making an intermediate stop near Pier 60 in the center of the beach district. Trolley runs Monday through Sunday from 10am to midnight. The ride is free as of press time, but a small fare (probably 10¢) may be instituted later in 1991–92.

BY FERRY

The **Clearwater Express,** Drew Street Dock, Clearwater (tel. 442-RIDE), is a ferry service connecting downtown Clearwater with Clearwater Beach (making stops at both the north and south ends of the beach). Ferries operate hourly Monday to Friday from 10am to 5pm, more frequently on weekends. Fare is $1.50. Service is also available from Clearwater and Clearwater Beach to neighboring Caladesi Island at $6.95 per round-trip.

BY TAXI

Taxis in St. Petersburg do not normally cruise the streets looking for fares, but they do line up at public loading places such as hotels and bus and train depots. If you need a taxi, it is best to ask at your hotel or call either **Yellow Cab** (tel. 821-7777) or **Independent Cab** (tel. 327-3444). Along the beach, the major cab company is **BATS Taxi,** 5201 Gulf Blvd., St. Petersburg Beach (tel. 367-3702). In the Clearwater area, call **Clearwater Yellow Cab** (tel. 799-2222).

BY CAR

RENTALS

Renting a car is the way to go in the St. Petersburg area. You really need a car to reach various attractions, hotels, and restaurants, especially in the evening hours.

All major firms are represented at the airports and in the St. Pete area, including Avis (tel. 813/867-6662), Budget (tel. 813/530-0441), Hertz (tel. 813/573-9156), and National (tel. 813/530-5491). Local car-rental companies include Phoenix Rent-A-Car (tel. 813/360-6941) and Lindo's (tel. 813/367-3779).

Rental rates, although always changing, are very competitive and can often be $100 a week or less with unlimited mileage, depending on the time of year. You can also rent a great variety of vehicles in this area, from economical subcompact cars to classy convertibles and sports cars such as the Le Baron (available from Avis).

Note: Under a new Florida law, rental-car agencies are required to charge drivers 50¢ per car per day (or part of a day) to help finance drug education for young people and for law enforcement. This rule applies to all rentals up to a maximum of 30 days.

PARKING

Parking is plentiful in downtown St. Petersburg, with most streets providing both free and metered parking (25¢ an hour). Meter rules are strictly enforced (maximum two hours, 8am to 6pm on weekdays).

Parking lots and garages charge an average of 50¢ to $1 per hour and from $2 to $5 all day.

Along the beach strip, meters are the rule, with a charge of 25¢ per half hour, enforced daily 9am to 5pm.

DRIVING RULES

It is legal to turn on red at traffic lights, after coming to a complete stop. Pedestrians in crosswalks have the right of way; automobiles must stop if someone is in a crosswalk.

The speed limit in most downtown or beach areas is 25 or 30 mph, unless otherwise indicated. Seat belts are mandatory for the driver and front-seat passenger; children under five must be in protective seats.

CAUSEWAYS AND BRIDGES

The St. Petersburg mainland (downtown) is connected to St. Petersburg Beach and the other Gulf beaches via a series of causeways and bridges. Some are free and others require a toll (in each direction). Here is a run-down, from the most southerly point northward:

Pinellas Bayway (50¢) links St. Petersburg (54th Ave. S.) with St. Petersburg Beach (Gulf Blvd.).

St. Petersburg Beach Causeway (free) links St. Petersburg (S. Pasadena district) with St. Petersburg Beach (Corey Ave.).

Treasure Island Causeway (35¢) links St. Petersburg (Central Ave.) with Treasure Island (Gulf Blvd.).

Tom Stewart Causeway (free) links St. Petersburg (38th Ave. N.) with Madeira Beach (Gulf Blvd.).

Park Boulevard Causeway (30¢) links Pinellas Park/ Seminole area (north of St. Petersburg) with Indian Shores (Gulf Blvd.).

Indian Rocks Bridge (free) links Largo area and Rte. 688 (north of St. Petersburg) with Indian Rocks Beach (Gulf Blvd.).

Belleair Causeway (free) links Largo/Belleair Bluffs area and Rte. 686 (north of St. Petersburg) with Belleair Shore, Belleair Beach, and Sand Key Beach/Park (Gulf Blvd.).

Clearwater Pass Bridge (75¢) links north end of Sand Key Island (Gulf Blvd.) to southern tip of Clearwater Beach (Gulfview Blvd.).

Memorial Causeway (free), links downtown Clearwater and Rte. 60 with Clearwater Beach and Marina (Gulfview Blvd. and Mandalay Ave.).

Note: Plans call for replacing Clearwater Pass Bridge, an old structure that is sometimes closed without advance warning, with a new bridge; construction could start as early as 1992. The construction may cause further delays. In any case, the speed limit of 15 mph across the bridge is *strictly* enforced.

 ST. PETERSBURG

Area Code   813.

Airports   See "Orientation: Arriving," above in this chapter.

Auto Rentals   See "Getting Around," above in this chapter.

Baby-sitters   With a few hours' advance notice, most hotels can arrange for baby-sitters. Otherwise, call the Family Care Referral Service (tel. 527-7386).

Buses   See "Getting Around," above in this chapter.

Business Hours   Most businesses are open Monday to Friday from 9am to 5pm, shops and stores from 9am to 6pm or later. Banks are open Monday to Friday from 9am to 4pm; some banks are open Friday until 6pm and others are open on Saturday mornings.

Car Rentals   See "Getting Around," above in this chapter.

Climate   See "When to Go" in Chapter 2.

Currency and Exchange   See Chapter 3, "For the Foreign Traveler."

Dentist   For 24-hour emergency services or referrals, call **Pinellas County Dental Society** (tel. 323-2992).

Doctor   Most hotels have a doctor on call; if not, contact the **Pinellas County Physician Information Line** (tel. 585-PHIL). The **Bayfront Medical Center,** in downtown St. Petersburg, operates a doctor referral service (tel. 893-6112). Along the beach strip, there are several walk-in medical offices including **The Doctors Inn,** 13495 Gulf Blvd., Madeira Beach (tel. 391-4100); the **Wayside Medical Clinic,** 2113 N. Gulf Blvd., Indian Rocks Beach (tel. 596-4631); and **Doctors' Walk-in Clinic,** 37 Baymount St., Clearwater Beach (tel. 461-4644).

Documents Required   See Chapter 3, "For the Foreign Traveler."

Driving Rules   See "Getting Around," above in this chapter.

Drugstores   **Eckerd Drugs** is the leading pharmacy chain in the area, with many stores throughout downtown and the beaches, including a 24-hour branch at the Tyrone Gardens Shopping Center, 900 58th St. N., St. Petersburg (tel. 345-9336). For more locations, consult the "yellow pages" under "Pharmacies."

Embassies/Consulates   See Chapter 3, "For the Foreign Traveler."

Emergencies   Dial 911 (free at any pay phone).

Eyeglasses   Many national optical chains operate in the St. Petersburg area, including **LensCrafters, Pearle Vision Center,** and **Sterling Optical.** For exact locations, consult the yellow pages under "Optical Goods: Retail."

Hairdressers/Barbers   Hair-care businesses for men and women are plentiful, with some of the best shops located in department stores such as Maas Brothers, Sears, and J. C. Penney, all shopping malls, and at the larger full-service hotels such as the Don CeSar and Breckenridge. Chains with several locations include **Fantastic Sam's, Joseph's, ManTrap,** and **Silver Sissors.** For locations nearest to you, consult the "yellow pages" under "Barbers," "Beauty Salons," and "Hair Styling."

Holidays See "When to Go" in Chapter 2, and also Chapter 3, "For the Foreign Traveler."

Hospitals Bayfront Medical Center, 701 6th St. S., St. Petersburg (tel. 823-1234); **St. Anthony's Hospital,** 601 12th St. N., St. Petersburg (tel. 825-1000); **Humana Hospital,** 6500 38th Ave. N., St. Petersburg (tel. 384-1414); and **Morton F. Plant Hospital,** 323 Jeffords St., Clearwater (tel. 462-7000).

Information See "Orientation: Tourist Information," above in this Chapter.

Laundry/Dry Cleaning Most hotels supply same-day laundry and dry cleaning service. Reliable local firms include **Pillsbury Cleaners,** 1800 4th St. N. (tel. 822-3456) and five other locations; **Rogers Cleaners and Laundry,** 1700 Central Ave. (tel. 822-3869) and 2018 4th St. N. (tel. 894-0706).

Luggage Storage/Lockers Both Tampa International Airport and St. Petersburg/Clearwater Airport have coin-operated public lockers for luggage storage.

Libraries The **St. Petersburg Central Library** is at 3745 9th Ave. N., St. Petersburg (tel. 893-7724), with five branches spread throughout the city. In addition, other convenient libraries are located at 365 73rd Ave., St. Petersburg Beach (tel. 360-0438), and at 100 N. Osceola Ave., Clearwater (tel. 462-6800).

Liquor Laws The legal drinking age is 21. No liquor may be sold prior to 1pm on Sunday. All alcoholic beverages are available in liquor stores; beer and wine are also sold in grocery stores. It is unlawful to consume liquor in public places such as beaches or streets or to have an open container of alcohol in any moving vehicle. In St. Petersburg, most lounges serve alcohol until 2am.

Lost Property If article is lost or found at a hotel, restaurant, shop, or attraction, contact the management; if lost or found in public areas, contact the police.

Mail Main post office is 3135 1st Ave. N., St. Petersburg (tel. 323-6516), open Monday through Friday from 8am to 5:30pm, Saturday from 8am to 12:30pm.

Maps See "Orientation," above in this chapter.

Money See Chapter 3, "For the Foreign Traveler."

Newspapers/Magazines The *St. Petersburg Times* is the city's award-winning daily newspaper; the best periodical covering the area is *Tampa Bay Life,* a monthly magazine.

Photographic Needs Eckerd Express Photo Services offer one-hour processing at several St. Petersburg area locations including 7900 Gateway Mall, St. Petersburg (tel. 579-4257); Dolphin Village, 4685 Gulf Blvd., St. Petersburg Beach (tel. 360-0818); and 467 Mandalay Ave., Clearwater Beach (tel. 796-1854). For general camera supplies or repairs, contact **Southern Photo**

Technical Service, 1750 9th Ave. N., St. Petersburg (tel. 896-6141).

Police: See "Emergencies," above. To report lost or stolen goods, call 893-7560 (St. Petersburg) or 587-6200 (Pinellas County).

Radio/TV: Local **radio** broadcasters include WFLA-AM 970 (ABC), WSUN-AM 620 (CBS), WTKN-AM 570 (NBC), WLFF-AM 680 (AP and Wall Street Journal), WEND-AM 760 (Financial Broadcasting Network), WGUL-AM 860 (Mutual Radio Network), and WRXB-AM 1590 (National Black Network); WAMA-AM 1500 provides Spanish-language programs, and WTIN-AM 1520 carries news for tourists in the area.

The local **TV stations** are WTSP-TV Channel 10 (ABC), WTVT-TV Channel 13 (CBS), WFLA-TV Channel 8 (NBC), WFTS-TV Channel 28 (Fox), WTOG-TV Channel 44 (independent), WEDU-TV Channel 3 (PBS), and WUSF-TV Channel 16 (PBS).

Religious Services There are hundreds of houses of worship in the St. Petersburg area; inquire at the front desk of your hotel or consult the "yellow pages" under "Churches," "Religious Organizations," and "Synagogues."

Rest Rooms All hotels, restaurants, and attractions have rest rooms available for customers. A unique and historic (dating to 1927) public comfort station is located downtown on the approach to the Pier, next to the Waterfront Historical Museum.

Safety Be mindful of money and valuables in public places; do not leave wallets or purses unattended on the beach; lock car doors and trunks at all times.

Shoe Repairs Two handy downtown locations are **Bill's Shoe Service,** 454 1st Ave. N. (tel. 822-3757), and **Holmes Shoe Repair,** 17 6th St. N. (tel. 898-7930). Others are listed under "Shoe Repairing" in "yellow pages".

Taxes Airport, $6 departure tax for international flights; hotel, 10%; restaurant, 7%; sales, 7%.

Taxis See "Getting Around," above in this chapter.

Time Zone Eastern. For more information, see Chapter 3, "For the Foreign Traveler."

Tipping For good restaurant service, 15% is usual; some establishments automatically add 12% to 18% to a bill (be sure to check). It is customary to leave $1 to $2 per person a day for hotel housekeeping staff; tip bellmen and doormen as services are provided. Tip taxi drivers 10% to 15%; porters at airports, $1 per bag.

Transit Information Dial 530-9911.

Weather Dial 894-6666.

CHAPTER 5

ST. PETERSBURG ACCOMMODATIONS

As a city surrounded by bays and beaches and as a developing commercial center, St. Petersburg offers a great variety of accommodations. From full-service hotels catering to businesspeople to sprawling surf-and-sand resorts or informal mom-and-pop motels, you are bound to find something to fit both your style and your budget. The lodgings that we have selected here represent a sampling of what we consider to be the best—in hotel and motel categories, as well as bed-and-breakfast and hostels.

A stay in "the St. Petersburg area" can mean many types of locations. It can mean downtown (along the bayfront), or north or south of the city center in residential or industrial areas. To most people, however, a stay in St. Petersburg means heading west to the Gulf beach strip—St. Petersburg Beach, Treasure Island, the Island of Sand Key, and Clearwater Beach.

Rates are at their highest during the high season, from December or January through April. If you want to stay on the beach during this period, you can sometimes expect to see "minimum stay" requirements of three to five nights. Rates are also set per room or unit, so that you'll pay the same price for single or double occupancy.

On the plus side, many units, particularly along the beach, offer much more than an average room—usually with small kitchens, minibars, refrigerators, and often separate living, dining, and sleeping rooms. This is ideal if you want to make your own breakfast or lunch.

Better rates are offered during June, July, and August, but if you want the best of bargains, plan to come during May, September, October, or November, when rates are as much as 50% lower than in the high season. And the hotels catering to businesspeople, primarily in downtown St. Petersburg and its business corridors, offer lower rates on weekends throughout the year.

(F) FROMMER'S SMART TRAVELER— HOTELS

VALUE-CONSCIOUS TRAVELERS SHOULD TAKE ADVANTAGE OF THE FOLLOWING:

1. Low prices during off-season months: May, September, October, and November
2. Reduced-rate package deals that may apply for the time you want to stay
3. Low weekends rates at hotels downtown and along business corridors

QUESTIONS TO ASK IF YOU'RE ON A BUDGET

1. Is there a parking charge? In St. Petersburg, this is usually free, but some places charge for valet service.
2. Is the 10% hotel tax included in the price quoted?
3. Is Continental breakfast included in the quoted price?
4. Is there a surcharge on local and long-distance telephone calls? At some hotels, local calls are free.
5. Is there a discount for cash payment?

The rates that we specify below give you the spectrum—ranging from the lowest in the off season to the highest in the peak months. A room that will cost you $125 in February might set you back only $65 or $75 in May.

In addition, at all times of the year you'll pay an extra **10% tax** on the price of a room—7% for Florida state and county taxes and 3% resort tax. Tipping is normally at your own discretion for daily maid service, etc., unless otherwise specified.

The following guidelines apply for high-season room prices (per night, double occupancy) in the St. Petersburg area hotels. In the low season, almost *all* properties have rooms in the moderate or budget range.

Very Expensive	Over $175
Expensive	$125–$175
Moderate	$65–$125
Inexpensive	Under $65

Reservations are a *must* in the high season and certainly recommended at other times, although you'll often find a special offer on the spot in the low-season months, if you don't mind shopping around. Better yet, shop around by phone before you travel by using the toll-free reservations numbers provided by most hotels.

1. DOWNTOWN

For a city of over 250,000 inhabitants, St. Petersburg has surprisingly few world-class hotels or major chain properties. Not that there aren't many places to stay—there are hundreds of apartments and boardinghouses for retirees throughout the city, but for the most part, these establishments cater to seniors who stay the entire winter season, or even year round.

St. Pete's accommodations for vacationers, like its attractions, are spread out in all directions. In addition to the downtown area near the bayfront, you'll find good hotels in the areas to the north and south. There are also dozens of small family-run motels along major routes, such as U.S. 19, U.S. Alt. 19, and U.S. 92. See "South of Downtown" and "North of Downtown," below, for information on accommodations in these areas.

The listings below represent the best choices for short-term vacationers.

Expensive Hotels

PRESIDENTIAL INN, 100 2nd Ave. S. (P.O. Box 57306), St. Petersburg, FL 33701. Tel. 813/823-7552. 30 rooms. A/C TV TEL   **Directions:** On the bayfront, at the corner of 1st Street S., oppsite the Al Lang Stadium.

$ Rates (including Continental breakfast): $85–$130 single or double. AE, CB, DC, MC, V.   **Parking:** Free adjacent covered self-parking.

An unusual concept, this hotel occupies the fifth floor of City Center, a 12-story office complex. It caters primarily to business travelers, but discriminating vacationers who prefer a quiet out-of-the-way setting consider this a real find.

Guest rooms, each with a different view of the bay or city, are individually decorated with traditional "Old Europe"–style furnishings, dark woods, silk wall hangings, and tasteful artworks; bathrooms have separate phone extensions, plush terry cloth robes, and eight have private whirlpools.

Dining/Entertainment: Guests have access to the President's Club, a private dining room on the 10th floor of the building.

Services: Laundry valet service, secretarial service, and limousine service at supplementary charge.

Facilities: Living room–style lounge/reading room.

ST. PETERSBURG HILTON AND TOWERS, 333 1st St. S., St. Petersburg, FL 33701. Tel. 813/894-5000, or toll free 800/HILTONS. Fax 813/823-4797. 333 rooms. A/C TV TEL **Directions:** On the bayfront, opposite the Bayfront Center and Al Lang Stadium, between 4th Avenue S. and 3rd Avenue S.

$ Rates: $65–$125, single or double; $104–$134 for concierge level, single or double. AE, CB, DC, MC, V. **Parking:** Free outdoor self-parking, or valet parking ($2).

The downtown area's largest hotel, this 15-story tower is within walking distance of major attractions such as the Pier and Dalí Museum. A favored choice for business travelers, it is also an ideal place to stay if you plan to attend concerts or sporting events. The high ceiling and soft lighting of the lobby reflects the tone of this well-maintained hotel, with a rich decor of marble, crystal, and tile, antiques and artwork, leafy potted trees and plants.

The guest rooms, with wide-windowed views of the bay, are accessible by computer-card keys and furnished with traditional dark woods and floral fabrics, one king-size or two double beds, and an executive desk. The 15th-floor concierge-level rooms also provide shoeshine machines, personal bathrobes, and a mini TV/radio in each bathroom.

Dining/Entertainment: Charmene's is the hotel's full-service restaurant specializing in Continental cuisine. For light fare, try the First Street Deli; for a quiet drink with a piano background, settle into Brandi's Lobby Bar; and for a lively evening, it's Wings lounge with a biplane suspended from the ceiling.

Services: Room service, concierge desk, valet laundry service, baby-sitting service.

Facilities: Outdoor heated swimming pool, patio deck, Jacuzzi, sauna, gift shop, meeting rooms, car rental desk.

Moderate Hotels

BEACH PARK MOTEL, 300 Beach Drive NE, St. Petersburg, FL 33701. Tel. 813/898-6325. 26 units. A/C TV TEL **Directions:** On the bayfront, across from Straub Park and the Fine Arts Museum.
$ Rates: $35-$40 single, $40-$65, double. MC, V. **Parking:** Free outdoor parking.

A well-maintained two-story motel right in the heart of downtown with views of the Bayfront or the Pier. Guest rooms have one or two double beds, or one king-size bed, with a decor of light woods and bright Florida colors. Each has a small balcony or sitting area; 11 have small kitchenettes. There are no dining facilities, but dozens of eateries are within walking distance.

THE HERITAGE, 234 3rd Ave. N., St. Petersburg, FL 33701. Tel. 813/822-4814 or toll free 800/283-7829. 71 rooms. A/C TV TEL **Directions:** Three blocks north of Central Avenue, at the corner of 2nd Street N.
$ Rates (including Continental breakfast): $50–$75 single, $70–$95 double. AE, CB, DC, MC, V. **Parking:** Free, outdoors.

With a sweeping veranda, French doors, and tropical courtyard, this hotel in the heart of downtown has the feel of a Southern mansion. Situated on a quiet street in a residential neighborhood, yet within three blocks of the business district or bayfront, the Heritage dates back to the early 1920s. Previously known as the Martha Washington, it was completely restored in the late 1980s. Furnishings include period antiques in the public areas and in the guest rooms.

Dining/Entertainment: The Heritage Grille, with a unique decor of light woods, modern art, and an antique wooden bar from the Jefferson Davis mansion, offers a creative menu of "nouveau American" light regional cuisine.

Services: Room service, valet laundry service.

Facilities: Outdoor heated swimming pool, Jacuzzi, meeting rooms.

BED-AND-BREAKFAST

BAYBORO BED AND BREAKFAST, 1719 Beach Dr. SE, St. Petersburg, FL 33701. Tel. 813/823-4955. 3 rooms and 1 suite, all with private bath. A/C TV   **Directions:** South to 22nd Avenue S.; turn left and proceed east five blocks to Tampa Bay; turn left on Beach Drive SE; house is on the left.

$ Rates (includes Continental breakfast): $60–$65 single or double; $60 for one-bedroom suite for minimum three-day booking. MC, V.   **Parking:** Free, outdoors.

This city of beautiful old homes is surprisingly short on good bed-and-breakfast inns. This little gem, the pride and joy of proprietors Gordon and Antonia Powers, is situated in a residential area a few minutes south of Bayboro Harbor and the Port of St. Petersburg. A grand three-story Victorian, it looks right out onto the bay opposite Lassing Park, a stretch of natural terrain with a small beach. An Old South ambience prevails here, from the wide veranda with rockers and a swing to the cozy upstairs bedrooms with antique beds and armoires, fine linens, lace and embroidery, and quilts. Each guest room has a different view and an individual theme and decor (the Yellow Room, the Rose Room, the Captain's Room); there is also an apartment-size suite with separate sitting area and kitchen. Breakfast is served each day in the dining room or on the veranda. Smoking is permitted, on the veranda, but not in the house.

HOSTELS

ST. PETERSBURG AYH HOSTEL, 326 1st Ave. N., St. Petersburg, FL 33701. Tel. 813/822-4141. 32 beds. **Directions:** One block north of Central Avenue, between 3rd and 4th streets N.

$ Rates: $10 per person for AYH members; $28–$38 single, $32–$42 double for nonmembers. No credit cards.

Located in the heart of the city opposite Williams Park, this hostel is housed in the McCarthy Hotel, an eight-story landmark built in the 1920s as the Dennis Hotel, now listed in the National Register of Historic Places. Restored recently, it is equipped with an up-to-date fire alarm and sprinkler system and 24-hour security. The public areas include a clubby lobby, common kitchen, TV room, paperback library, and guest laundry. Bedrooms are basic; linen rental ($1 per day) is required for those without sleepsacks. Air conditioners, TVs, refrigerators and microwave ovens can also be rented at supplementary charges.

ST. PETERSBURG INTERNATIONAL HOSTEL, 215 Central Ave., St. Petersburg, FL 33701. Tel. 813/822-4095. 71 rooms.   **Directions:** Between 2nd and 3rd streets N.
$ Rates: $10 per person including linen.

This hostel is housed in the former Detroit Hotel, the city's first, built in 1888. It is now part of Jannus Landing, a complex of shops and restaurants along the main thoroughfare of the city. The public areas could use some refurbishing, but the clientele seems content. Bedrooms are Spartan but have lockers; some have air conditioning and adjoining bathrooms. Guest facilities include a laundry, common kitchen, and bicycle rentals.

2. SOUTH OF DOWNTOWN

A largely residential area and the home of Eckerd College, this section of St. Petersburg has a number of standard motels along the I-275 and U.S. 19 corridors. The advantage of staying in this area is that you'll have ready access to the Sunshine Skyway Bridge, linking St. Petersburg with Bradenton, Sarasota, and points south, and to the Pinellas Bayway, a causeway connecting the city of St. Petersburg with St. Petersburg Beach.

EXPENSIVE HOTEL

DAYS INN MARINA BEACH RESORT, 6800 34th St. S., St. Petersburg, FL 33711. Tel. 813/867-1151, or toll free 800/227-8045 or 800/325-2525. Fax 813/864-4494. 157 units, 6 suites. A/C TV TEL   **Directions:** Take I-275 south to Pinellas Point Drive (exit 3).
$ Rates: $49–$94 single or double; $75–$196 suites. AE, CB, DC, MC, V.   **Parking:** Free, outdoors.

Located on the southern tip of the city this sprawling two-story motel seems to have it all. Offering quick access to downtown, it sits in a tropical setting on 14 acres along the Tampa Bay shoreline just north of the Skyway Bridge. For good measure, it is also a year-round base of the Annapolis Sailing School.

Guest rooms have an airy decor with light woods, pastel tones, ceiling fans, plants, and private balconies or patios. Suites also offer kitchenettes. The highest-priced rooms face the bay, while others have views of the garden or pool.

Dining/Entertainment: Seafood restaurant, poolside bar, and snack bar.

Bayboro Bed & Breakfast **13**

Beach Park Motel **14**

Bilmar Beach
 Resort Hotel **1**

Bon-Aire Motel **9**

Breckenridge
 Resort Hotel **6**

Captain's Quarters Inn **2**

Colonial Gateway Inn **3**

Days Inn Island
 Beach Resort **4**

Days Inn Marina
 Beach Resort **12**

The Don CeSar **10**

The Heritage **18**

Passe-A-Grille
 Beach Motel **11**

Presidential Inn **15**

Sandpiper Beach Resort **5**

St. Petersburg
 AYH Hostel **17**

St. Petersburg Beach
 Hilton Inn **8**

St. Petersburg Hilton
 & Towers **14**

St. Petersburg International
 Hostel **16**

Tradewinds **7**

↑ To Tampa

(19)

2nd Ave. N.
0th Ave. N.
6th Ave. N.

62nd Ave. N.
58th Ave. N.
54th Ave. N.
50th Ave. N.
46th Ave. N.
42nd Ave. N.
40th Ave. N.
38th Ave. N.
34th Ave. N.
30th Ave. N.
26th Ave. N.
22nd Ave. N.
17th Ave. N.
13th Ave. N.
9th Ave. N.
5th Ave. N.

62nd Ave. N.

40th Ave. N.

55th St. N.
49th St. N.
40th St. N.
34th St. N.
31st St. N.
28th St. N.
16th St. N.
9th St. N.
4th St. N.
1st St. N.

Coffeepot Bayou

(19)

22nd Ave. N.

Crescent Lake

(595) (375)

ST. PETERSBURG

Central Ave.
3rd Ave. S.

Fairfield Ave.

9th Ave. S.

13th Ave. S.

17th Ave. S.

22nd Ave. S.

26th Ave. S.
30th Ave. S.
34th Ave. S.
38th Ave. S.

Mirror Lake

Florida Suncoast Dome

(175)

Al Lang Stadium

Albert Whitted Airport

The Pier

17 **18** **19**

16

15

14

52nd St. S.
48th St. S.
46th St. S.
31st St. S.
28th St. S.
25th St. S.
22nd St. S.
19th St. S.
16th St. S.
13th St. S.
12th St. S.
9th St. S.
7th St. S.
4th St. S.
2nd St. S.

13

Big Bayou

Clam Bayou

Lakeview Country Club

Lake Maggiore

Lake Maggiore Park

Boyd Hill Nature Park

37th St. S.
31st St. S.
34th St. S.

45th Ave. S.

Little Bayou

54th Ave. S.
58th Ave. S.
Royhanna Dr. 62nd Ave. S.

Pinellas Point Dr.

(19)
(275)

↓ **12**

Airport ✈

Facilities: Private bayside beach, two heated outdoor swimming pools, Jacuzzi, five tennis courts, fishing pier, marina, shuffleboard and volleyball courts, game room, children's playground, meeting rooms, coin-operated laundry.

3. NORTH OF DOWNTOWN

Almost a dozen fine hotels are clustered north of downtown St. Petersburg on Route 688 (Ulmerton Road), just after you cross over the Howard Frankland Bridge on I-275 heading south. Called the "gateway" area, this section is an entry corridor for traffic heading to St. Petersburg from the airport, from Tampa, and from points north, and the site of several large office parks, including Gateway Industrial Park. The St. Petersburg–Clearwater Airport is also smack in the middle of this busy hub. This hotel strip is wedged between north St. Petersburg and south Clearwater. The establishments listed here actually have Clearwater addresses, but, for all practical purposes, their location is most readily identified as "north St. Petersburg." For these reasons, we are describing these hotels here rather than in the Clearwater section, which, for the most part, concentrates on beachside accommodations.

And why would you want to stay on the northern rim of St. Petersburg, rather than downtown or near the beaches? First, there's the location: This is an ideal base if you want to fan out in several directions, dividing your time between St. Petersburg and Tampa attractions, all within a half hour's drive from this central point. Then there are the prices: Even the best choices fall into the moderate range. And since all of these hotels are geared primarily to weekday business traffic, you can also find some good bargains here on weekends or at other times (such as holiday periods) when business travel is low.

MODERATE HOTELS

COURTYARD BY MARRIOTT, 3131 Executive Drive at Ulmerton Rd., Clearwater, FL 34622. Tel. 813/572-8484, or toll free 800/321-2211. Fax 813/572-6991. 149 rooms. A/C TV TEL **Directions:** On Route 688, just west of the Howard Frankland Bridge.
$ Rates: $68 single, $78 double. **Parking:** Free, outdoors.

Opened in late 1989, this is one of the newest hotels along this strip. Set back from the road, it follows the usual layout for hotels in this chain, with guest rooms surrounding a central well-landscaped courtyard and lobby with café/lounge. Most of the bedrooms, furnished in light woods and pastel colors, have one king-size bed, but about one-third have two double beds.

Facilities: Outdoor heated swimming pool, indoor whirlpool, exercise room, coin-operated guest laundry.

DAYS INN, 3910 Ulmerton Rd., Clearwater, FL 34622. Tel. 813/573-3334 or toll free 800/325-2525. Fax 813/573-3334, ext. 163. 120 rooms. A/C TV TEL   **Directions:** On Route 688, one-half mile west of the Showboat Dinner Theater.
$ Rates (including Continental breakfast and free local phone calls)· $35–$65 single, $35–$75 double. AE, DC, DISC, MC, V. **Parking:** Free, outdoors.
A modern four-story hotel, short on frills but offers good value. Guest rooms, with standard furnishings, have two double beds or one queen-size bed, and some have sofa sleepers or recliners. Decor emphasizes contemporary sea-patterned fabrics and Florida art. There are no dining facilities on the premises, but a 24-hour restaurant is adjacent.
Facilities: Outdoor heated swimming pool, sundeck, meeting rooms.

HOLIDAY INN, 3535 Ulmerton Rd., Clearwater, FL 34622. Tel. 813/577-9100, or toll free 800/HOLIDAY. Fax 813/573-5022. 174 rooms. A/C TV TEL   **Directions:** On Route 688, next to Showboat Dinner Theater.
$ Rates: $51–$106 single, $61–$116 double. AE, CB, DC, DISC, MC, V.   **Parking:** Free, outdoors.
This five-story hotel is the largest along this busy strip, but set back from the main traffic flow. The high-ceilinged atrium-style lobby is impressive. Guest rooms are equally contemporary, with light colors and woods, most with two double beds and standard amenities. Some rooms have a king-size bed, work area, and a large desk.
Dining/Entertainment: Cascades Restaurant, on the lobby level, specializing in buffets; Club Marbles lounge, with live entertainment Tuesday through Saturday.
Services: Complimentary shuttle to Tampa airport.
Facilities: Outdoor heated swimming pool, whirlpool, lighted tennis court, exercise room, car-rental desk, gift shop, coin-operated guest laundry.

RADISSON INN, 3580 Ulmerton Rd., Clearwater, FL 34622. Tel. 813/573-1171 or toll free 800/333-3333. Fax 813/573-1171, ext. 402. 123 rooms. A/C TV TEL   **Directions:** On Route 688 directly across from the Showboat Dinner Theater.
$ Rates: $64–$104 single, $74–$114 double. AE, CB, DC, MC, V.   **Parking:** Free, outdoors.
Originally built as a top-of-the-line Comfort Inn, this three-story hotel has a futuristic architecture with geometric designs, wide columns, concealed lighting, and glass-walled elevators. The bedrooms, each with a king- or queen-size bed, have sand and sea tones, light woods, modern art, and large work areas with desks. Most rooms have patios or balconies that overlook a lushly landscaped central courtyard or the pool.

Dining: Girard's, a two-tiered café and lounge serving American dishes.

Facilities: Outdoor heated swimming pool, whirlpool, exercise room, meeting rooms.

INEXPENSIVE HOTELS

HAMPTON INN, 3655 Hospitality Lane at Ulmerton Road, Clearwater, FL 34622. Tel. 813/577-9200 or toll free 800/HAMPTON. Fax 813/572-8931. 118 rooms. A/C TV TEL **Directions:** On Route 688, just west of the Showboat Dinner Theater.

$ Rates (including Continental breakfast and free local phone calls): $44–$54 single, $49–$59 double. AE, CB, DC, DISC, MC, V. **Parking:** Free, outdoors.

Situated next to the Holiday Inn, in a convenient location, the Hampton Inn has limited services. It does have well-equipped contemporary guest rooms as well as outdoor heated swimming pool, whirlpool, sauna, lighted tennis court, exercise room, and coin-operated guest laundry. Restaurants are adjacent and nearby.

LA QUINTA INN, 3301 Ulmerton Rd., Clearwater, FL 34622. Tel. 813/572-7222 or toll free 800/531-5900. Fax 813/572-0076. 118 rooms. A/C TV TEL **Directions:** On Route 688 just east of the Showboat Dinner Theater.

$ Rates (including Continental breakfast): $46–$51 single, $51–$56 double. AE, CB, DC, DISC, MC, V. **Parking:** Free, outdoors.

This well-kept three-story hotel, decorated in the Spanish theme characteristic of this popular chain, offers contemporary-style rooms all with a choice of bed sizes and standard appointments. There is no dining facility on the premises, but a 24-hour restaurant is adjacent. Facilities on site include outdoor heated swimming pool, sauna, Jacuzzi, and exercise room.

4. ST. PETERSBURG BEACH

VERY EXPENSIVE HOTELS

THE DON CeSAR, 3400 Gulf Blvd., St. Petersburg Beach, FL 33706. Tel. 813/360-1881 or toll free 800/247-9810. Fax 813/360-1881, ext. 584. 227 rooms and suites. A/C TV TEL **Directions:** Take Pinellas Bayway via toll bridge west to Gulf Boulevard (Rte. 699).

$ Rates: $115–$215 single or double, $210–$545 suites, $600–$800 penthouse suites. AE, CB, DC, MC, V. **Parking:** Free, outdoors.

Often referred to as the Pink Palace, this local landmark sits majestically on 7½ acres of beachfront, rising to 8 and 10 stories in separate wings. A blend of Moorish and Mediterranean architecture and fairy-tale whimsy, it was built in 1928 by Thomas Rowe, a successful land speculator born in Boston but reared in Ireland—hence the structure's castlelike turrets, towers, and trim. Rowe named the hotel after his favorite hero, Don Caesar de Bazan, a character in the English opera *Maritana*. In its heyday, "the Don" was frequented by F. Scott Fitzgerald, Babe Ruth, Lou Gehrig, and countless other celebrities, but then it fell on hard times. Eventually restored and totally refurbished in the 1980s (for a reputed $15 million), it is today in a class by itself—on the National Register of Historic Places, and a showcase of classic high windows and archways, crystal chandeliers, marble floors, and original art works.

Guest rooms, most of which offer spectacular views of the Gulf of Mexico or Boca Ciega Bay, are first-rate, with high ceilings, traditional furnishings, marble bathrooms, and a decor blending rich tones of rose, teal, mauve, and sea green. Some rooms have balconies, and, for ultimate luxury, there are two penthouse suites with private terraces.

Dining/Entertainment: The King Charles Restaurant is the place to splurge on a gourmet dinner (see Chapter 5, "St. Petersburg Dining"). Other choices include Le Jardin, for seafood; Zelda's, a café by day and a lively music lounge at night; and the Beachcomber Bar and Poolside Grill for light snacks and drinks served outdoors.

Services: 24-hour room service, concierge desk, valet laundry service, children's program.

Facilities: Beach, outdoor heated swimming pool, Jacuzzi, exercise room, saunas, whirlpools, resident masseuse, lighted tennis courts, volleyball, gift shops, meeting rooms, and rentals for watersports.

TRADEWINDS, 5500 Gulf Blvd., St. Petersburg Beach, FL 33706. Tel. 813/367-6461 or toll free 800/237-0707. Fax 813/360-3848. 381 rooms and suites. A/C TV TEL **Directions:** Take Pinellas Bayway to Route 699. Turn right at light and head north; hotel is at 55th Avenue.

$ Rates: $82–$227 single or double, $134–$329 for one-bedroom suites. AE, CB, DC, DISC, MC, V. **Parking:** Free valet or self-parking.

This six-story hotel, opened in 1985, sits amid 13 acres of beaches, sand dunes, and tropical gardens, with rambling brick paths, meandering channels of water, boardwalks, Victorian gazebos, and wooden footpaths. Guests can glide along the waterways in motorized gondolas to their rooms or to dinner.

Bedrooms, which look out on the Gulf or the extensive grounds, have every up-to-date convenience, from computer-card keys to wet bars, coffee makers, toasters, contemporary furnishings, and private balconies. Suites have one, two, or three bedrooms, a separate living room, and kitchen with full appliances.

Dining/Entertainment: The top spot is the Palm Court (see Chapter 5, "St. Petersburg Dining"); dinner reservations include a complimentary gondola cruise. Other choices include the Flying Bridge, a casual beachside floating restaurant and bar; Reflections, a waterside piano lounge with fireplace and patio; the Fountain Square Deli; and Picnic Island, with gas grills for barbecues.

Services: Room service, valet laundry service, lifeguard, children's program.

Facilities: Three heated outdoor swimming pools, enclosed heated pool, saunas, whirlpools, paddleboats, fitness room, tennis, paddle tennis, racquetball, basketball, croquet, chess and checkers on a 7-by-7-foot board, bicycles, putting green, hammocks, beach and water volleyball, shuffleboard, game room, general store.

EXPENSIVE HOTELS

ST. PETERSBURG BEACH HILTON INN, 5250 Gulf Blvd., St. Petersburg Beach, FL 33706. Tel. 813/360-1811, or toll free 800/HILTONS. Fax 813/360-6919. 152 units. A/C TV TEL **Directions:** Take Pinellas Bayway to Route 699, turn right at light and head north; hotel is on left between 52nd and 53rd avenues.

$ Rates: $80–$145 single or double. AE, CB, DC, DISC, MC, V. **Parking:** Free, covered and outdoors.

Set back from the main road, this 11-story hotel stands out along the beachfront with a circular facade, a glass-walled elevator, and a revolving rooftop lounge. Guest rooms are furnished in contemporary light woods, bright colors, and some rattan touches, all with private balconies and expansive views of the Gulf of Mexico or Boca Ciega Bay.

Dining/Entertainment: C. Chan's Restaurant on the lobby level features mesquite-grilled steaks and seafoods. Schooner's Beach Bar and Grill serves snacks by the pool, and the revolving Bali Hai Lounge on the rooftop is the place to go for sunsets from every angle as well as for drinks and entertainment into the wee hours (Tues–Sun).

Services: Room service, lifeguard, valet laundry service.

Facilities: Outdoor heated swimming pool, whirlpool, game room, meeting rooms, and beach rentals for parasailing and water sports.

SANDPIPER BEACH RESORT, 6000 Gulf Blvd., St. Petersburg, FL 33706. Tel. 813/360-5551 or toll free 800/237-0707. Fax 813/360-3848. 159 rooms and suites. A/C TV TEL **Directions:** Take Pinellas Bayway to Route 699; turn right at light and head north; hotel is on the left at 60th Avenue.

$ Rates: $65–$166 single or double; $90–$218 suites. AE, CB, DC, DISC, MC, V. **Parking:** Free.

A well-landscaped tropical courtyard separates the two wings of this six-story hotel, set back from the main road with the older wing sitting right on the beachfront and the newer wing slightly to the side.

Rooms in the older wing have the best views of the beach, but rooms in the newer wing have private balconies. Pleasantly furnished with light woods, pastel tones, and touches of rattan, most units have two double beds (some have one king- or queen-size bed) as well as coffee makers, toasters, small refrigerators, and wet bars. Suites have separate living rooms with sofa bed and full kitchen.

Dining/Entertainment: Piper's Patio is a casual café with indoor and outdoor seating; the Sandbar offers frozen drinks and snacks by the pool. Also part of the hotel is the Brown Derby, a local chain restaurant and lounge.

Services: Room service, concierge desk, valet laundry service, child care.

Facilities: Beachfront heated swimming pool, enclosed heated swimming pool, two air-conditioned courts for racquetball, handball, and squash, volleyball, exercise room, shuffleboard, game room, gift shop/general store.

MODERATE HOTELS

BON-AIRE MOTEL, 4350 Gulf Blvd., St. Petersburg Beach, FL 33706. Tel. 813/360-5596. 80 rooms. A/C TV TEL **Directions:** Take Pinellas Bayway to Route 699, turn right at light and head north; motel is on the left between 43rd and 44th avenues.
$ Rates: $36–$130 single or double. MC, V. **Parking:** Free.
A sprawling motel complex with more than a dozen wings, this beachfront property offers a wide choice of size and type of accommodations, including basic motel rooms; half or full efficiency units with kitchenettes; deluxe apartments with separate bedroom and living room; and various other combinations. Rooms with waterfront views are the most in demand and command the highest rates. Some units can accommodate families of up to eight persons.

Facilities: Two outdoor heated pools, sundeck/terrace, barbecue grills, four shuffleboard courts, car-rental desk, coin-operated laundry.

BRECKENRIDGE RESORT HOTEL, 5700 Gulf Blvd., St. Petersburg Beach, FL 33706. Tel. 813/360-1833 or toll free 800/828-3371; toll free in Fla. 800/392-5700. Fax 813/367-2162. 196 units. A/C TV TEL **Directions:** Take Pinellas Bayway to Route 699; turn right at light and head north; hotel is on left at 57th Avenue.
$ Rates: $78–$125 single or double. AE, CB, DC, DISC, MC, V. **Parking:** Free.
Directly on the beach, and set back from the main road, this striking seven-story rectangular resort offers unobstructed views of the water for many miles. Guest rooms have kitchenettes, light wood furnishings, étagères, and lots of shelf and cabinet space. Some units have extra sofa beds or trundle beds.

Dining/Entertainment: The Surfside Restaurant frequently offers all-you-can-eat buffet-style dinners; the Beach Deli and poolside Tiki Hut are good for snacks and drinks, and the Peacock Lounge has nightly music for dancing.

Facilities: Outdoor heated swimming pool, two lighted tennis courts, hair salon, gift shop, game room, and rentals for cabanas and water-sports equipment.

COLONIAL GATEWAY INN, 6300 Gulf Blvd., St. Petersburg Beach, FL 33706. Tel. 813/267-2711 or toll free 800/237-8918; in Fla. 800/282-5245. Fax 813/367-7068. 200 units. A/C TV TEL   **Directions:** Take Pinellas Bayway to Route 699; turn right at light and head north; hotel is on left at 63rd Avenue.

$ Rates: $70–$110 single or double. AE, CB, DC, DISC, MC, V. **Parking:** Free.

Spread over a quarter mile of beachfront, this -shaped complex of one- and two-story units is a favorite with families. Rooms, most of which face the pool and a central landscaped courtyard, are contemporary, with light woods and beach tones; about half of the units are efficiencies with kitchenettes.

Dining/Entertainment: Sweden House restaurant is well known for its breakfast and dinner buffets; Etchings Lounge is a popular nightspot for music and occasional comedy shows; and the Swigwam beach bar offers light refreshments.

Facilities: Outdoor heated swimming pool, children's pool, shuffleboard, game room, parasail and water-sports rentals.

DAYS INN ISLAND BEACH RESORT, 6200 Gulf Blvd., St. Petersburg Beach, FL 33706. Tel. 813/367-1902, or toll free 800/544-4222 or 800/325-2525. Fax 813/367-4422. 101 rooms. A/C TV TEL   **Directions:** Take Pinellas Bayway to Route 699; turn right and head north; hotel is on left at 62nd Avenue.

$ Rates: $89–$149 single or double. AE, CB, DC, DISC, MC, V. **Parking:** Free.

Formerly the Beachcomber but now under the Days Inn banner, this two-story beachfront complex is being renovated and expanded as we go to press. Guest rooms have picture-window views of the beach or of a central courtyard with the pool, lush greenery, and fountains. About half of the units currently have kitchenettes.

Dining: An informal beach bar has long been a tradition here, and a new VIP sports bar and restaurant has just been added.

Facilities: Outdoor heated swimming pool, shuffleboard, game room, rental equipment for windsurfing and water sports.

INEXPENSIVE HOTELS

PASS-A-GRILLE BEACH MOTEL, 709 Gulf Way, St. Petersburg Beach, FL 33706. Tel. 813/367-4726 or toll free 800/537-3269; toll free in Fla. 800/544-4184. 25 studio efficiencies, 4 one-bedroom units, 1 two-bedroom unit. A/C TV **Directions:** Take Pinellas Bayway to Route 699; turn left at light and take Pass-A-Grille Way south to 7th Avenue; turn right, go one

block to Gulf Way; hotel is between 7th and 8th avenues on the right.
$ Rates: $37–$65 for studios and one-bedrooms, $60–$80 for two-bedroom units. MC, V. **Parking:** Free.

Situated across the street from the wide and sandy beachfront, this two-story motel is one of the few in the mostly residential strip at the southern tip of St. Pete Beach. Units have basic motel decor, with light woods and rattan furnishings, and most have small kitchenettes. It's ideal for those who prefer a quiet little stretch of seafront, yet close enough to the action of Gulf Boulevard. The complex includes a small café, and the popular Hurricane Restaurant is just a block away.

5. TREASURE ISLAND

MODERATE HOTEL

BILMAR BEACH RESORT HOTEL, 10650 Gulf Blvd., P.O. Box 9548, Treasure Island, FL 33706. Tel. 813/360-5531 or toll free 800/826-9724. Fax 813/360-2362. 69 rooms, 110 efficiencies with one or two bedrooms. A/C TV TEL **Directions:** From downtown St. Petersburg, take Central Avenue west; continue straight over Treasure Island Causeway to Treasure Island and Gulf Boulevard; turn left and hotel is on right.
$ Rates: $58–$90 single or double; $66–$125 for one-bedroom efficiencies; $110–$165 for two-bedroom efficiencies. AE, CB, DC, MC, V. **Parking:** Free.

Stretching for over 500 feet along the beachfront, this huge hotel stands out on the Treasure Island strip, with a complex of three-, four-, and eight-story buildings standing side-by-side. Most of the units have balconies or patios and many have kitchenettes.

Dining: An Old English theme dominates the decor and menu at the Grog Shoppe Restaurant and Lounge; light fare is also available outdoors at Don's Beach Bar.

Services: Room service, baby-sitting service.

Facilities: Two outdoor heated swimming pools, two sundecks, rooftop miniature golf, meeting rooms.

INEXPENSIVE HOTEL

CAPTAIN'S QUARTERS INN, 10035 Gulf Blvd., Treasure Island, FL 33706. Tel. 813/360-1659. 7 units. A/C TV TEL **Directions:** From downtown St. Petersburg, take Central Avenue west; continue straight over Treasure Island Causeway to Treasure Island and Gulf Boulevard; turn left and travel south for six blocks; hotel is on right.
$ Rates: $45–$60 single or double, $60–$70 for one-bedroom apartment. MC, V. **Parking:** Free.

In the endless row of motels along this small island, this is a real find—well-kept accommodations on the Gulf at inland rates. It is owned and operated by Ralph and Cathy Bassett, former opera singers, who completely remodeled and refurbished all of the units in 1989 with a nautical theme. Six of the rooms are efficiencies with new mini-kitchens (including microwave oven, coffeemaker, and wet bar or sink), and one unit has a separate bedroom and a full kitchen. The complex sits on 100 yards of beachfront and quiet tropical gardens, a much favored vantage point for watching the sun set each evening.

Facilities: Outdoor solar-heated freshwater swimming pool, sundeck, guest barbecues, library, guest laundry.

6. THE ISLAND OF SAND KEY

MADEIRA BEACH

EXPENSIVE HOTEL

HOLIDAY INN, 15208 Gulf Blvd., Madeira Beach, FL 33708. Tel. 813/392-2275, or toll free 800/HOLIDAY. Fax 813/392-2275, ext. 143. 147 rooms. A/C TV Tel **Directions:** Take Tom Stewart Causeway (Rte. 666) to Gulf Boulevard (Rte. 699), turn right and go one block; hotel is directly on the left.

$ Rates: $56–$136 single, $66–$146 double. AE, CB, DC, DISC, MC, V. **Parking:** Free.

Well-maintained and dependable, it sits on 600 feet of Gulf beach, on the north end of the Madeira strip. Guest rooms are contemporary in style, most with two double beds, some with one king-size bed. All have balconies or patios, with full beach views or side views.

Dining/Entertainment: Maxie's Restaurant overlooks the pool and the Gulf and frequently offers seafood buffets; Maxie's Lounge enjoys the same views and is popular at sunset; try the Tiki Bar by the pool for snacks and tropical beverages.

Services: Room service, valet laundry service, baby-sitting service.

Facilities: Outdoor heated swimming pool, lighted tennis court, meeting room, and rentals of cabanas, beach lounge chairs, and water-sports equipment.

INEXPENSIVE HOTEL

AU-RENDEZVOUS MOTEL, 160 145th Avenue, Madeira Beach, FL 33708. Tel. 813/347-5330. 9 units. A/C TV **Directions:** From downtown St. Petersburg, take Tom Stewart Causeway (Rte. 666) to Gulf Boulevard (Rte. 699); turn left and go five blocks, then turn left onto 145th Avenue; motel is mid-block on the left.

$ Rates: $40–$50 single or double for one-bedroom units; $45–$70 for two-bedroom units. No credit cards accepted. **Parking:** Free.

A half-block from Gulf Boulevard, this small family-run motel, though not on the beach, is within two blocks of the Gulf beach to the west and Boca Ciega Bay to the east. The Pesovinck family, owners since 1989, have refurbished each room with new carpeting and furniture, tiled bath with shower, and fully equipped kitchen and dining area. The guest units surround a central courtyard, with orange trees, gardens, and shuffleboard court.

NORTH REDINGTON BEACH

EXPENSIVE HOTEL

NORTH REDINGTON BEACH HILTON, 17120 Gulf Blvd., N. Redington Beach, FL 33708. Tel. 813/391-4000, or toll free 800/HILTONS or 800/447-SAND. Fax 813/391-4000, ext. 7777. 125 rooms. A/C MINIBAR TV TEL **Directions:** Take Tom Stewart Causeway (Rte. 666) to Gulf Boulevard (Rte. 699), make a right, and go north to hotel.

$ Rates: $84–$124 single or double. AE, CB, DC, DISC, MC, V. **Parking:** Free.

This six-story Hilton is one of the newest full-service hotels along the Redington Beach/Shores strip. Set on 250 feet of beachfront, surrounded largely by private homes and condominiums, it is built so that every room has a balcony and enjoys a water view, either of the Gulf of Mexico or of Boca Ciega Bay. Even-numbered rooms face the Gulf, and odd-numbered units look out on the bay. Guest rooms, accessible by computer-card keys, are decorated in pastel tones, with extra-large bathrooms, separate dressing areas, and full-length mirrored closets.

Dining/Entertainment: The multilevel Jasmine's offers outdoor and indoor dining (see Chapter 6, "St. Petersburg Dining). The poolside Tiki Bar is popular each evening for its sunset-watching festivities.

Services: Room service, valet laundry service.

Facilities: Outdoor heated swimming pool, sundeck, meeting rooms.

INDIAN ROCKS BEACH

MODERATE HOTEL

ALPAUGH'S GULF BEACH MOTEL APARTMENTS, 68 Gulf Blvd., Indian Rocks Beach, FL 34635. Tel. 813/595-2589. 16 rooms. And 1912 Gulf Blvd., Indian Rocks Beach, FL 34635. Tel. 813/595-9421. 17 rooms, 1 cottage. A/C TV TEL. **Directions:** Take Route 688 west to Gulf Boulevard; turn left for first location and right for second location.

$ Rates: $52–$74 single or double at either property. At 1912 Gulf Blvd., a one-bedroom cottage ($64–$78) and some two-bedroom suites ($70–$90) are available. MC, V. **Parking:** Free.

A long-established tradition in the Indian Rocks area, these two family-oriented motels are owned by Bob and Kay Alpaugh. Both properties sit beside the beach, with grassy central courtyard areas and fountains on each site. The rooms offer homey motel-style furnishings, and all units have a kitchenette and dining area. Units facing the courtyards are less expensive than Gulf-front units. Facilities at each location include coin-operated laundry, lawn games, picnic tables, and shuffleboard.

INEXPENSIVE HOTEL

PELICAN EAST & WEST, 108 21st Ave., Indian Rocks Beach, FL 34635. Tel. 813/595-9741. 8 units. A/C TV. **Directions:** Take Route 688 west to Gulf Boulevard; turn north and go to 21st Avenue; units are on right and left side of street.
$ Rates: $25–$50 single or double at Pelican East, $40–$70 single or double at Pelican West. MC, V. **Parking:** Free.
"P.D.I.P." ("Perfect Day in Paradise") is the motto at this dependable motel complex owned and operated for over 20 years by Mike and Carol McGlaughlin. Depending on your budget, you have a choice of two settings. Pelican East, which has four units, each with bedroom and separate kitchen, offers the best rates, but it is on the bay side of the road, 500 feet from the beach and with no water views. Pelican West sits right on the Gulf beachfront, offering four apartments, each with living room, bedroom, kitchen, and small patio, and unbeatable views of the Gulf. Either choice gives you access to the beach in a quiet, mostly residential neighborhood, but close to restaurants and shops in either direction.

BELLEAIR BEACH

MODERATE HOTEL

BELLEAIR BEACH RESORT MOTEL, 2040 Gulf Blvd., Belleair Beach, FL 34635. Tel. 813/595-1696. 42 units. A/C TV. **Directions:** Take the Belleair Causeway to Gulf Boulevard, turn right at light; hotel is ten blocks north, on the left between 20th and 21st streets.
$ Rates: $39–$65 single or double for motel rooms; $45–$69 for standard efficiencies; $55–$82 for Gulf-front efficiencies; $49–$72 for one-bedroom apartments. AE, MC, V. **Parking:** Free.
Belleair is undoubtedly the most unspoiled of all the beaches on Sand Key Island, with only a handful of motels discreetly placed along a mile-long corridor of spectacular and secluded Gulf-front homes. Shaded by leafy foliage and palms, this two-story complex is set back from the road, and sits right on the beach. The well-kept units, about two-thirds of which are equipped with kitchens, face either the central courtyard and outdoor pool or the Gulf. Other facilities include a patio sundeck, shuffleboard, barbecue grills, picnic tables, and coin-operated guest laundry.

7. CLEARWATER BEACH

EXPENSIVE HOTELS

ADAM'S MARK CARIBBEAN GULF RESORT, 430 S. Gulf-view Blvd., Clearwater Beach, FL 33515. Tel. 813/443-5714 or toll free 800/231-5858. Fax 813/443-5714, ext. 2490. 207 rooms. A/C TV TEL **Directions:** Take Route 60 and Memorial Causeway west to Clearwater Beach; turn left at Mandalay Avenue, then bear right to Gulfview Boulevard.

$ Rates: $92–$154 single or double. **Parking:** Free.

Sitting just south of the Clearwater public beach, this 14-story property makes good use of limited ground space. The building is divided into three sections—the lobby, restaurant, and lounges are on the ground floor, then there are three levels of parking, and the bedrooms occupy the upper floors. It does not have its own beach, but all of its rooms have balconies that overlook the Gulf waters.

Dining/Entertainment: Calico Jack's restaurant has rattan chairs and lots of leafy plants; Jack's Place lounge offers live music as well as backgammon tables; for outdoor refreshment, try the Calypso Galley or the Tiki Bar, both of which also offer steel drum music.

Services: Room service, valet laundry service.

Facilities: Outdoor heated swimming pool, whirlpool, children's pool, sundeck, game room, meeting rooms.

CLEARWATER BEACH HOTEL, 500 Mandalay Ave., Clearwater Beach, FL 34630. Tel. 813/441-2425 or toll free 800/292-2295. Fax 813/449-2083. 157 units. A/C TV TEL **Directions:** Take Route 60 and Memorial Causeway west to Clearwater Beach; turn right at Mandalay Avenue.

$ Rates: $75–$150, single or double; $100–$190 for suites. AE, CB, DC, MC, V. **Parking:** Free valet or self-parking.

Dating back more than 75 years but renovated and updated in 1988, this is one of the few hotels on Clearwater Beach that offers an "old world" atmosphere. The complex, which directly overlooks the Gulf, consists of the main six-story building plus smaller two- and three-story wings. The guest rooms, many of which have balconies, are decorated with floral fabrics and light woods or caned pieces, mirrored closets, separate vanities; some have small kitchens. The types of rooms vary, and so do the rates, according to location and views.

Dining/Entertainment: The Dining Room offers a Continental menu and views of the Gulf, as does the Schooner Lounge with its nautical decor, a classic oasis with cherry-wood bar and brass foot rail; outdoor service is provided at the Cabana Beach Bar.

Services: Room service, valet laundry service.

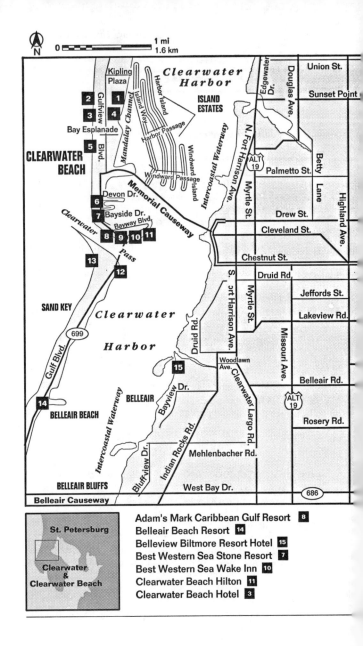

Adam's Mark Caribbean Gulf Resort 8
Belleair Beach Resort 14
Belleview Biltmore Resort Hotel 15
Best Western Sea Stone Resort 7
Best Western Sea Wake Inn 10
Clearwater Beach Hilton 11
Clearwater Beach Hotel 3

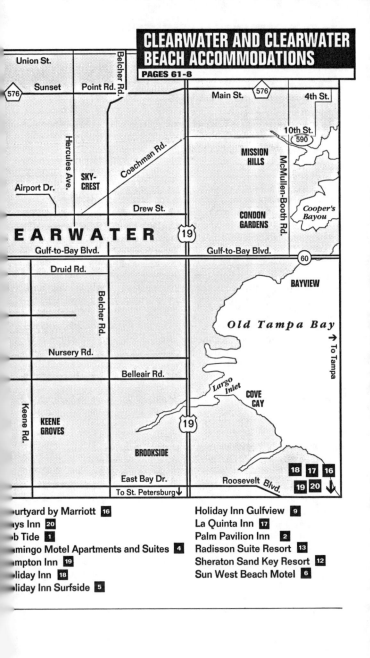

Courtyard by Marriott **16**
Days Inn **20**
Ebb Tide **1**
Flamingo Motel Apartments and Suites **4**
Hampton Inn **19**
Holiday Inn **18**
Holiday Inn Surfside **5**

Holiday Inn Gulfview **9**
La Quinta Inn **17**
Palm Pavilion Inn **2**
Radisson Suite Resort **13**
Sheraton Sand Key Resort **12**
Sun West Beach Motel **6**

Facilities: Heated outdoor swimming pool, sundeck, library, meeting rooms.

CLEARWATER BEACH HILTON, 715 S. Gulfview Blvd., Clearwater Beach, FL 34630. Tel. 813/447-9566 or toll free 800/HILTONS. Fax 813/447-9566, ext. 2168. 210 rooms, 7 suites. A/C TV TEL **Directions:** Take Route 60 and Memorial Causeway west to Clearwater Beach; turn left at Mandalay Avenue, and bear right onto Gulfview Boulevard.

$ Rates: $79–$165 single or double, $205–$325 for one-bedroom suites, $305–$425 for two-bedroom suites. AE, CB, DC, DISC, MC, V. **Parking:** Free.

Situated on the southernmost end of the beach strip and next to the Sand Key Bridge, this beachfront hotel is a favorite spot for watching the boat traffic between the Gulf and Clearwater Harbor. The complex consists of a 10-story tower and a 2-story beachfront lanai wing. The guest rooms, which have balconies or patios, are a pleasant blend of light woods, pastel tones, sea art, and plants. Units on the upper floors that offer a Gulf view cost more than rooms on the lower levels or those with views of the boulevard. Some rooms have refrigerators, and the one- and two-bedroom suites have parlor/sitting rooms.

Dining/Entertainment: The main restaurant indoors is Pippindale's, while Lane's Landing offers drinks and live music on a tropical outdoor deck by the pool. Other choices are the Barefoot Deli and The Cafe for outdoor dining.

Services: Room service, valet laundry service, baby-sitting service.

Facilities: Outdoor heated swimming pool, children's pool, playground, gift shop, meeting rooms, water-sport equipment rentals.

HOLIDAY INN GULFVIEW, 521 S. Gulfview Blvd., Clearwater Beach, FL 34630. Tel. 813/447-6461 or toll free 800/HOLIDAY. Fax 813/447-6461, ext. 132. 288 rooms. A/C TV TEL Take Route 60 and Memorial Causeway west to Clearwater Beach; turn left at Mandalay Avenue, then bear right onto Gulfview Boulevard.

$ Rates: $51–$156 single, $61–$166 double. AE, CB, DC, DISC, MC, V. **Parking:** Free.

At the south end of Clearwater Beach, this property overlooks Clearwater Pass and the Gulf of Mexico, but is not directly on the beach. The guest rooms, spread over a seven- and a nine-story wing, have fabrics in sea tones, light woods, and two double beds or one king-size bed. Most have balconies.

Dining/Entertainment: The main dining room, Currents, is especially popular for Friday-night seafood buffets; other outlets include the Coffee Shop, the poolside Tiki Bar, and Fanny's Lounge for music and dancing.

Services: Room service, valet laundry service.

Facilities: Outdoor heated swimming pool, children's pool, gift shop, barber and beauty salons, game room, car rental desk, meeting rooms.

HOLIDAY INN SURFSIDE, 400 Mandalay Avenue, Clearwater Beach, FL 34630. Tel. 813/461-3222 or toll free 800/HOLIDAY. Fax 813/461-0610. 427 rooms. A/C TV TEL **Directions:** Take Route 60 west and Memorial Causeway to Clearwater Beach; turn right onto Mandalay Avenue; hotel is on the left.

$ Rates: $70–$151 single, $80–$161 double. AE, CB, DC, DISC, MC, V. **Parking:** Free valet or self-parking.

This nine-story hotel dominates the north end of the Clearwater Beach strip, with 10 acres of beachfront property. It is also a center for water-sports equipment rentals and beach events and tournaments. The guest rooms, most of which have balconies, are decorated in tones of sea green or sandy beige, with light wood furniture. The largest rooms offer king-size beds and separate work or sitting areas.

Dining/Entertainment: The main restaurant is Reflections, while the Sand Bar offers snacks and drinks; the Lobby Bar has a piano lounge, and the Surf Club is a multilevel state-of-the-art disco.

Services: Room service, concierge desk, valet laundry service.

Facilities: Outdoor heated swimming pool, sundeck, volleyball, gift shop, car-rental desk, meeting rooms, and equipment rentals for windsurfing, parasailing, and other water sports.

RADISSON SUITE RESORT, 1201 Gulf Blvd., Clearwater Beach, FL 34630. Tel. 813/596-1100 or toll free 800/333-3333. Fax 813/595-4292. 220 suites. A/C MINIBAR TV TEL **Directions:** Take the Belleair Causeway to Gulf Boulevard, turn right and follow Gulf for approximately three miles to the top of Sand Key Island; hotel is on the right.

$ Rates: $99–$175 single or double. AE, CB, DC, DISC, MC, V. **Parking:** Free valet or self-parking.

Although technically at the northern tip of Sand Key Island, this 10-story all-suite hotel is considered part of the Clearwater Beach corridor. It is situated next to the Shops at Sand Key, a new bayside complex of 35 shops and two restaurants including the Clearwater Beach branch of the famous Tampa-based Spanish restaurant the Columbia. Opened in early 1990, this hotel is an expansive $40 million 7-acre property overlooking Clearwater Harbor, with the Gulf of Mexico just across the street.

Each suite, accessible by computer-card key, has a bedroom with balcony offering harbor views, as well as a complete living room, with sleep sofa, wet bar, and entertainment center/VCR/tape deck. The decor, of mostly pink and teal tones, includes mirrored closets, miniblinds, and bathrooms with cultured marble accoutrements.

Dining/Entertainment: On the lobby level, the Harbor Grille specializes in Florida seafood and Black Angus beef as well as pastas and stir-fried dishes at moderate prices; the Harbor Lounge, with indoor and outdoor seating, features a piano bar, while Kokomo's by the pool offers light fare and tropical drinks.

Services: Room service, laundry valet service, shuttle to Sand Key Park and beaches, child care.

Facilities: Outdoor heated free-form swimming pool with waterfalls, sundeck, sauna, exercise room, waterfront boardwalk, meeting rooms, and planned 60-slip marina.

SHERATON SAND KEY RESORT, 1160 Gulf Blvd., Clearwater Beach, FL 33515. Tel. 813/595-1611 or toll free 800/325-3535. Fax 813/596-8488. 390 rooms. A/C TV TEL **Directions:** Take the Belleair Causeway to Gulf Boulevard, turn right, and follow Gulf for approximately three miles to the top of Sand Key Island; hotel is on the left.

$ Rates: $69–$148 single or double. AE, CB, DC, DISC, MC, V. **Parking:** Free.

Situated along 32 Gulf-front acres of Sand Key Island's northern tip, this nine-story resort overlooks a 650-foot beach and is a favorite with water-sports enthusiasts. It is one of the largest properties in the area and plans call for it to double in size by 1992.

Guest rooms currently offer standard beach-toned decor with light wood furniture; accessibility is via computer-card keys. Despite the high-rise layout, ground-floor accommodations are available near the pool. All units have a balcony or patio with views of the Gulf or the harbor.

Dining/Entertainment: Rusty's Restaurant, just off the lobby, serves breakfast and dinner; for lighter fare, try the Island Cafe, at the east end of the lobby, or the Sundeck or Gazebo Bar outdoors; the rooftop Sky Lounge offers live music for dancing or comedy shows Monday through Saturday.

Services: Valet laundry service, baby-sitting service.

Facilities: Outdoor heated fresh-water swimming pool, Jacuzzi, three lighted tennis courts, volleyball court, gift shop, newsstand, game room, children's pool, playground, meeting rooms, rooms equipped for disabled guests, and rentals for paddle boats, sailboats, windsurfers, cabanas, umbrellas, and snorkeling equipment.

MODERATE HOTELS

BEST WESTERN SEA STONE RESORT, 445 Hamden Drive, Clearwater Beach, FL 34630. Tel. 813/441-1722 or toll free 800/444-1919, 800/528-1234. Fax 813/449-1580. 108 units. A/C TV TEL **Directions:** Take Route 60 west and Memorial Causeway to Clearwater Beach; at Mandalay Avenue, bear left onto Coronado Drive; at Brightwater Drive, make a left and then the next right onto Hamden Drive.

$ Rates: $45–$88 single or double, $88–$166 suites (suite rates include complimentary breakfast and cocktail hour). AE, CB, DC, DISC, MC, V. **Parking:** Free.

Formerly two properties, known individually as the Best Western Sea Stone Suites and the Gulfview Inn, this is now one resort on the bayfront, connected by a pool and sundeck. The focus is on the Sea Stone Suites, a six-story building of classic Key West–style architecture, newly opened in 1988 with 43 one-bedroom suites. A few steps away, the older five-story Gulfview wing has been revamped with a matching exterior and 65 refurbished bedrooms. The suites have kitchenettes and a living room.

Dining/Entertainment: Marker 5 Restaurant is on the lobby level of the suite complex, offering indoor and outdoor seating, and a lounge.

Facilities: Heated outdoor swimming pool, Jacuzzi, boat dock, coin-operated guest laundry, meeting rooms.

BEST WESTERN SEA WAKE INN, 691 S. Gulfview Blvd., Clearwater Beach, FL 34630. Tel. 813/443-7652 or toll free 800/444-1919, 800/528-1234. Fax 813/449-1580. 110 units. A/C TV TEL **Directions:** Take Route 60 west and Memorial Causeway to Clearwater Beach; turn left at Mandalay Avenue, then bear right to Gulfview Boulevard.

$ Rates: $52–$109 single or double, $60–$119 for efficiency units. AE, CB, DC, DISC, MC, V. **Parking:** Free.

This six-story property is on the southern tip of the strip, with its own beach. Its relatively small size provides a homey atmosphere but with all the modern and up-to-date amenities of a larger complex. Renovated in early 1990, it offers rooms with views of the water or of the boulevard; most have balconies and some have small kitchens.

Dining/Entertainment: Lenora's Restaurant, with inside and outdoor seating, is especially popular at sunset and for its menu of dishes prepared at the table; Lenora's Lounge offers nightly music, and the outdoor Tiki Bar serves snacks and tropical drinks.

Services: Valet laundry service, children's program.

Facilities: Outdoor heated swimming pool, sundeck, gift shop, meeting rooms, cabana rental.

INEXPENSIVE HOTELS

EBB TIDE, 621 Bay Esplanade, Clearwater Beach, FL 34630. Tel. 813/441-4421. 17 units. A/C TV TEL **Directions:** Take Route 60 west and Memorial Causeway to Clearwater Beach; turn right onto Mandalay Avenue, go six streets north, and turn right onto Bay Esplanade.

$ Rates: $40–$72 single or double, for one bedroom; $65–$100 for up to four guests for two bedrooms (three-day minimum). MC, V. **Parking:** Free.

Situated in the quiet northern end of Clearwater Beach in a mostly residential area, this two-story motel overlooks the bay, with its own fishing pier and boat dock. The rooms are furnished with standard motel-style pieces including two beds, plus some comfortable Florida-style rockers, rattan furniture, and tiled bathrooms. Each apartment has a balcony or patio that overlooks the bay as well as the on-site gardens. Facilities include outdoor swimming pool, shuffleboard, and barbecue grills.

**FLAMINGO MOTEL APARTMENTS AND SUITES, 450 N.
Gulfview Blvd., Clearwater Beach, FL 34630. Tel. 813/
441-8019.** 34 units. A/C TV **Directions:** Take Route 60 and
Memorial Causeway west to Clearwater Beach, turn right onto
Mandalay Avenue, go one block north to Papaya Street and turn
left; then turn right onto Gulfview Boulevard; hotel office is on left.
$ Rates: $25–$80 single or double. DISC, MC, V. **Parking:**
Free.

On a quiet street in the northern section of the beach strip, this
two-story multiwing motel has been owned and operated by the
Fletcher/Tiernan family for over 30 years. It sits on 160 feet of
beachfront, with two buildings directly on the Gulf and another
smaller building with two cottages, outdoor pool, and sundeck on
the opposite side of the street. Most units have kitchenette facilities
and can accommodate up to four adults. The rates depend on the
location and size of rooms. In addition to the pool, facilities include a
whirlpool, exercise room, barbecue grills, shuffleboard, and children's playground.

**PALM PAVILION INN, 18 Bay Esplanade, Clearwater
Beach, FL 34630. Tel. 813/446-6777.** 30 units. A/C TV
TEL **Directions:** Take Route 60 and Memorial Causeway west
to Clearwater Beach, turn right onto Mandalay Avenue, and go six
streets north; hotel is on left, next to the firehouse.
$ Rates: $38–$95 single or double, $55–$110 for efficiencies. AE,
CB, DC, MC, V. **Parking:** Free.

A stroll along the beachfront is bound to draw your attention to this
three-story art deco building, recently restored and artfully trimmed
in pink and blue. The lobby and guest rooms are also art deco.
Rooms in the front of the house face the Gulf, and those in the back
face the bay; four units have kitchenettes. Facilities include a rooftop
sundeck, direct access to the beach, and complimentary coffee in the
lobby.

**SUN WEST BEACH MOTEL, 409 Hamden Dr. S., Clearwa-
ter Beach, FL 34630. Tel. 813/442-5008.** 14 units. A/C
TV TEL **Directions:** Take Route 60 and Memorial Causeway
west to Clearwater Beach; at Mandalay Avenue, turn left onto
Coronado Drive; at Brightwater Drive make a left and then left
again onto Hamden.
$ Rates: $38–$58 single or double, $43–$75 for efficiencies. MC,
V. **Parking:** Free.

Overlooking the bay and yet only a two-block walk from the
Gulf beach, this modern one-story motel is a good value at any
time of year, thanks to careful maintenance by owners Allan
and Linda McLean. The rooms, which face either the bay or the
outdoor heated pool and sundeck, have contemporary resort-style
furnishings including ceiling fans; nine rooms are efficiency units with
small kitchens, and about half have extra sleep sofas. Facilities
include fishing/boating dock, shuffleboard, and guest laundry room.

8. NEARBY WORLD-CLASS RESORTS AND SPAS

VERY EXPENSIVE/EXPENSIVE

BELLEVIEW BILTMORE RESORT HOTEL, 25 Belleview Blvd., Belleair, FL 34616. Tel. 813/442-6171 or toll free 800/237-8947; toll free in Fla. 800/282-8072. Fax 813/441-4173. 310 rooms, 40 suites. A/C TV TEL   **Directions:** Take Route 60 west to downtown Clearwater; at Fort Harrison Avenue, turn left and drive south 1 mile to Belleview Boulevard; take a right and follow to entrance.

$ Rates: $65–$175 single, $80–$190 double, $145–$290 suites. AE, CB, DC, DISC, MC, V. **Parking:** Free.

Perched on a high bluff above Clearwater Bay, this massive multigabled white clapboard Victorian hotel enjoys an out-of-the-way setting amid lofty native pines, water oaks, cabbage palms, palmettos, citrus, orchids, holly, and jacarandas. Opened in 1897 with great fanfare by railroad magnate Henry Plant, it became almost overnight the favored western-Florida oasis for steel magnates, industrial barons, company presidents, and international celebrities such as the Duke of Windsor. Today, almost a century later, the "white Queen of the Gulf" is a landmark—beautifully preserved, restored, and expanded. Listed on the National Register of Historic Places, it is the largest occupied wooden structure in the world—with a fair sprinkling of Tiffany stained-glass windows, crown moldings, crystal chandeliers, and brass fixtures, not to mention its red-carpeted outdoor veranda.

The high-ceilinged guest rooms, many of which have paddle fans as well as air conditioning, are decorated in Queen Anne style, with dark wood period furniture including four-poster beds, armoires, and rich fabrics. Ever anxious to keep up with the times, the hotel has recently added a new European-style health spa with fitness instructors, masseuses and masseurs, cosmetologists, and nutritionists on staff. The complex also includes a full-service Cabana Club on Sand Key Island overlooking 500 feet of Gulf beach.

Dining/Entertainment: The main restaurants are the huge Tiffany Room, named for its skylight of original Tiffany glass, the Terrace Cafe for snacks, and the clubby Victoria's Parlor and Lounge.

Services: Complimentary shuttle service to the Cabana Club on the beach, room service, valet laundry service, and baby-sitting service.

Facilities: Two 18-hole championship golf courses on site and access to a third course; golf school, six tennis courts, pro shop, indoor and outdoor heated swimming pools, Jacuzzi, steam rooms, sauna, Swiss showers, workout gym, jogging and walking trails, shuffleboard, volleyball, croquet, bicycle rentals, boating, gift shop, florist, hair salon, fashion boutique, jewelry shop, newsstand, meeting rooms.

INNISBROOK, P.O. Drawer 1088, Tarpon Springs, FL 34688. Tel. 813/942-2000 or toll free 800/456-2000. Fax 813/942-2000, ext. 5004. 1000 units. A/C MINIBAR TV TEL **Directions:** From St. Petersburg, take U.S. 19 north, about 8 miles past the intersection of Route 60. The complex is south of Klosterman Road between U.S. 19 and U.S. 19A; there are entrances on U.S. 19 and on Klosterman.

$ Rates: $80–$173 single or double; $111–$207 for one-bedroom suites, $154–$335 for two-bedroom suites. Two-, three-, and five-night packages and meal plans available. AE, CB, DC, MC, V. **Parking:** Free.

Situated on 1,000 acres of rolling hills in upper Pinellas County, this sprawling resort sits between two very busy thoroughfares, yet it is in a world by itself. No traffic sounds are heard, just the sounds of birds and the peaceful hum of rustling natural foliage, the ripples of the lakes, the stirring of nearby wildlife. All this, and world-class golf and tennis facilities too (it's the home of the Innisbrook Golf Institute and the Australian Tennis Institute).

Accommodations are spread throughout the complex in 28 three-story mansard-roofed lodges, each named for a famous golf course around the world (from St. Andrews and Royal Aberdeen, to Augusta and Pine Valley). All units have balconies or patios, and are nestled around the resort's three golf courses, one of which (the Copperhead Course) is ranked among the top courses in the world. Each unit also has a fully equipped kitchen and living area, and the larger layouts have one or two separate bedrooms.

Dining/Entertainment: Each golf clubhouse offers a full-service dining room, a café-style facility for light meals, and a bar/lounge with evening entertainment. For gourmet meals, the top spot is the Vintage Dining Room in the Island Clubhouse; for mesquite-grilled or barbecued dishes, try the Copperhead Corral and Lounge, while the Sandpiper Dining Room is known for its elaborate buffet meals. (*Note:* Meals and lounge services are only available to overnight guests).

Services: Complimentary on-site tram service and beach-shuttle service, airport shuttle service ($15), concierge desk, room service, valet laundry service, children's activity program, baby-sitting service.

Facilities: One 27-hole championship golf course and two 18-hole championship courses, practice tee, driving range, six outdoor heated swimming pools, health club, three clubhouses and pro shops, and a tennis and racquetball center with 18 courts (seven lighted), children's play area, game room, fishing-rod and bicycle rentals, jogging track, nature trails, flower arranging and handcraft workshops, gift shops, men and women's hair salons, meeting rooms.

SAFETY HARBOR SPA AND FITNESS CENTER, 105 N. Bayshore Dr., Safety Harbor, FL 34695. Tel. 813/726-1161 or toll free 800/237-0155. Fax 813/726-4268. 212 rooms. A/C TV TEL **Directions:** Take U.S. 19 north to Route 60 and

turn right (east); after 1 mile, turn left onto Bayshore
Boulevard, which eventually becomes Bayshore Drive, and
travel north for 2 miles; the spa is on the right.

$ **Rates:** $165–$222 single, $242–$330 double (includes all meals
and unlimited daytime tennis and on-site golf driving range). Four-
and seven-day fitness packages, tennis packages, and beauty
makeover plans, available, as well as two-night fitness or beauty
weekends. AE, CB, DC, MC, V. **Parking:** Free.

Founded in 1926 and completely renovated in the late 1980s, this
modern 35-acre spa on Old Tampa Bay is not just another artificial
fitness complex—it is a health resort built around five natural
sulfur-filled springs, reputed to have been discovered in 1539 by
Hernando de Soto and named Espíritu Santo or "Springs of the Holy
Spirit." For many centuries, believers seeking cures were drawn to
these mineral waters.

Today you can not only soak in or sip the natural waters, but also
take part in a program of up to 35 different activities. The regimen
includes swimming, rowing, walking, tennis, golf, and bicycling, as
well as water exercise, low-impact aerobics, calisthenics, and circuit
weight training. One of the newest options is BoxAerobics, a rigorous
training workout similar to the program used by professional boxers;
guests often find themselves working out alongside world-class
fighters.

Most of the accommodations are in a six-story main building and
three-story wing, all with patios or balconies overlooking the bay; 20
additional rooms with kitchenettes are available across the street in a
newly renovated building. Rooms are decorated in tropical style, with
original artwork, rattan furnishings, and brilliant colors.

Dining/Entertainment: Enjoy nutritious 900-calorie-a-day international spa cuisine or order à la carte in the skylit dining room
with an exotic bird mural. Other choices include a juice bar and a
lounge where evening concerts, movies, lectures, and seminars are
held.

Services: Complimentary airport shuttle, room service, valet
laundry service.

Facilities: Heated indoor and outdoor swimming pools, Finnish
saunas, Turkish steam baths, Jacuzzis, seven clay tennis courts,
exercise equipment, golf driving range, full-time medical staff,
on-premises Lancôme Skin Care Institute, quit-smoking program,
meeting rooms, fashion boutique, gift shop/newsstand, and coin-
operated guest laundries.

ST. PETERSBURG DINING

From elegant candlelit dining rooms to panoramic waterfront restaurants or casual cafés, St. Petersburg has a wide variety of good eating experiences. There is plenty of international fare—from Japanese steakhouses to Swiss fondue places, as well as the cuisines of Italy, France, Germany, Spain, Scandinavia, and all parts of the U.S., especially regional Southern dishes.

But, most of all, the St. Petersburg area is outstanding for seafood—fresh from Gulf waters and beyond. You'll have a choice of local favorites like grouper, pompano, snapper, stone crabs, or rock shrimp, as well as piscatorial delights from other shores, such as Maine lobster, Louisiana crawfish, and crab legs and salmon from the Northwest. Many restaurants sell so much seafood that they operate their own fishing boats, and literally take the day's catch from the dock to the kitchen in a matter of hours. Fresher fish is hard to find anywhere. Stick with the daily specials and you'll always have something to rave about.

Before you set out to satisfy your appetite, here are some points to remember:

Reservations: Particularly for dinner, reservations are always advised and often required at the more elegant establishments. However, a good number of the moderate or inexpensive restaurants do not take reservations. They base their operations on high volume, requiring a first-come, first-served policy. You might have to stand in line, but it's usually well worth the wait.

Taxes: All restaurant charges are subject to 7% state and county tax.

Tipping: Many of the older and more formal restaurants in the St. Petersburg area add a gratuity or service charge to the bill, usually

15% to 18%. If this is the case, it will be clearly stated on the menu. Always ask if you are in doubt.

Alcoholic Beverages: Most restaurants serve cocktails, wine, and other alcoholic beverages with meals, and many also have separate bar/lounge areas. If a place serves only beer and wine, or does not serve alcoholic beverages but permits guests to bring their own, this is specified in our description.

Prices: In dollar terms, St. Pete–area restaurants run the gamut —you can spend $50 and up for a dinner at the top spots, or confine the tab to under $10 with no problem at all. For the restaurants we describe, we have used the following guidelines for average prices of most entrées on the menu:

Very Expensive	Over $25
Expensive	$17–$25
Moderate	$10–$17
Inexpensive	Under $10

In the majority of St. Petersburg–area restaurants, the price of an entrée includes a house salad or soup, breads or rolls, vegetables, and potato, rice, or pasta. To estimate the price of a complete meal with appetizer, dessert, coffee, tax, and tip, you can usually double the cost of the entrée. So, if your entrée is $12, a complete dinner will probably be around $24 for one or about $50 for two.

"Early-Bird" Dining: Like many Florida cities, St. Petersburg is a great exponent of the "early-bird dinner"—a three- or four-course evening meal at a set price, usually costing $5.95 to $9.95 and served between 3:30pm and 6:30pm. Menu choices may be limited, but by being an "early bird," you can sample even the most expensive restaurants and rarely pay more than $10 for a complete dinner. As a rule, such specials and rates change often, so we have not specified early-bird prices for the restaurants we describe. The best strategy is to inquire about early-bird policies when calling for a reservation. Although most restaurants are eager to feature these special prices to draw customers before peak dining hours, a few places may not tell you about early-bird specials unless you ask.

1. DOWNTOWN

EXPENSIVE

BASTA'S CANTINA D'ITALIA RISTORANTE, 1625 4th St. S. Tel. 894-7880.
   Cuisine: NORTHERN ITALIAN/CONTINENTAL. **Reservations:** Suggested, especially for dinner. **Directions:** South of Central Avenue, between 16th and 17th avenues S.
$ **Prices:** Entrées $5.95–$9.95 at lunch, $13.95–$19.95 at dinner. AE, CB, DC, MC, V.

Open: Mon–Fri 11am–3pm and 5–10pm, Sat 5–10pm.

Situated southwest of the Dalí Museum, this classy little enclave is slightly off the beaten track but worth a detour. The decor, a blend of art deco and Mediterranean influences, is capped with fine linens and soft lighting.

The main attraction, of course, is the food, and chef/owner Frank Basta earns frequent accolades for using natural ingredients and fresh herbs, making all pastas on the premises, and cooking all food to order. His specialties include seafood Porto Fino (lobster, shrimp, clams, scallops, and crab legs poached in white sauce over angel hair pasta), and filet mignon Napoléon (filet of beef topped with mozzarella cheese, mushrooms, and herbs, and sprayed with brandy), as well as veal saltimbocca, shrimp scampi, lobster tails, steak Diane, and rack of lamb.

PETER'S PLACE, 200 Central Ave. Tel. 822-8436.

Cuisine: AMERICAN/INTERNATIONAL. **Reservations:** Strongly advised, especially for dinner. **Directions:** on 2nd level of Barnett Tower, between 2nd and 3rd avenues.

$ Prices: Entrées $4.95–$9.95 at lunch, $11.95–$19.95 at dinner. AE, MC, V.

Open: Tues–Sat 11:30am–2pm and 6–9pm.

For almost 20 years at its original Beach Drive location, this award-winning restaurant was *the* place to dine in downtown St. Petersburg. As we go to press, it is moving to more spacious quarters in the city's tallest building, and owner Peter Kersker is trading his former cozy café-style setting for a bold Egyptian palace theme. The decor includes 13-foot-high ceilings, a skylight 32 feet above the floor, wall murals with hieroglyphics and exotic desert landscape scenes, and furnishings with leopard, zebra, and giraffe motifs. The menu promises to be more "American," but no doubt Peter will continue to offer some of his tried-and-true international favorites, such as Madras curry shrimp (from India), veal piccata (from Italy), baked stuffed shrimp with crabmeat (from Florida), baked breast of capon stuffed with Brie, almonds, and apple-raisin chutney (from England), or roast duckling with Amaretto and brandied peaches (from France). Lunch items range from salads and chilled seafood platters to charbroiled burgers, crêpes, and pastas. Also serves afternoon tea, Sunday brunch, and weekday breakfasts. Call for latest details when you visit.

MODERATE

THE COLUMBIA, 800 2nd Ave. NE. Tel. 822-8000.

Cuisine: SPANISH. **Reservations:** Recommended for dinner. **Directions:** Follow signs to the Pier; restaurant is on the fourth floor.

$ Prices: Entrées $4.95–$8.95 at lunch, $8.95–$16.95 at dinner. AE, CB, DC, MC, V.

Open: Mon–Sat 11am–11pm, Sun noon–11pm.

Opened in 1988, this branch of the landmark Tampa restaurant occupies a prime position in the St. Pete Pier complex. Although it may lack some of the charm and antique decor of the original location, it excels by offering unequaled views of the Gulf of Mexico and the St. Petersburg skyline. See Chapter 10, "Tampa Dining: Ybor City," for a description of the cuisine.

FROMMER'S SMART TRAVELER—RESTAURANTS

QUESTIONS TO ASK IF YOU'RE ON A BUDGET

1. Do you serve an "early bird" dinner? If so, what are the prices and the hours of service?
2. Is the service charge included in the bill's total?
3. Is the 7% state and county tax included in the total?
4. Do you have any specials today? What are the prices?
5. (If you're traveling with kids) Is there a children's menu?

INEXPENSIVE

ALESSI CAFE AT THE PIER, 800 2nd Ave. NE. Tel. 894-4659.
   Cuisine: AMERICAN.   **Reservations:** Not needed, except for large parties.   **Directions:** Follow signs to the Pier; restaurant is on the ground level, on the left in the rear.
$ Prices: Entrées $4.95–$11.95, lunch or dinner. AE, MC, V.
   Open: Mon–Thurs 11am–11pm, Fri–Sat 11am–midnight, Sun 11:30am–10pm.
This casual, waterside setting combines a raw bar, a café, and an outdoor daiquiri bar. The all-day menu features creative salads (such as Mediterranean spinach, chicken tarragon, or seafood Caesar), French-bread pizzas, sandwiches, burgers, ribs, seafood, steaks, and chicken dishes (from char-grilled to Szechuan-style).

CHA CHA COCONUTS, 800 2nd Ave. NE. Tel. 822-6655.
   Cuisine: AMERICAN.   **Reservations:** Not necessary.   **Directions:** Follow signs to the Pier; take elevator to the fifth floor.
$ Prices: Entrées $3.95–$7.95 lunch or dinner. AE, CB, DC, MC, V.
   Open: Mon–Thurs 11am–midnight, Fri–Sat 11am–1am, Sun noon–11pm.
Billed as a tropical bar and grill, this informal spot sits on the top floor of the Pier complex, offering panoramic views of both the Gulf of Mexico and the St. Petersburg skyline. It's a great vantage point from which to watch the fishermen and boaters or to sip a tropical

drink as the sun sets. Live music is usually on tap after dark and the menu is appealing at any hour of the day—burgers, fish sandwiches, chowders and chilis, and finger foods such as peel-and-eat shrimp, oysters on the half-shell, and chicken wings. All items on the menu are also available for take-out. For other locations (see "Clearwater Beach," below in this chapter, and Chapter 10, "Tampa Dining: Harbour Island.")

2. SOUTH OF DOWNTOWN

MODERATE

LEVEROCK'S, 4801 37th St. S. Tel. 864-3883.
   Cuisine: SEAFOOD. **Reservations:** Not accepted. **Directions:** Take U.S. 19 south to 46th Avenue S. and turn right; go one block to 37th Street S. and turn left.

$ **Prices:** Entrées $3.95–$6.95 lunch, $6.95–$12.95 dinner. AE, CB, DC, MC, V.

   Open: Daily 11:30am–10pm.

Dating back to 1948 and synonymous with the freshest of seafoods at affordable prices, Leverock's now operates four fish houses, each unique in its way, in the St. Petersburg area. In our view, this location (the newest) on the Maximo Moorings is the best. Wide floor-to-ceiling windows frame views of Boca Ciega Bay and the yachts along the docks. If you like seafood, you won't be disappointed here (the chain has its own fleet of fishing boats). You may have to wait on line at busy times.

Selections range from 10 different shrimp dishes, to salmon Wellington, grouper Florentine, halibut stir-fry, and crab-stuffed turbot, to a "captain's platter" of shrimp, scallops, fish, crab legs, and Danish lobster tails. Only Caribbean lobster tails, surf-and-turf, and king crab legs are slightly higher than the general entrée price range. Steaks, chicken cordon bleu, and baby back ribs round out the menu. The lunch choices include burgers, salads, and sandwiches (don't miss Leverock's version of the traditional "club," stuffed with tender bay shrimp).

Surprisingly, the original Leverock's is not on the water at all, but north of downtown St. Petersburg at 7000 U.S. 19 at Park Boulevard, Pinellas Park (tel. 526-9188), convenient if you are traveling between St. Pete and Tampa. The other two locations are on the water and are described under our listings for St. Petersburg Beach and Madeira Beach (see "St. Petersburg Beach" and "Island of Sand Key," below in this chapter).

ST. PETE FISH HOUSE, 1080 Pasadena Ave. S. Tel. 345-4670.

Cuisine: SEAFOOD. **Reservations:** Not accepted, except for parties of 10 or more. **Directions:** Take 5th Avenue N. west to Pasadena Avenue; turn left and restaurant is at junction of Pasadena Avenue and Gulfport Boulevard.

$ Prices: Entrées $2.95–$6.95 at lunch, $7.95–$14.95 at dinner, with lobster and crab at market price. CB, DC, MC, V.

Open: Daily 11:30am–10pm.

Situated next to the Pasadena Shopping Center, this is a large restaurant with five dining rooms. A favorite with fish-lovers since 1974, it does not offer any spectacular waterside views, but the Corey Avenue Causeway to St. Petersburg Beach is less than a half-mile to the south and many of the windows do look out onto well-tended gardens. The decor is nautical with fish tanks, ship's wheels, and paintings of sea scenes.

The menu offers an extensive array of seafood, from catfish to crab or clams, from sole or scrod to salmon and snapper. All dishes are cooked to order—your choice of broiled, fried, baked, blackened, or sautéed. In addition, there are a dozen different shrimp dishes and at least three kinds of lobster (Maine, Caribbean, Danish). You can also create your own platters by selecting different kinds of seafood. Steaks, prime ribs, ham, chicken, and barbecued ribs are also available. The lunch choices are similar, but also include seafood salads, fish sandwiches, and burgers. Worth noting is the fact that this restaurant has one of the most extensive "early-bird" menus in the entire St. Pete/Tampa area, offering not just three or four choices, but over 20 entrée selections, pegged at about half the normal dinner prices.

INEXPENSIVE

TED PETERS' FAMOUS SMOKED FISH, 1350 Pasadena Ave. S. Tel. 381-7931.

Cuisine: SMOKED SEAFOOD. **Reservations:** Not accepted. **Directions:** Take 5th Avenue N. west, turn left at Pasadena Avenue, and restaurant is south of the Pasadena Shopping Center, on the approach to the Corey Avenue Causeway leading to St. Petersburg Beach.

$ Prices: Entrées $3.95–$7.95, lunch or dinner. No credit cards.

Open: Wed–Mon 11:30am–7:30pm.

Your nose tells you when you are near this rustic little roadside stand and its adjacent smokehouse—aromas of smoking fish fill the air. The menu is limited, basically just smoked mackerel or mullet, but people drive for miles to get their fill. It's totally informal and casual, with seating at picnic tables or along the counter. The smoked fish is served with German potato salad. If you feel like something lighter, there are sandwiches filled with smoked-fish spreads. The spreads are so popular that they are also sold by the quart. Burgers are also available, as is beer and wine.

3. NORTH OF DOWNTOWN

MODERATE

PEPIN'S, 4125 4th St. N. Tel. 821-3773.
　　Cuisine: SPANISH. **Reservations:** Recommended. **Directions:** North of downtown, between 41st and 42nd avenues N.
$ Prices: Entrées $4.95–$9.95 at lunch; $10.95–$17.95 at dinner. AE, MC, V.
　　Open: Mon–Fri 11am–11pm, Sat 5–11pm, Sun 5–10pm.

A mainstay of fine dining along the busy Fourth Street corridor, this inland restaurant was the first of two current locations (the other is on the beach strip at Indian Shores). The setting is reminiscent of an Iberian villa, with lots of red tones and dark wrought-iron trim.

　　The menu reflects the restaurant's motto of *"Al pan, pan y al vino, vino,"* which roughly translated means food in its purest form, with no artificial ingredients or additives. The bread is freshly baked on the premises every morning, the fish comes from nearby waters, and the meats are aged and cut daily. Specialties include Spanish favorites such as salmon Almendrina (with orange mustard sauce), paella, and chicken with yellow Valencia rice, as well as local and international fare, from whole Florida lobster and pompano en papillote, to Châteaubriand and rack of lamb. Tapas, which can be a meal in themselves at lunch, range from $3.95 to $5.95.

ARIGATO JAPANESE STEAKHOUSE, 3600 66th St. N. Tel. 343-5200.
　　Cuisine: JAPANESE. **Reservations:** Recommended on weekends. **Directions:** Northwest of downtown, near the Tyrone Boulevard shopping area.
$ Prices: Entrées $7.95–$16.95. AE, MC, V.
　　Open: Mon–Sat 5–10pm, Sun 4–9pm.

A fun place for adults and kids alike, this is a typical Japanese steakhouse where the chef is also the star performer. Groups of 10 guests sit around a teppanyaki table for each meal. You may not know all the people at your table as the meal begins, but such formalities certainly don't prevent you from sharing a memorable dining experience. A chef assigned to your table then prepares hibachi steak, sukiyaki chicken, shrimp, lobster, scallops, or whatever you order right before your eyes, with a dash of spice and a flash of cutlery. A favorite selection is ichiban, a mix of filet mignon, shrimp, and chicken. In all, seven courses are served, including appetizer, soup, salad, fried rice, and vegetables.

　　Other locations in the area include one at 1500 U.S. 19 N. (tel. 799-0202), Clearwater, and one in Tampa (see Chapter 10, "Tampa Dining").

FAT JACQUE'S CAJUN CAFÉ, 11270 4th St. N. Tel. 578-0158.

    Cuisine: CAJUN/CREOLE. **Reservations:** Recommended
Directions: North of downtown, between 112th and 113th avenues N., in the Paragon Crossing Shopping Center.

$ Prices: Entrées $4.95–$13.95 lunch or dinner. AE, MC, V.

    Open: Mon–Sat 11am–midnight, Sun 10am–midnight.

Located between the approaches to the Gandy and Howard Frankland bridges, this popular eatery adds a touch of New Orleans to a growing business/residential sector of the city. The decor is bright and airy, with lots of hanging plants, wrought-iron fixtures, Tiffany-style lamps, and brass trim. Specialties include shrimp Creole, deep-fried crawfish tails, grilled redfish, crawfish étouffé, roast Cajun duck, red beans and rice, and blackened "catch of the day." In addition, there is a "light" menu for those who want to ease up on cholesterol and calories, with such choices as Caribbean fruit platter, shrimp melt, spicy chicken salad, and quiche of the day. Pasta, burgers, and sandwiches are also available, including hot roast beef po-boys, club croissants, and Louisiana-style muffalatta (salami and ham on a round hard roll).

As we go to press, a companion restaurant of the same name and style is opening along the Gulf strip at 9550 Blind Pass Rd., St. Petersburg Beach (tel. 367-8384); a third location is in Tampa (see Chapter 10, "Tampa Dining").

MELTING POT, 2221 4th St. N. Tel. 895-6358.

    Cuisine: SWISS. **Reservations:** Recommended **Directions:** North of downtown, between 21st and 22nd avenues N., and two blocks north of Sunken Gardens.

$ Prices: Entrées $8.95–$14.95. AE, MC, V.

    Open: Sun–Thurs 5–11pm, Fri–Sat 5pm–midnight.

The fondue craze of the past is alive and thriving at this rustic chalet-style spot. The menu is simple, with emphasis on bubbling pots of Swiss and cheddar cheeses and baskets filled with bite-size pieces of bread, fruit, and vegetables. You simply skewer a piece of bread, a grape, green bean, or various other choices, and then submerge and coat it with the creamy melted cheeses.

For variety, fondue-style cooking is also available using chicken, beef, or seafood, accompanied by a selection of spicy and piquant dipping sauces. Top off the meal with a selection from a variety of white and dark chocolate fondues for dessert ($4.95–$9.95 for two to four people).

OUTBACK STEAKHOUSE, 4088 Park St. Tel. 384-4329.

    Cuisine: AUSTRALIAN/AMERICAN. **Reservations:** Not accepted. **Directions:** Northwest of downtown, at the junction of Tyrone and Bay Pines boulevards.

$ Prices: Entrées $6.95–$15.95. AE, DC, MC, V.

    Open: Sun–Thurs 4:30–10:30pm, Fri–Sat 4:30–11:30pm.

If you're a *Crocodile Dundee* fan, you're sure to enjoy this casual, come-as-you-are Aussie-theme restaurant. In fact, you'll probably

St. Petersburg

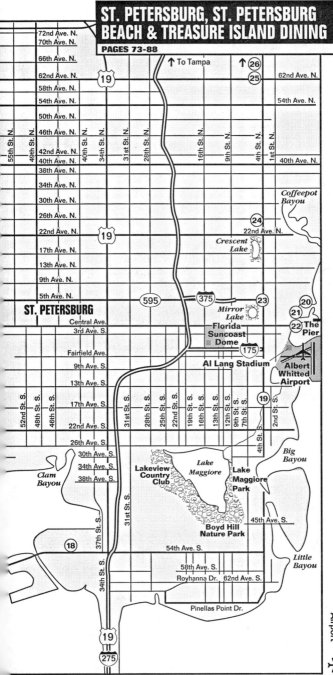

catch yourself saying "G'day" before the meal's end. The menu
features such down-under dishes as chicken and ribs grilled "on the
barbie," Jackeroo pork chops, the Melbourne (a hefty porterhouse
steak), Brisbane shrimp sautée, and "Botany Bay fish o' the day." The
libation list includes lots of imported beers and wines from Australia.

Farther north, between St. Pete and Clearwater, there is another
location at 3690 E. Bay Dr., Largo (tel. 538-9499), and there are
branches both north and south of Tampa Airport (see Chapter 10,
"Tampa Dining").

**THE WATERFRONT STEAK HOUSE, 8800 Bay Pines Blvd.
N. Tel. 345-5335.**
    Cuisine: AMERICAN. **Reservations:** Not accepted. **Di-
rections:** Follow Tyrone Boulevard north toward the causeway to
Madeira Beach; restaurant is between Lighthouse Point Marina
and Veterans Memorial Park.
$ Prices: Entrées $3.95–$6.95 at lunch, $6.95–$15.95 at dinner.
AE, CB, DC, MC, V.
    Open: Daily 11:30am–10pm.

    A prime waterfront location, this restaurant was taken over in
early 1990 by the Leverock's group, known primarily for fine
seafood at moderate prices. The company decided not to
convert it into another seafood house, but to put the focus on choice
Western beef, at affordable prices. So, if you've enjoyed any of the
Leverock's other locations for seafood, this place is the ideal
alternative when you have a craving for beef. Best of all, it's not just
another steakhouse setting—there are expansive views of Boca Ciega
Bay from every table.

The menu features three different cuts of prime rib, two sizes of
filet mignon, and four types of steaks, plus chopped steak, beef
kebabs, and four variations of surf-and-turf. Just for variety, baby
back ribs, chicken, and two or three seafood items round out the
menu. Alaskan crab legs and lobster are also available, at higher
prices.

INEXPENSIVE

**FOURTH STREET SHRIMP STORE, 1006 4th St. N. Tel.
822-0325.**
    Cuisine: SEAFOOD. **Reservations:** Not accepted. **Di-
rections:** Between 10th and 11th avenues N.
$ Prices: Entrées $3.99–$8.99, lunch or dinner. No credit cards.
    Open: Tues–Thurs 11:30am–8pm, Fri 11:30am–9pm, Sat
11:30am–8:30pm; and Mon (Jan–Apr only) 11:30am–8pm.

    An Old Florida–style fish market and restaurant, offering
seafood at rock-bottom prices. Step inside and take a seat at
one of the two dining rooms; there are no views of the water,
but lots of nautical memorabilia, from fish nets and crab traps to
three-dimensional fish art. Whimsical murals, old St. Petersburg
street signs, and sports pennants round out the eclectic decor.

The tablecloths, utensils, and glasses are plastic and the plates are made of paper, but the seafood is the real thing—heaping servings of fresh grouper, smelts, or frogs' legs, shrimp of all sizes, oysters, and crab. Many of the main courses come with mallets, so you can crack open the crustaceans on your own. The most expensive dish is the "Tuesday-night special": all-you-can-eat snow crab ($10.99). Full dinners, platters, and baskets of fish are available throughout the day, as are seafood sandwiches, beef burgers, chicken wings, and steaks. Beer and wine available.

HOOTERS, 2901 Tyrone Blvd. Tel. 343-4947.
   Cuisine: AMERICAN. **Reservations:** Not accepted. **Directions:** Northwest of downtown, opposite the Tyrone Square Mall shopping center.
$ **Prices:** Entrées $2.95–$12.95 lunch or dinner. AE, MC, V.
   Open: Mon–Fri 11am–midnight, Sat 11am–1am, Sun noon–10pm.

Though located along a busy shopping corridor and far from the beaches, this establishment maintains a year-round beach-party atmosphere. For a description of the decor and the menu, see the entry for the original Hooters in Clearwater under "Nearby Dining," below in this chapter. For branches in Tampa, see Chapter 10, "Tampa Dining."

PEP'S SEA GRILL, 7610 4th St. N. Tel. 521-1655.
   Cuisine: SEAFOOD. **Reservations:** Not accepted. **Directions:** North of downtown, between 76th and 77th avenues N., near the Gateway Mall Shopping Center.
$ **Prices:** Entrées $5.95–$9.95. No credit cards.
   Open: Mon–Sat 4–10:30pm, Sun noon–9pm.

Located about a mile south of Gandy Boulevard and the Gandy Bridge approach, this is a small, almost dinerlike eatery, with a cheery art deco decor. It is known for serving fresh seafood at rock-bottom prices. The menu items vary with the local catch, but specials often include salmon and snow crab, stone crabs, and a hearty one-pound shrimp feast. Beer and wine available.

   Another branch is located in St. Petersburg Beach at 5895 Gulf Blvd. (tel. 367-3550).

4. ST. PETERSBURG BEACH

VERY EXPENSIVE

KING CHARLES, 3400 Gulf Blvd. Tel. 360-1881.
   Cuisine: FRENCH/CONTINENTAL. **Reservations:** Required. **Directions:** On south end of the St. Petersburg Beach strip in the Don CeSar Hotel, fifth floor.
$ **Prices:** Entrées $19–$29. AE, CB, DC, MC, V.
   Open: Tues–Sat 6–10pm.

Overlooking the Gulf of Mexico from a high vantage point, this restaurant is quite a departure from the usual beachfront eateries. Wide windows and panoramic views are a prime draw, of course, but there is also the serenity of a more formal atmosphere, somewhat like that of the great châteaux or villas of Europe, with fine china and linens, fresh flowers, crystal chandeliers, and a harpist playing in the background. This is one of the few "dress-up" spots along the beach, with jackets required for men.

Specialties include rack of lamb, veal chops, lobster medallions, Norwegian salmon, sliced breast of wild duck, chateaubriand, chicken Veronique, and rainbow fettuccine, all prepared to your exact requirements. Both the chefs and the serving staff have won countless awards and strive to make every meal a memorable dining experience.

EXPENSIVE

THE PALM COURT, 5500 Gulf Blvd. Tel. 360-0061 or 367-6461, ext. 58.
Cuisine: FRENCH/AMERICAN. **Reservations:** Required for dinner. **Directions:** In the center of St. Petersburg Beach at 55th Avenue, on the ground floor of the TradeWinds Resort Hotel.
$ **Prices:** Entrées $4.95–$9.95 lunch, $15.95–$24.95 dinner. AE, CB, DC, DISC, MC, V.
Open: Mon–Sat 11:30am–2pm and 5:30–10pm, Sun 10am–2pm and 5:30–9pm.

For a romantic evening, nothing quite compares to this unique spot, set amid 13 beachfront acres of gardens and sand dunes, with rambling brick paths, meandering channels of water, boardwalks, Victorian gazebos, and wooden footpaths. If you wish, before dinner you can reserve your own private gondola (at no extra charge) for a cruise around the hotel's waterways, leading up to the restaurant entrance.

The cuisine is a blend of creative "new American" style with French influences and the freshest Florida ingredients. You'll dine on such specialties as veal Kentucky (veal chop in savory morel and bourbon sauce), roast lamb Virginia Highlands (lamb chops with apple brandy and pâté en croûte in a zinfandel sauce), grouper Biscayne (broiled grouper with sauce of dark rum, lime, lobster chunks, and cream), or perhaps roast duckling in a Gruyère glaze, filet of salmon in saffron champagne sauce, or prosciutto and lamb d'amore (lamb and ham in a creamy vodka sauce). Lunch is also available, with lighter fare such as salads, pastas, burgers, and pita sandwiches.

MODERATE

HURRICANE, 807 Gulf Way. Tel. 360-9558.
Cuisine: SEAFOOD. **Reservations:** Not accepted. **Directions:** From downtown, take the Pinellas Bayway to Gulf

Boulevard, turn left at the Don CeSar and go south to 8th Avenue, turn right and right again onto Gulf Way; restaurant is between 8th and 9th avenues.

$ Prices: Entrées $1.95–$3.95 at lunch, $6.95–$17.95 at dinner. MC, V.

Open: Daily 8am–1am.

If you're a fan of Florida black grouper or even if you've never tasted it before, here's *the* spot to try it. Overlooking Pass-A-Grille beach, this informal indoor-outdoor restaurant serves more than 5,000 pounds of grouper in an average week.

Entrées range from Cajun grouper and grouper Alfredo to grouper parmigiana, grouper au gratin, grouper Oscar, or grouper almondine, to name a few. And if you tire of grouper, there's always crab legs and claws, shrimp, scallops, and swordfish, as well as barbecued ribs and steaks. Lunch offers a choice of nine different grouper sandwiches, grouper chowders, and grouper salads, as well as conch fritters, barbecued shrimp, and burgers. The most popular eating times seem to be around sunset, when the view from the outside deck is mesmerizing, and after 9pm, when there's a live jazz band inside.

KINJO, 4615 Gulf Blvd. Tel. 367-6762.

Cuisine: JAPANESE. **Reservations:** Not accepted. **Directions:** In the center of St. Petersburg Beach, at 46th Avenue, in the Dolphin Landing shopping center.

$ Prices: Entrées $8.95–$19.95. AE, CB, DC, MC, V.

Open: Sun–Thurs 5–10pm, Fri–Sat 5–11pm.

A glass elevator whisks you to the second floor of this modern restaurant overlooking Boca Ciega Bay. Seating, which is both Western-style (at tables) and tatami-style (on the floor), is on a first-come, first-serve basis, so it is wise to arrive early.

The menu offers a selection of sushi and sashimi, acclaimed as first-rate by local newspaper critics, as well as a variety of beef, chicken, seafood, and vegetables cooked according to your preference (teppanyaki-style on a grill, deep-fried as tempura, or stir-fried).

LEVEROCK'S, 10 Corey Ave. Tel. 367-4588.

Cuisine: SEAFOOD. **Reservations:** Not accepted. **Directions:** On the north end of St. Petersburg Beach, to the right of the entrance to the Corey Avenue Causeway.

$ Prices: Entrées $3.95–$6.95 lunch, $6.95–$12.95 dinner. AE, CB, DC, MC, V.

Open: Daily 11:30am–10pm.

One of four Leverock's in the St. Petersburg area, all known for fresh seafood at affordable prices, this location is convenient to both downtown and the beaches, so it's understandably popular. Situated overlooking Boca Ciega Bay, it offers lovely waterside views. The only drawback is waiting on line at peak dining times, so get here early.

For a description of the menu, see "South of Downtown," earlier in this chapter.

SILAS DENT'S, 5501 Gulf Blvd. Tel. 360-6961.
    Cuisine: REGIONAL/SEAFOOD. **Reservations:** Recommended. **Directions:** At 55th Avenue, opposite the Trade-Winds Resort.
$ Prices: Entrées $7.95–$19.95. AE, CB, DC, DISC, MC, V.
    Open: Mon–Thurs 5–10pm, Fri–Sat 5–11pm, Sun noon–10pm.
With a rustic facade of driftwood and an interior of palm fronds and cedar poles, this restaurant seeks to replicate the home of a popular local folk hero, Silas Dent. Known as the "hermit of Cabbage Key," he inhabited a nearby island for many years earlier this century and often rowed his boat over to St. Pete Beach, to the delight of the local residents.

The menu aims to reflect Silas's diet of local fish and vegetation, using such ingredients as alligator, amberjack, grouper, and squid, as well as current favorites, such as Dungeness crab and lobster tails, seafood fettuccine, coconut shrimp, sea bass with dill sauce, scallops primavera, and Jamaica paella, as well as prime ribs, filet mignon, and chicken Silas (stuffed with oysters). Added attractions are a resident clown performing a little tableside magic (Tues–Sat from 7:30pm) and live music usually on tap in the lounge.

SUMMER'S LANDING, 5100 Gulf Blvd. Tel. 360-4949.
    Cuisine: AMERICAN. **Reservations:** Recommended, especially at dinner. **Directions:** In the center of the St. Pete Beach strip, next to the Hilton Inn.
$ Prices: Entrées $3.95–$5.95 at lunch, $6.95–$19.95 at dinner. AE, MC, V.
    Open: 11:30am–10pm.
Set back from the main road, this beach house–style restaurant overlooks the Gulf and offers great views. The menu, which presents seafood in creative ways, includes orange-almond flounder, salmon Wellington, shrimp Dijon, blackened grouper, and snapper florentine. There are also fish choices from afar such as mahimahi, Australian lobster tails, and Alaskan king crab. Steaks, barbecued ribs, and chicken are also offered, as well as create-your-own combinations. The lunch menu lists mainly sandwiches, salads, and daily fresh fish specials.

INEXPENSIVE

DOE-AL'S, 85 Corey Circle. Tel. 360-7976.
    Cuisine: REGIONAL. **Reservations:** Recommended. **Directions:** At the north end of St. Pete Beach, to the right of the entrance to the Corey Avenue Causeway.
$ Prices: Entrées $3.25–$7.75 lunch, $7.50–$8.50 dinner. AE, CB, DC, MC, V.
    Open: Mon–Sat 11:30am–4pm and 4:30–9:30pm, Sun noon–8pm.
A tradition in the area for over 20 years, this informal and homey spot offers Southern food at its finest and heartiest. Dinner choices include broiled, barbecued, or fried chicken, country fried steak, barbecued beef or short ribs, pork chitterlings, pork ribs, fresh ham, and fried

shrimp or catfish, all served family-style with salad, hot corn bread, and fresh vegetables (such as collard greens, black-eyed peas, and sweet potatoes). The lunch menu offers smokehouse sandwiches (barbecued beef, pork, or ribs), pastas, salads, Cajun red beans and rice, country burgers, fried chicken, and old-fashioned chicken pot pie. Beer and wine available.

WOODY'S WATERFRONT, 7308 Sunset Way. Tel. 360-9165.
Cuisine: AMERICAN. **Reservations:** Not accepted. **Directions:** At the north end of St. Pete Beach, between 73rd and Corey avenues on the Gulf.
$ Prices: $2.95–$6.95. No credit cards.
Open: Tues–Sun 11am–2am.
Nestled beside the beach, this is a casual café and beach bar with indoor and outdoor patio seating, ideal for lunch, a cooling tropical drink, or late-night snack. The simple menu offers sandwiches, burgers, chicken wings, fried shellfish, and the ubiquitous grouper (fried, grilled, or blackened).

5. TREASURE ISLAND

MODERATE

CAPTAIN KOSMAKOS, 9610 Gulf Blvd. Tel. 367-3743.
Cuisine: AMERICAN/INTERNATIONAL. **Reservations:** Recommended. **Directions:** Follow Blind Pass Road north from St. Pete Beach; restaurant is on the bay side at 96th Avenue.
$ Prices: Entrées $7.95–$19.95. AE, CB, DC, MC, V.
Open: Daily 3pm–1am.
The setting is eye-catching—a large glass building on concrete stilts, with the restaurant on the upper level overlooking the waters between St. Pete Beach and Treasure Island. There are two big and open dining rooms, which are sometimes noisy.

But the big draw is the food, an eclectic blend of American, Greek, and Italian dishes, all served in hefty portions. The menu includes Florida grouper and snapper, Maryland crabcakes, Alaskan crab legs, Maine lobster, and pan-fried squid, as well as chicken cacciatore, veal marsala or parmesan, shrimp Creole, shish-kebab, pasta, prime rib, and steaks.

INEXPENSIVE

THE BANK 1890'S RESTAURANT, 11595 Gulf Blvd. Tel. 360-2221.
Cuisine: AMERICAN. **Reservations:** Accepted only for large parties. **Directions:** At the north end of Treasure Island, between 115th and 116th avenues.

Prices: $3.49 breakfast, $3.99 lunch, $6.99 dinner (subject to change). MC, V.
Open: Mon–Sat 8–11am, 11:30am–3pm, and 4–9pm, Sun 8–11am, 11am–2pm, and 3–9pm.

It's hard to beat the value at this bayside eatery. Just step in, pay the cashier, take a table, and make as many trips as you wish to the all-you-can-eat buffet table. The dinner spread changes nightly but often includes carved roast beef, chicken, fish, soups, pastas, salad bar, dessert bar, and more. On some nights (usually Tues–Fri), the price is slightly higher ($9.95), but the menu includes unlimited snow crab as well. Entertainment is on tap in the lounge after 8pm at no extra charge.

6. THE ISLAND OF SAND KEY

MADEIRA BEACH

MODERATE

BALLOON PALACE, 14995 Gulf Blvd. Tel. 393-2706.
  Cuisine: AMERICAN. **Reservations:** Not accepted.
  Directions: Just south of the entrance to the Tom Stewart Causeway (S.R. 666), in the Madeira Commons shopping center.
$ Prices: Entrées $2.95–$6.95 lunch, $8.95–$16.95 dinner. AE, MC, V.
  Open: Daily 11am–11pm.
Launched in the spring of 1989, this relatively new restaurant is a fun spot with a beach-party atmosphere. The decor is dominated by dozens of models and miniatures of hot-air balloons.

The menu is straightforward, with emphasis on steaks, barbecued ribs, local seafoods, and the house specialty, Buffalo-style chicken wings. Servings range from a five-piece taster portion to 20 pieces or more, with extra sauce or celery on the side. You can also get a take-out bucket of 50 wings for beach parties. Lunch items include pizza fingers, peel-and-eat shrimp, nachos, salads, beer-battered grouper fingers, burgers, and sandwiches.

FRIENDLY FISHERMAN, 150 128th Ave. Tel. 391-6025.
  Cuisine: SEAFOOD. **Reservations:** Not accepted. **Directions:** At the southern tip of Madeira Beach, on the boardwalk at John's Pass.
$ Prices: Entrées $2.95–$5.95 lunch, $6.95–$19.95 dinner. MC, V.
  Open: Sun–Thurs 7am–10pm or 11pm, Fri–Sat 7am–midnight.
The centerpiece of John's Pass Village, this restaurant is the outgrowth of a busy fishing business launched over 50 years ago by Capt. Wilson Hubbard, who is indeed a "friendly fisherman" and hence the name. You'll often see the captain checking the catch brought in by his vessels or strolling from table to table making sure that customers

are happy—you'll recognize him by his yachting cap and his red-and-green socks, a trademark. The restaurant offers indoor and outdoor seating, with waterside views in both cases.

The menu leans toward seafood, brought in fresh daily by the captain's own fleet, and served smoked, steamed, fried, or broiled. Dinner choices range from amberjack and mullet to stone crabs, shrimp, grouper, snapper, and flounder, as well as lobster tails, and four kinds of surf-and-turf. Lunch choices are seafood samplers, sandwiches, and salads, as well as burgers and smoked meats.

LEVEROCK'S, 565 150th Ave. Tel. 393-0459.
   Cuisine: SEAFOOD. **Reservations:** Not accepted. **Directions:** East of Gulf Boulevard, to the right of the entrance to the Tom Stewart Causeway.
$ Prices: Entrées $3.95–$6.95 lunch, $6.95–$12.95 dinner. AE, CB, DC, MC, V.
   Open: Daily 11:30am–10pm.

Situated off the main beach stretch on the marina overlooking Boca Ciega Bay, this is one of four Leverock's in the St. Petersburg area. All are known for fresh seafood at affordable prices, and are understandably very popular, even though the no-reservations policy can often mean standing in line to wait for a table.

For a menu description, see "South of Downtown," above in this chapter.

INEXPENSIVE

OMI'S BAVARIAN INN, 14701 Gulf Blvd. Tel. 393-9654.
   Cuisine: GERMAN. **Reservations:** Recommended. **Directions:** In the center of Madeira Beach, four blocks south of the Tom Stewart Causeway, on the bay side.
$ Prices: Entrées $5.75–$12.45. MC, V.
   Open: Tues–Sat 4:30–9:30pm, Sun 4–8pm.

This little restaurant is a small patch of Germany on the Gulf. You won't find much seafood here, but you will have a choice of various schnitzels, sauerbraten and schweinebraten (roast pork), chicken paprikash, beef goulasch, Bavarian bratwurst, and stuffed pepper. Beer and wine available including many European imports.

NORTH REDINGTON BEACH

EXPENSIVE

THE WINE CELLAR, 17307 Gulf Blvd. Tel. 393-3491.
   Cuisine: CONTINENTAL. **Reservations:** Highly recommended. **Directions:** On the bay side, about two miles north of the Tom Stewart Causeway, between 173rd and 174th avenues.
$ Prices: Entrées $9.50–$24.50. AE, CB, DC, MC, V.
   Open: Tues–Sat 4–11pm, Sun 4–10pm.

Considered by locals to be the top choice in the St. Pete area despite its lack of a view of the water. With its culinary reputation, it doesn't need views. There are seven dining rooms, each with a distinctive European theme, such as a village boulevard of shops, a wine vault, or a skylit conservatory.

With tuxedoed waiters and live background music, this is an atmosphere conducive to a big splurge. Why not start your meal by indulging in fresh Russian caviar ($45 for two ounces), Swedish smoked salmon ($6.75 a serving), or perhaps a hearty soup (Hungarian goulasch or Swiss cheese soup, $3.75). The entrées present the best of Europe and the United States, with such dishes as North Carolina rainbow trout, red snapper Waleska, frogs' legs provençale, various cuts of prime rib, wienerschnitzel, beef Wellington, rack of lamb, chateaubriand, and a unique combination of "tail and quails" (lobster tail with two Georgia quails). There are also vegetarian and low-calorie dishes and a nightly "surprise dinner" when the chef selects a "culinary adventure" from appetizer through dessert.

MODERATE

JASMINE'S CAFE, 17120 Gulf Blvd. Tel. 391-4000.
   Cuisine: AMERICAN. **Reservations:** Recommended. **Directions:** On the Gulf side, just under two miles north of the Tom Stewart Causeway, at the N. Redington Beach Hilton, between 171st and 172nd avenues.
$ Prices: Entrées $3.95–$8.95 lunch, $4.95–$15.95 dinner. AE, CB, DC, DISC, MC, V.
   Open: 11:30am–2:30pm, 5–10pm.

This casual hotel restaurant has a tropical atmosphere, with indoor and outdoor seating overlooking the Gulf of Mexico. The menu strives to be different, with a creative selection of local and international favorites, such as shrimp Diane, nutty filet (skewered filet mignon rolled in Dijon mustard and crushed peanuts and charbroiled), snapper milanese, ginger scallops, chicken and mushroom strudel, Southern-fried chicken, Key lime chicken (marinated in lime and char-broiled), barbecued ribs, and steaks. Lunch items range from sandwiches and salads to design-your-own omelets, seafood, and pastas. Even if you can't dine here, it's worth stopping by for a drink and the nightly "sunset ceremony" on the deck.

REDINGTON SHORES

EXPENSIVE

LOBSTER POT, 17814 Gulf Blvd. Tel. 391-8592.
   Cuisine: SEAFOOD. **Reservations:** Highly recommended. **Directions:** On the Gulf side, about 2.5 miles north of the Tom Stewart Causeway, between 178th and 179th avenues.
$ Prices: Entrées $11.75–$21.50. AE, CB, DC, MC, V.
   Open: Mon–Thurs 4:30–10pm, Sat 4:30–10:30pm, Sun 4–10pm.

Don't judge this restaurant by its exterior. Housed in a rustic-looking building with a plain exterior and no waterside views, it has a charming nautical decor inside with fine linens, crystal, and candlelight. Above all, you'll quickly discover why this spot is considered a benchmark among the Gulf Coast's seafood houses.

First and foremost this is a lobster house, with 22 varieties of lobster offerings, including specimens from Maine, Florida, South Africa, and Denmark, tails or whole, in sauces and au naturel, all sold at market prices. In addition to lobster, there is a wide selection of grouper, snapper, salmon, swordfish, shrimp, scallops, crab, and even Dover sole, prepared simply or in elaborate sauces. If you can't decide, try one of the dishes designed "for those who want it all," such as lobster potpourri, bouillabaisse, and Neptune's delight. Filet mignon, steaks, and chicken round out the menu.

INEXPENSIVE

THE FRIENDLY TAVERN, 18121 Gulf Blvd. Tel. 393-4470.
   Cuisine: AMERICAN. **Reservations:** Not accepted. **Directions:** About 3 miles north of Tom Stewart Causeway, between 181st and 182nd avenues.
$ Prices: Entrées $1.95–$7.95. AE, MC, V.
   Open: Daily 11am–1am

Situated opposite a public beach, this indoor-outdoor spot is convenient for casual dining after a swim or a walk on the beach. You can watch the traffic go by on Gulf Boulevard as you sip a tropical drink or try some finger foods such as fried vegetables or cheese sticks. Other items on the menu include beer-steamed shrimp (sold by the pound or half-pound), plus burgers, hot dogs, sandwiches, chili, soups, and steaks. Seafood salads are worth trying, especially the "in-crab-able" crab salad plate. To quench a thirst, there are also 50 beers from 14 countries.

SHELLS, 17855 Gulf Blvd. Tel. 393-8990.
   Cuisine: SEAFOOD. **Reservations:** Not accepted. **Directions:** On the bay side, about 2½ miles north of Tom Stewart Causeway, between 178th and 179th avenues.
$ Prices: Entrées $4.95–$12.95. No credit cards.
   Open: Sun–Thurs 4–10pm, Fri–Sat 4–11pm.

Shells is a local institution. The first Shells restaurant opened in Tampa in 1985 and this location followed soon after, as have over twenty other branches in Florida and beyond. This is one of the nicer settings, overlooking Boca Ciega Bay. For a description of the decor and the menu, see Chapter 10, "Tampa Dining: Airport and West Shore."

Other branches in the St. Pete area include 1290 34th St. N., St. Petersburg (tel. 321-6020), and 3138 U.S. 19 N., Clearwater (tel. 789-3944).

INDIAN SHORES

EXPENSIVE

LE POMPANO, 19325 Gulf Blvd. Tel. 596-0333.
   Cuisine: FRENCH/CONTINENTAL. **Reservations:** Recommended. **Directions:** Take the Park Boulevard Causeway (S.R.

694) west to Gulf Boulevard; turn right and restaurant is three blocks north on the Intracoastal Waterway side.

$ Prices: Entrées $10.95–$22.95. AE, CB, DC, MC, V.

Open: daily 4–10pm.

Started in 1973 by chef-owner Michel Denis and his wife, Clarine, as a small 50-seat bistro at Redington Shores, this restaurant gradually expanded to its present location and 200-seat capacity. Set back from the road, it offers wide-windowed views of the "Narrows" of the Intracoastal Waterway and a bright and airy California-style decor of wood-paneled walls, hanging plants, book-filled shelves, and contemporary art.

Entrees include filet of sole amandine or Veronique, veal Cordon Bleu, roast duckling à l'orange, chicken Oscar, sautéed sweetbreads, Châteaubriand, rack of lamb for two, and, of course, a signature dish of filet of pompano en papillote. This is one place you'll also want to save room for dessert—lots of flambé choices including bananas Foster, cherries jubilee, crêpes Suzette, as well as fruit fondues and profiterolles (averaging $7 for two persons).

MODERATE

PEPIN'S ON THE BEACH, 19519 Gulf Blvd. Tel. 596-9100.

Cuisine: SPANISH. **Reservations:** Recommended. **Directions:** Take the Park Boulevard Causeway (S.R. 694) west to Gulf Boulevard; turn right and restaurant is five blocks north on the Intracoastal Waterway side.

$ Prices: Entrées $10.95–$17.95. AE, MC, V.

Open: Mon–Sat 5–11pm, Sun. 5–10pm.

Set back from main road, this contemporary-style hacienda overlooks the waters of The Narrows, along the Intracoastal Waterway. Like its companion restaurant inland (see "North of Downtown," above in this chapter), it conveys the ambience of an Iberian villa.

The menu here also reflects the Pepin corporate motto of *"Al pan, pan y al vino, vino,"* which roughly translated means food in its purest form, with no artificial ingredients or additives. The bread is freshly baked on the premises every morning, the fish is picked from nearby waters, and the meats are aged and cut daily. Specialties include a tempting array of tapas ($3.95–$5.95) and Spanish-accented main courses such as salmon Almendrina (with orange mustard sauce), paella, and chicken with yellow Valencia rice, as well as local and international fare, from whole Florida lobster and pompano en papillote, to Châteaubriand and rack of lamb.

SCANDIA, 19829 Gulf Blvd. Tel. 595-5525.

Cuisine: SCANDINAVIAN. **Reservations:** Recommended. **Directions:** Take Park Boulevard (S.R. 694) west to Gulf Boulevard; turn right and restaurant is eight blocks north on the Intracoastal Waterway side.

$ Prices: Entrées $4.95–$7.95 at lunch, $9.95–$17.95 at dinner. AE, CB, DC, MC, V.

Open: Mon–Sat 11:30am–3pm, 4–9pm, Sun noon–8pm.

Unique in decor and menu along the Gulf coast, this Chalet-style restaurant brings a touch of Hans Christian Andersen to the beach strip. There are five cozy dining rooms, four downstairs and one in an upstairs loft, all decorated with Delft pottery, paintings of Denmark, chiming clocks, and other handcrafted bric-a-brac.

The menu offers Scandinavian favorites, from smoked salmon and pickled herring to roast pork, sausages, schnitzels, and Danish lobster tails, as well as a few international dishes such as curried chicken, surf-and-turf, roast leg of lamb, and local seafood choices—jumbo or rock shrimp, scallops, grouper, flounder, and more. Many of the items served—red cabbage, sausage, soups, salad dressings, and baked goods—are also available for purchase in the adjacent shop.

INEXPENSIVE

HUNGRY FISHERMAN, 19915 Gulf Blvd. Tel. 595-4218.
  Cuisine: SEAFOOD. **Reservations:** Not accepted. **Directions:** Take Park Boulevard (S.R. 694) west to Gulf Boulevard; turn right and restaurant is nine blocks north on the Intracoastal Waterway side.
$ Prices: Entrées $2.95–$5.95 at lunch, $4.95–$12.95 at dinner. No credit cards.
  Open: daily 11:30am–10pm.

There's nothing fancy about this restaurant, but you'll regularly see people lined up outside the door. It has to be doing something right, and in this case, the secret is serving a tremendous variety of fresh seafood at remarkably low prices. With the exception of multi-item seafood platters and steaks, all dinner entrées come in well below the $10 mark. The menu includes over 40 seafood choices from white fantail Gulf shrimp to Alaskan salmon, grilled halibut, grouper, snapper, Danish lobster tails, Dungeness crab, frogs' legs, and deep-sea scallops. The lunch menu offers much of the same, as well as seafood platters, salads, and casseroles, beef or fish burgers. Get there early.

INDIAN ROCKS BEACH

EXPENSIVE

LA CAVE, 1701 N. Gulf Blvd. Tel. 595-6009.
  Cuisine: FRENCH/CREOLE. **Reservations:** Recommended. **Directions:** Take Route 688 west to Gulf Boulevard and turn right; restaurant is just over 1 mile north, between 17th and 18th avenues, on the Intracoastal Waterway side.
$ Prices: Entrées $10.95–$22.95. AE, MC, V.
  Open: Mon–Sat 5–10, Sun (Jan–May only) 5–9.

A favorite for over 20 years in this area, this restaurant has no water views, but it does offer the indoor charms and aromas of a small and intimate French country inn.

The menu includes beef chasseur, steak au poivre, veal Cordon Bleu, duck à la moutarde, shrimp Creole, grouper poached in court bouillon, lobster sautéed and flambéed in brandy, and a signature dish of "boeuf et brisant" (filet mignon and African lobster tail in lime Creole sauce and spinach à la crème). Beer and wine available.

MODERATE

MURPH'S, 2208 Gulf Blvd. Tel. 596-7401.
   Cuisine: SEAFOOD. **Reservations:** Not accepted. **Directions:** Take Route 688 west to Gulf Boulevard and turn right; restaurant is a little over 1 mile north, on the Gulf side between 22nd and 23rd avenues.
   $ Prices: Entrées $3.95–$4.95 lunch, $3.99–$12.99 dinner. AE, MC, V.
   Open: Daily 11:30am–10pm.
An informal indoor-outdoor spot, not directly on the beach, but within viewing distance of the Gulf from the tables on the outside deck (also a prime spot to watch sunsets). The emphasis is on local seafoods, cooked to order over an open wood-fired grill, or blackened, steamed, or fried. Choices include grouper, snapper, swordfish, tuna, and "catch of the day." If you don't mind a little work, try the you-peel-'em shrimp or seasonal specials of Florida lobster and stone crab claws. Top the meal with Key lime pie (a family recipe) available by the slice for $2; if you become addicted, buy a whole pie for $12. Lunch items include fish sandwiches, burgers, gumbo soups, and salads. Beer and wine available.

INEXPENSIVE

CRABBY BILL'S, 401 Gulf Blvd. Tel. 595-4825 or 593-1819.
   Cuisine: SEAFOOD. **Reservations:** Not accepted. **Directions:** Take Route 688 west to Gulf Boulevard, turn left; restaurant is one block south on the Intracoastal Waterway side.
   $ Prices: Entrées $1.95–$9.95. No credit cards.
   Open: Sun–Thurs 11am–10pm, Fri–Sat 11am–11pm.
As the name implies, crabs are the specialty here—steamed blue crabs, garlic crabs, stone crab claws, snow crabs, soft-shell crabs, and crab cakes. The atmosphere is informal and the walls are lined with handmade posters announcing the daily specials. Bushel baskets of salted crackers, plastic cutlery, paper plates, wooden mallets, and stacks of paper napkins are standard fare at every picnic-style table, while country music plays in the background. But the seafood is first-rate and people don't mind waiting or sharing a table to get in on the action.

Besides crab, you can indulge in heaping platters of oysters, clams, or mussels on the half-shell, fried or steamed shrimp, as well as seafood gumbo and oyster stews. If you prefer a fork to a mallet, generous portions of fish are also available, from flounder, grouper, tuna, and amberjack to marlin or mahimahi. Lobster is also offered (at slightly higher prices), and there are token choices of pasta, burgers, ribs, and chicken wings. The menu is the same throughout the day, so come early and avoid the crowds. Above all, don't miss this spot—it's a real Florida Gulf Coast experience.

7. CLEARWATER BEACH

EXPENSIVE

BOB HEILMAN'S BEACHCOMBER, 447 Mandalay Ave. Tel. 442-4144.

Cuisine: AMERICAN. **Reservations:** Recommended. **Directions:** Take Route 60 west over Memorial Causeway to Mandalay; turn right and restaurant is two blocks north on the right.

$ Prices: Entrées $4.95–$12.95 lunch, $8.95–$21.95 dinner. AE, DC, MC, V.

Open: Mon–Sat 11:30am–11pm, Sun noon–10pm

Even though it doesn't have any water views, this restaurant has become a mainstay after 40 years. The decor in the two dining rooms features unusual murals and lots of leafy plants.

The menu presents a wide variety of fresh seafood, from Everglades frogs' legs to Maine lobsters, as well as Atlantic sole and the best of the local catch. Beef is also a specialty here, with aged steaks and prime ribs much in demand. One of the most popular items on the menu is in a class by itself—"back-to-the-farm" fried chicken from an original 1926 recipe.

THE PELICAN, 470 Mandalay Ave. Tel. 442-3151.

Cuisine: CONTINENTAL. **Reservations:** Recommended. **Directions:** Take Route 60 west over Memorial Causeway to Mandalay; turn right and restaurant is two blocks north on the left.

$ Prices: Entrées $4.95–$7.95 lunch, $8.95–$22.95 dinner. AE, DC, MC, V.

Open: Mon–Thurs 11:30am–10:30pm, Fri–Sat 10:30am–11:30pm, Sun 4–10:30pm.

Though not directly overlooking the water, this has been a favorite since 1938. With three contemporary-style dining rooms, most with large windows overlooking a lush tropical garden, and live piano music in the background, the big draw is the food, which is consistently first-rate.

The most celebrated dish on the menu is jumbo stuffed shrimp, made with a "house secret" recipe, but other choices are equally appealing, from veal Marsala to filet of grouper Grand Marnier, duck à l'orange, soft-shell crabs, frogs' legs, and sautéed sweetbreads, to prime ribs and surf-and-turf. Lunch choices range from sandwiches, salads, and soups to burgers and steaks.

MODERATE

THE COLUMBIA, 1241 Gulf Blvd. Tel. 596-2828.

Cuisine: SPANISH. **Reservations:** Recommended. **Directions:** From Clearwater Beach, take toll bridge south to Sand Key; restaurant is next to the Radisson Hotel on the harbor side.

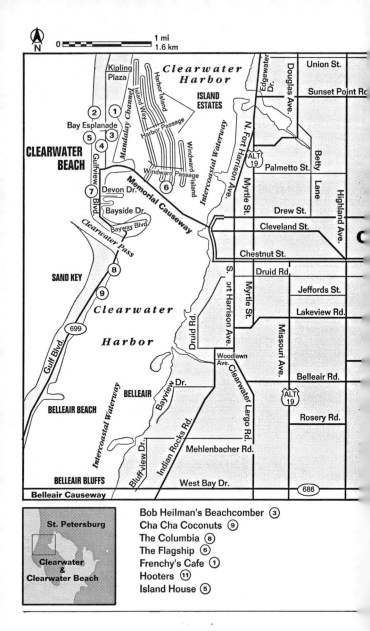

0 |====== 1 mi
        1.6 km

N

Kipling Plaza

Clearwater Harbor

ISLAND ESTATES

② ①
Bay Esplanade
⑤ ③
④

Island Way

Mandalay Channel

Harbor Island

Harbor Passage

Intracoastal Waterway

CLEARWATER BEACH

Gulfview Blvd.

⑦ Devon Dr.

Bayside Dr.

Bayway Blvd.

Windward Island

Windward Passage

⑥

Memorial Causeway

Edgewater Dr.

Douglas Ave.

Union St.

Sunset Point Rd

N. Fort Harrison Ave.

Myrtle St.

Betty Lane

Palmetto St.

Highland Ave.

Drew St.

Clearwater Pass

Cleveland St.

Chestnut St.

SAND KEY

⑧

⑨

(699)

Clearwater

Harbor

Gulf Blvd.

S. ort Harrison Ave.

Druid Rd.

Myrtle St.

Druid Rd.

Jeffords St.

Lakeview Rd.

Missouri Ave.

Woodlawn Ave.

Clearwater Largo Rd.

Belleair Rd.

ALT 19

Rosery Rd.

Intracoastal Waterway

BELLEAIR

Bayview Dr.

BELLEAIR BEACH

Bluffview Dr.

Indian Rocks Rd.

Mehlenbacher Rd.

BELLEAIR BLUFFS

West Bay Dr.

(686)

Belleair Causeway

St. Petersburg

Clearwater & Clearwater Beach

Bob Heilman's Beachcomber ③
Cha Cha Coconuts ⑨
The Columbia ⑧
The Flagship ⑥
Frenchy's Cafe ①
Hooters ⑪
Island House ⑤

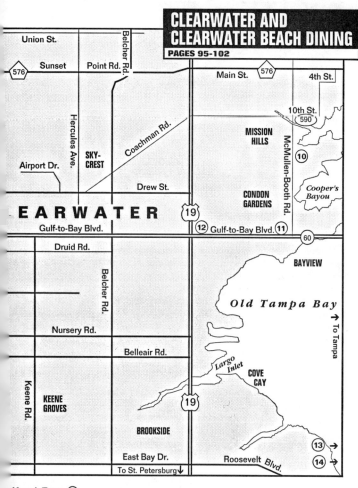

Kapok Tree ⑩
94th Aero Squadron ⑭
The Pelican ②
Rajan's ④
Seafood and Sunsets at Julie's ⑦
Tio Pepe ⑫
Whiskey Joe's ⑬

$ Prices: Entrées $4.95–$7.95 lunch, $5.95–$13.95 dinner. AE, CB, DC, MC, V.

Open: Daily 11am–11pm.

Situated just south of the main Clearwater Beach strip, this restaurant is the newest offshoot of the famous Tampa landmark. This branch manages to meld the old and the new with great success—lovely wide-windowed views of Clearwater Harbor and a decor of dark woods, old Spanish tiles, Don Quixote prints, and intricate wrought ironwork. See Chapter 10, "Tampa Dining: Ybor City," for a description of the cuisine.

THE FLAGSHIP, 20 Island Way. Tel. 443-6210.

Cuisine: SEAFOOD. **Reservations.** Recommended. **Directions:** Take Route 60 west to Memorial Causeway, turn right at Island Way.

$ Prices: Entrées $4.95–$7.95 lunch, $6.95–$21.95 dinner. AE, MC, V.

Open: Sun–Thurs 11:30am–10pm, Fri–Sat 11:30am–10:30pm.

Reopened in late 1989 after an earlier fire, this is one of the area's best-known dining spots. Located just east of the main beach strip, it sits on the waterfront in a well-landscaped 2-acre setting, next to the Clearwater Marine Science Center.

The menu is similar at lunch and dinner, with a wide variety of seafood as well as chicken, beef, and pastas; sandwiches and salads are available at lunch. The seafood selections include a half dozen daily specials ranging from amberjack to mahimahi and scrod to salmon, all cooked to order—blackened, char-broiled, broiled, or fried. Other choices range from snow crab, lobster tails, and shrimp in various styles, to prime ribs (in the evening only).

RAJAN'S, 435 Mandalay Ave. Tel. 443-2100.

Cuisine: SEAFOOD. **Reservations:** Recommended. **Directions:** Take Route 60 west across Memorial Causeway to Mandalay Avenue and turn right; restaurant is two blocks north on the right.

$ Prices: Entrées $2.95–$5.95 lunch, $7.95–$17.95 dinner. AE, DC, MC, V.

Open: Mon–Sat 11:30am–11pm, Sun noon–10pm.

Named for its owners (Ray and Jan), this is an informal Florida-style eatery across the street from the beach. Using a seafood-by-the-seashore theme, the menu offers several types of oysters, as well as soft-shell or stone crabs, butterflied shrimp, scallops scampi, grouper Oscar, and salmon hollandaise. You can also make your own platters with a choice of two or three types of seafood. Steaks and chicken round out the dinner menu, and at lunch you can also order seafood sandwiches, croissant-wiches, soups, burgers, and omelets.

SEAFOOD & SUNSETS AT JULIE'S, 351 S. Gulfview Blvd. Tel. 441-2548.

Cuisine: SEAFOOD. **Reservations:** Not accepted. **Directions:** Take Route 60 across the Memorial Causeway; keep left, follow road to end, and turn left onto Gulfview Boulevard; restaurant is on the left opposite public beach.

$ Prices: Entrées $2.95–$6.95 at lunch, $6.95–$16.95 at dinner.
AE, MC, V.
Open: Daily 11am–10pm.

A Key West–style atmosphere prevails at this beach house eatery on the main thoroughfare. And yes, there is a Julie (Julie Tiernan), who is usually on the scene. Seating is indoors or on an umbrella-shaded patio, ideal for watching the beach traffic go by during the day and for sunset-viewing each evening. And just to make sure no one misses this spectacular sight, sunset time is posted on a blackboard every day.

Dinner items range from Florida lobster tails, stone crabs, conch, grouper and other fish (prepared char-broiled, blackened, fried, or broiled) to steaks, surf-and-turf, and chicken. On Tuesday and Saturday, don't miss Ryan's red-tide stew, a variety of fish and vegetables in a Manhattan chowder base. In addition, sandwiches, salads, burgers, fish-and-chips, you-peel-'em shrimp, and other finger foods are sold throughout the day, to go or to stay. Beer and wine available.

INEXPENSIVE

CHA CHA COCONUTS, 1241 Gulf Blvd., Clearwater. Tel. 596-6040.
   Cuisine: AMERICAN. **Reservations:** Not necessary. **Directions:** From Clearwater Beach, take toll bridge south to Sand Key; restaurant is next to Radisson Hotel on the left.
$ Prices: Entrées $3.95–$7.95, lunch or dinner. AE, CB, DC, MC, V.
   Open: Mon–Thurs 11am–midnight, Fri–Sat 11am–1am, Sun noon–11pm.

This informal tropical bar and grill sits beside the Columbia restaurant overlooking Clearwater Harbor, with both indoor and outdoor deck seating along the boardwalk. It's a great vantage point from which to watch the passing sailboats and yachts or to sip a tropical drink as the sun sets. Live music is usually on tap after dark. See the entry for Cha Cha Coconuts and under "Downtown," above in this chapter. For the Tampa branch, see Chapter 10, "Tampa Dining: Harbour Island."

FRENCHY'S CAFE, 41 Baymount St. Tel. 446-3706.
   Cuisine: SEAFOOD: **Reservations:** Not accepted. **Directions:** Off Mandalay Avenue, across the street from the Clearwater Beach Hotel.
$ Prices: Entrées $2.75–$15.95. No credit cards.
   Open: Mon–Thurs 11:30am–11pm, Fri–Sat 11:30am–midnight, Sun 1pm–11pm.

A casual eatery nestled on a side street across from the beachfront, this is Clearwater Beach at its most relaxed. A U-shaped bar dominates the small interior, with a sprinkling of square tables, booths, nautical fixtures, and an overworked jukebox.

Ignore the noise and come for the grouper burgers, famous in their own right, as are the "crabby shrimp" sandwiches. Other items on the menu range from smoked fish spreads and crackers to oysters, mussels, and clams in the shell, as well as Greek-style salads and Louisiana shrimp gumbo soup, boiled shrimp, and Florida stone-crab claws. A second location is two blocks away at 419 East Shore Drive (tel. 442-6411).

ISLAND HOUSE, 452 Mandalay Ave. Tel. 442-2373.

Cuisine: SEAFOOD/GREEK. **Reservations:** Recommended.
Directions: Take Route 60 west across Memorial Causeway to Mandalay and turn right; restaurant is one block north on left.
$ Prices: Entrées $6.95–$12.95. AE, MC, V.
Open: Tues–Sun 4–11pm.

A local favorite since 1963, this restaurant is run by the Houllis family, who have incorporated many recipes from Greece into the menu. The choices include Greek salads, moussaka, Greek spaghetti (spaghetti with browned butter, sautéed onions, and Romano cheese), and lamb and seafood kebabs.

In addition, there is a wide variety of seafood, from pan-fried catfish to mountain trout, snow crab, frogs' legs, conch-and-squid combo, and surf-and-turf. Steaks and prime ribs are also featured. Children are particularly welcome here, and each youngster who finishes his or her dinner gets a free balloon.

8. NEARBY DINING

MODERATE

KAPOK TREE, 923 McMullen Booth Rd., Clearwater. Tel. 726-0504.

Cuisine: AMERICAN. **Reservations:** Recommended. **Directions:** Take Route 60 to McMullen-Booth Road; go north just under 1 mile and restaurant is on right.
$ Prices: Entrées $5.95–$6.95 lunch, $9.95–$19.95 dinner. AE, CB, DC, DISC, MC, V.
Open: Daily noon–10pm.

Situated next to the Ruth Eckerd Hall Performing Arts Center, this restaurant is about seven miles east of the Clearwater Beach area and well worth a slight detour. A local landmark, it opened originally in 1957, with seating for 125, on the site of a former orange grove. It has since grown to a capacity of 1,750 and is one of the largest restaurants in the world, with gardens, cascading fountains, statuary, an art gallery, a promenade lined with gift shops, and, in the middle of it all, a 135-foot blooming kapok tree. The dining rooms are each decorated according to a different theme, from the Bordello or the Casino to the Patio, Terrace, or Grand Ballroom.

The menu is equally extensive, with a choice of 20 entrées including teriyaki chicken, coconut-fried shrimp, crab-stuffed flounder, tuna steak, grouper filet, prime ribs, and such specialties as veal

Kapok (with savory Italienne sauce and provolone cheese). Be sure to sample the corn fritters that are delivered to every table with powdered sugar. Lighter lunch fare ranges from salads and sandwiches to quiches, croissant-wiches, and burgers.

94TH AERO SQUADRON, 94 Fairchild Dr., Clearwater. Tel. 536-0409.

Cuisine: AMERICAN **Reservations:** Recommended. **Directions:** Off Roosevelt Boulevard between the St. Petersburg–Clearwater Airport and Boatyard Village.

$ Prices: Entrées $3.95–$7.95 lunch, $9.95–$19.95 dinner. AE, DC, MC, V.

Open: Mon–Thurs 11am–10pm, Fri–Sat 11am–11pm, Sun 10:30am–2:30pm, 4–10pm.

Overlooking Old Tampa Bay, this restaurant is designed to resemble a World War I French farmhouse. On the front lawn, you'll see an authentic 1917 Sopwith Camel, a collector's item, and inside there is a decor of sandbag walls, military artifacts and equipment, old pictures and posters, and antique bottles and books lining the four fireplaces. But that's only part of the setting—the building also overlooks the runways of the airport, so you can enjoy water views or watch the planes land as you dine.

The dinner menu offers steaks, prime ribs, farmhouse chicken, pastas, and stir-fry dishes, as well as a variety of local seafoods. Lunch items include soups (the beer-cheese soup is a specialty), sandwiches, and light and unusual entrées such as Florida alligator tail. It's a fun place for all ages, and a change from the beach scene.

TIO PEPE'S, 2930 Gulf-to-Bay Blvd., Clearwater. Tel. 799-3082.

Cuisine: SPANISH. **Reservations:** Recommended. **Directions:** Between McMullen-Booth Road and U.S. 19.

$ Prices: Entrées $3.25–$11.95 at lunch, $11.95–$19.95 at dinner. MC, V.

Open: Tues–Fri 11am–2:30pm and 5–11pm, Sat 5–11pm, Sun 4–10pm.

Situated along the busy thoroughfare between Clearwater Beach and Tampa Airport, this restaurant stands out beside the road with a tile roof and white-washed facade. The interior is equally Iberian with rich red tones, wrought-iron fixtures, and romantic little alcoves with tables for two. The aroma of freshly baked breads greets you as you enter.

The dinner menu offers Spanish specialties, such as gambas suprema (jumbo shrimp wrapped in bacon) or paella valenciana, as well as local and international dishes including whole Florida lobster, sea bass or sea trout broiled with lemon butter, pompano en papillotte, trout a la rusa, duckling with red currant sauce, pork chop in prune and garlic sauce, chateaubriand, and rack of lamb. Lunchtime features sandwiches, salads, and steaks, as well as daily specials that provide very good value, from Spanish beef stew to chicken and yellow rice.

INEXPENSIVE

HOOTERS, 2800 Gulf-to-Bay Blvd. Tel. 797-4008.
Cuisine: AMERICAN. **Reservations:** Not accepted. **Directions:** Between McMullen-Booth Road and U.S. 19.
$ Prices: Entrées $2.95–$12.95 lunch or dinner. AE, MC, V.
Open: Mon–Fri 11am–midnight, Sat 11am–1am, Sun noon–10pm.

This is the original Hooters; branches also thrive in St. Petersburg, (see "North of Downtown," above in this chapter) and Tampa (see Chapter 10, "Tampa Dining"). Though located along a busy thoroughfare between Clearwater Beach and Tampa Airport, and far from the surf and sand, it is a relaxed eatery. Step in and enjoy—the jukebox blares "golden oldies," the staff is clad in skimpy T-shirts and short shorts, and the finger-food menu is designed to give you a laugh or two.

Hooters is definitely not the choice for an evening of fine dining, but it is a fun place, especially if you're fond of chicken wings, steak sandwiches, steamed shrimp, or oyster roasts (oysters roasted in the shell and served with drawn butter). It's hard to spend more than $10 on a meal, but if you really want to splurge, there's one tongue-in-cheek selection designed for a group of friends: the "Gourmet Chicken Wing Dinner" (20 wing pieces with a bottle of Dom Perignon for $100).

WHISKEY JOE'S, 16100 Fairchild Drive, Clearwater. Tel. 536-6541.
Cuisine: AMERICAN. **Reservations:** Recommended. **Directions:** Off Roosevelt Boulevard in Boatyard Village, next to St. Petersburg–Clearwater Airport.
$ Prices: Entrées $3.95–$14.95. AE, MC, V.
Open: Sun–Thurs 11am–9pm, Fri–Sat 11am–10pm.

Overlooking Cross Bayou Canal off Old Tampa Bay, this restaurant is the centerpiece of Boatyard Village, a rustic complex of shops. It is a branch of the original Whiskey Joe's across the bay in (see Chapter 10, "Tampa Dining") and sports a similarly casual decor, with antiques, old pictures, bric-a-brac, and plastic tablecloths.

Besides the expansive views of the water, the big draw here is a 50-item salad bar, with just about everything from artichokes and asparagus tips to hearts of palm, nuts, beans, sprouts, cheeses, and fruits available as an accompaniment to your meal or as a main course. Other choices include sandwiches, burgers, fajitas, barbecued meats, prime ribs, steaks, chicken teryaki, and several variations of shrimp and grouper. The same menu is offered for lunch or dinner.

9. ST. PETERSBURG RESTAURANTS

BY CUISINE

AMERICAN

Alessi Café at The Pier (page 75)	I
Balloon Palace (page 88)	M
The Bank 1890's Restaurant (page 87)	I
Bob Heilman's Beachcomber (page 95)	E
Captain Kosmakos (page 87)	M
Cha Cha Coconuts (pages 75 and 99)	I
The Friendly Tavern (page 91)	I
Hooters (pages 83 and 102)	I
Jasmine's Café (page 90)	M
Kapok Tree (page 100)	M
94th Aero Squadron (page 101)	M
Peter's Place (page 74)	E
Outback Steakhouse (page 79)	M
The Palm Court (page 84)	E
Summer's Landing (page 86)	M
The Waterfront Steak House (page 82)	M
Whiskey Joe's (page 102)	I
Woody's Waterfront (page 87)	I

AUSTRALIAN

Outback Steakhouse (page 79)	M

CAJUN/CREOLE

La Cave (page 93)	E
Fat Jacque's Cajun Café (page 79)	M

CONTINENTAL

Basta's Cantina d'Italia Ristorante (page 73)	E
King Charles (page 83)	VE
The Pelican (page 95)	E
Le Pompano (page 91)	E
The Wine Cellar (page 89)	E

FRENCH

La Cave (page 93)	E
King Charles (page 83)	VE
The Palm Court (page 84)	E
Le Pompano (page 91)	E

GERMAN

Omi's Bavarian Inn (page 89)	I

GREEK

Island House (page 100)	I

INTERNATIONAL
Captain Kosmakos (page 87)   M
Peter's Place (page 74)   E

ITALIAN
Basta's Cantina d'Italia Ristorante (page 73)   E

JAPANESE
Arigato Japanese Steakhouse (page 78)   M
Kinjo (page 85)   M

LIGHT, CASUAL, AND FAST FOOD
Alessi Café at The Pier (page 75)   I
Balloon Palace (page 88)   M
Cha Cha Coconuts (pages 75 and 99)   I
Frenchy's Café (page 99)   I
The Friendly Tavern (page 91)   I
Hooters (pages 83 and page 102)   I
Hurricane (page 84)   M
Murph's (page 94)   M
Ted Peters' Famous Smoked Fish (page 77)   I
Whiskey Joe's (page 102)   I
Woody's Waterfront (page 87)   I

REGIONAL
Silas Dent's (page 86)   M
Doe-Al's (page 86)   I

SCANDINAVIAN
Scandia (page 92)   M

SEAFOOD
Crabby Bill's (page 94)   I
The Flagship (page 98)   M
Fourth Street Shrimp Store (page 82)   I
Frenchy's Cafe (page 99)
Friendly Fisherman (page 88)   M
Hungry Fisherman (page 93)   I
Hurricane (page 84)   M
Island House (page 100)
Leverock's (pages 76, 85, and 89)   M
Lobster Pot (page 90)   E
Murph's (page 94)   M
Pep's Sea Grill (page 83)   I
Rajan's (page 98)   M
St. Pete Fish House (page 76)   M
Seafood & Sunsets at Julie's (page 98)   M
Shells (page 91)   I
Silas Dent's (page 86)   M
Ted Peter's Famous Smoked Fish (page 77)   I

SPANISH
The Columbia (pages 74 and 95)   M
Pepin's (page 78)   M

Pepin's on the Beach (page 92)   M
Tio Pepe's (page 101)   M

STEAKHOUSES
Arigato Japanese Steakhouse (page 78)   M
Outback Steakhouse (page 79)   M
The Waterfront Steak House (page 82)   M

SWISS
Melting Pot (page 79)   M

SPECIALTY DINING

COOL FOR KIDS
Arigato Japanese Steakhouse (page 78)   M
Balloon Palace (page 88)   M
Crabby Bill's (page 94)   I
Fourth Street Shrimp Store (page 82)   I
Friendly Fisherman (page 88)   M
Hooters (page 102)   I
Island House (page 100)   I
Melting Pot (page 79)   M
Murph's (page 94)   M
94th Aero Squadron (page 101)   M
Outback Steakhouse (page 79)   M
Shells (page 91)   I
Silas Dent's (page 86)   M

DINING WITH A VIEW
Alessi Café at The Pier (page 75)   I
Captain Kosmakos (page 87)   M
Cha Cha Coconuts (pages 75 and page 99)   I
The Columbia (pages 74 and page 95)   M
The Flagship (page 98)   M
Friendly Fisherman (page 88)   M
Jasmine's Café (page 90)   M
King Charles (page 83)   VE
Leverock's (pages 76, 85, and 89)   M
Murph's (page 94)   M
94th Aero Squadron (page 101)   M
Pepin's on the Beach (page 92)   M
Le Pompano (page 91)   E
Seafood & Sunsets at Julie's (page 98)   M
Summer's Landing (page 86)   M
The Waterfront Steak House (page 74)   M
Whiskey Joe's (page 102)   I
Woody's Waterfront (page 87)   I

HOTEL DINING
Jasmine's Café (page 90)   M
King Charles (page 79)   VE
The Palm Court (page 84)   E

WEEKEND BRUNCHES

WHAT TO SEE AND DO IN ST. PETERSBURG

From downtown to the beaches, St. Petersburg is a city with a myriad of outdoor and indoor activities. It would take months to see and do it all, but if you only have a week or less, here are some suggestions to help you choose what is most appealing.

SIGHT-SEEING STRATEGIES

IF YOU HAVE 1 DAY

Explore the newly rejuvenated downtown area, starting with the Pier on Tampa Bay —browsing in the shops, touring the aquarium, sampling the variety of foods, and savoring the panoramic views. Continue to the nearby Museum of Fine Arts, the Waterfront Historical Museum, Beach Drive with its string of fine boutiques, and along the bayfront to the Dalí Museum. Walk through the city along the wide corridor of Central Avenue, ending at the newly built sports/entertainment center, the Florida Suncoast Dome.

IF YOU HAVE 2 DAYS

Do the downtown area and add a few more nearby attractions, from Sunken Gardens and the Haas Museum to Great Explorations or Ft. DeSoto Park. Take a relaxing boat cruise in the afternoon on Tampa Bay or Boca Ciega Bay, or go to the greyhound races, or perhaps a baseball game or concert.

IF YOU HAVE 3 DAYS

After taking in the downtown sights for the first two days, spend a full day on nearby St. Petersburg Beach or Pass-A-Grille Beach, with swimming and sunning and perhaps a little fishing or a parasail ride.

IF YOU HAVE 5 DAYS OR MORE

Branch out from St. Pete to the nearby beaches and visit the Suncoast Seabird Sanctuary at Indian Shores, John's Pass Village on Madeira Beach, Redington Long Pier at Redington Shores, Heritage Park at Largo, or the Marine Science Center of Clearwater. Spend a day or two exploring Treasure Island, Indian Rocks Beach, the Intracoastal Waterways, or Boca Ciega Bay.

Soak up the sunshine, cast a fishing line, board a cruise boat, watch the pelicans diving for dinner or the sandpipers scurrying on the water's edge, see the sun set from a different vantage point each evening, or just relax and have the time of your life in this Gulf Coast paradise.

1. THE TOP ATTRACTIONS

THE PIER, 800 2nd Ave. NE, St. Petersburg. Tel. 821-6164.

The focal point of the city's recent downtown rejuvenation, this is a festive waterfront sightseeing/shopping/entertainment complex that extends one-quarter of a mile into Tampa Bay. Dating back to 1889, it was originally built as a railroad pier, but over the years it was redesigned in various ways until it took its present shape of an inverted pyramid in 1988.

Today it is the city's prime playground, with five levels of shops and restaurants, plus an aquarium, nightclub, tourist information desk, observation deck, catwalks for fishing, boat docks, a small bayside beach, and watersport rentals. Best of all are the views—sweeping panoramas of the bay, the marina, and the St. Petersburg skyline. A free trolley service operates between the Pier entrance and the nearby parking lots.

Adjacent to the Pier is Straub Park, a scenic 36-acre waterfront park that runs along Beach Drive, between 1st and 5th avenues NE. It's ideal for a stroll after visiting the Pier, a place to sit on a bench and watch the swirl of activity.

Admission: Free to all the public areas and decks; donations welcome at the aquarium.

Open: Most shops Mon–Sat 10am–9pm, Sun noon–6pm; restaurants 11am–midnight; lounges 10am–1am; aquarium, Mon and Wed–Sat 10am–8pm, Sun noon–6pm. **Directions:** On Tampa Bay, downtown at the east end of 2nd Avenue NE.

FLORIDA SUNCOAST DOME, 1 Stadium Dr., St. Petersburg. Tel. 825-3100.

The skyline of St. Petersburg changed dramatically with the opening of this new $110 million slant-roofed dome in March 1990. An attraction in itself, it was built on a 66-acre downtown site to host major concerts, sports competitions, and

FROMMER'S FAVORITES —
ST. PETERSBURG EXPERIENCES

Swimming, Sunning, Shelling Take your choice, along 28 miles of wide, sandy, clean, and safe beaches.

Sunset Time Vivid vistas of red, pink, yellow, or golden hues on the western horizon—everywhere along the Gulf beaches.

Gliding above Gulf Waters Look down on St. Petersburg Beach from the heights of a parasail.

Casting a Line From a boat, shoreline, or pier, take your time and hook a grouper, snapper, or other "big catch" of the day.

Watching Wild Seabirds Soar into the Sky Marvel as previously injured birds take to the sky every day after being restored to health at the Suncoast Seabird Sanctuary.

Dining With the "Early Birds" Enjoy three or four courses of top-class cuisine at bargain-basement prices.

Music in the Air Listen to an open-air band concert at Williams Park in downtown St. Petersburg or watch live Shakespeare performances along the bayfront.

conventions and, foremost, as a home for a major-league baseball team. As we go to press, no team has yet signed on to play from this base, but city officials are working feverishly to make that a reality by the time you read this guidebook.

The stadium has a translucent roof that is the first cable-supported dome of its kind in the U.S. and the largest of its type in the world. The secret to the building's versatility is a series of moveable stands that slide, section by section, on pneumatic tires, then lower into place hydraulically. Seating capacities range from 12,000 to 55,000, depending on the event. In addition to sports and entertainment, the dome is also the venue for ethnic folk fairs, garden shows, and other general-interest daytime activities. On non-event days, guided tours are available.

Admission: $4–$30; varies according to event.

Open: Hours vary according to event. **Directions:** Downtown, between 10th and 16th streets S., off 1st Avenue S.

SALVADOR DALI MUSEUM, 1000 3rd St. S., St. Petersburg. Tel. 823-3767.

Nestled on Tampa Bay just south of the Bayfront Center and the Pier, this starkly modern museum houses the world's largest collection of works by the renowned Spanish surrealist.

Boyd Hill Nature Park 16

Clearwater Marine
  Science Center 1

Florida Suncoast Dome 12

Fort DeSoto Park 18

Grant Field 2

Great Explorations 15

Haas Museum Complex 8

Heritage Park 5

John's Pass Village
  and Boardwalk 7

Moccasin Lake
  Nature Park 3

Museum of Fine Arts 10

The Pier 13

St. Petersburg Waterfront
  Historical Society
  Museum 11

Salvador Dali Museum 14

Suncoast Seabird
  Sanctuary 6

Sunken Gardens 9

Sunshine Skyway Bridge 17

Yesterday's Air Force
  Museum 4

90

60

3 Courtney Campbell Causeway

275

To Tampa →

19

O l d

St. Petersburg-Clearwater International Airport

Howard Frankland Bridge

686

4

ater

T a m p a

688

Ulmerton Rd.

686

Gandy Bridge

92

275

B a y

693

Pinellas Park

694

74th Ave.

694

694

595

54th Ave.

49th St.

19

275

92

38th Ave.

9

Coffeepot Bayou

asure Island Causeway

ALT 19

Downtown

Central Ave.

10

St. Petersburg

11

S. Pasadena

8

Gulfport

375

13

12

St. Petersburg Beach Causeway

22nd Ave. S.

175

14

Albert Whitted Municipal Airport

15

Big Bayou

Bay

Lake Maggiore

Coquina Key

16

99

Long Key

ch

Pinellas Bayway

Little Bayou

54th Ave. S.

682

Bird Key

I n t r a   c o a s t a l

W a t e r   w a y

T a m p a

B a y

Cabbage Key

Bush Key

Shell Key

679

17

The Reefs

Madelaine Key

19

679

275

18

Mullett Key

Airport

✈

Assembled over a 40-year period, the collection was donated in 1982 by a Cleveland industrialist, A. Reynolds Morse, and his wife, Eleanor R. Morse, who were friends of Dalí and his wife, Gala. Although Dalí never set foot here himself, it is said that the St. Pete harbor site was chosen because of its resemblance to the artist's favorite Iberian haunt, the Bay of Cadaques.

Valued at over $150 million, the collection includes 93 oil paintings, over 100 watercolors and drawings, and 1,300 graphics, plus posters, photos, sculptures, and objets d'art, and a 2,500-volume library with works on Dalí and Surrealism. One of Dalí's masterworks, the wall-size painting *Columbus' Discovery of America,* is currently garnering a lot of attention, in conjunction with the 500th anniversary of that event.

You can see the museum at your leisure or join one of the guided tours that are conducted daily for the public (the schedule varies according to demand; call for exact times). The museum store offers over 100 reproductions of Dalí's work, as well as Dalí-related T-shirts, jewelry, books, and gift items.

Admission: $4 for adults, $2.50 for seniors and students, free for children under 8.

Open: Tues–Sat 10am–5pm, Sun noon–5pm; and Mon (Christmas through Easter only) noon–5pm. **Directions:** On Bayboro Harbor adjacent to the Bayboro Campus of the University of South Florida; well signposted from I-275 and other parts of downtown.

MUSEUM OF FINE ARTS, 255 Beach Dr. NE, St. Petersburg. Tel. 896-2667.

Resembling a Mediterranean villa on the waterfront, this museum houses a permanent collection of European, American, pre-Columbian, and Far Eastern art, with works by artists such as Fragonard, Monet, Renoir, Cézanne, and Gauguin.

Other highlights include period rooms with antiques and historical furnishings, plus a gallery of Steuben crystal, and world-class rotating exhibits. *Note:* On Tuesday (mid-November to mid-April), you can enjoy tea in the garden of the museum from 3 to 4pm; reservations required.

Admission: $2 suggested donation; "Tea in the Garden" fee is $3.

Open: Tues–Sat 10am–5pm, Sun 1–5pm; open till 9pm on third Thurs of month. Guided tours Tues–Fri 11am and 2pm, Sat–Sun 2pm. **Directions:** On the bayfront at the foot of the approach to the Pier, just north of 2nd Avenue NE.

FORT DeSOTO PARK, Route 679, St. Petersburg. Tel. 866-2662.

One of the oldest sections of St. Petersburg, this is the largest and most diverse park in the area, made up of five islands south of the mainland (Mullet Key, Madelaine Key, St. Jean Key, St. Christopher Key, and Bonne Fortune Key), all nestled between the waters of Tampa Bay and the Gulf of Mexico. With a total of 900 acres, seven miles of waterfront, and almost three miles of beaches, the islands are connected by roads and bridges. A public park for over

25 years, it also offers fishing piers, shaded picnic sites, a bird, and animal sanctuary, and 235 campsites.

Historical accounts indicate that Mullet Key gained significance from the visits by Juan Ponce de León, who anchored his ship here in 1513. However, the island is most often associated with Hernando de Soto, for whom Fort DeSoto, on the southwest tip of the island, is named.

Now listed on the National Register of Historic Places, this fort was built in 1898 as an artillery installation to protect Tampa Bay during the Spanish-American War. It was armed with 12-inch mortars, which, incidentally, never fired a single shot at any enemy. Today you can explore the fort; its lookout point offers great views, especially at sunset.

Admission: Free, except for tolls totaling 85¢.

Open: Sunrise to sunset. **Directions:** Take I-275 south to the Pinellas Bayway (exit 5) and follow signs.

SUNCOAST SEABIRD SANCTUARY, 18328 Gulf Blvd., Indian Shores. Tel. 391-6211.

Among the attractions outside the immediate downtown area, this one is well worth a special trip. Founded in 1971 by zoologist Ralph Heath, Jr., it is the largest wild bird hospital in the U.S., dedicated to the rescue, treatment, recuperation, and release of sick and injured wild birds.

Situated right on the edge of the beach, this facility daily treats an average of 15 seabirds that have been injured by a variety of causes, from fish hooks and fishing lines to gunshot wounds. Unfortunately, approximately 90% of all injuries are directly or indirectly attributable to humans. At any one time, there are usually in excess of 500 seabirds living at the sanctuary, from cormorants, white herons, and birds of prey to the ubiquitous brown pelican. Most of these birds are returned to their natural habitat when they are well, but some, particularly those who have lost an eye or a limb, remain in permanent residence; some of these produce offspring, which are then released.

Visitors are free to wander around this tree-lined open-air sanctuary, looking in on the bird hospital and various other facilities. You can also tag along as Ralph Heath or one of his staff takes a bucket of small fish down to the beach to feed the passing pelicans, often finding injured birds in the process. Tours of the entire operation are given on Tuesdays at 2pm.

Admission: Free, but donations are welcome.

Open: Daily 9am–dusk. **Directions:** North of downtown, take I-275 to Route 694 (exit 15) west. Cross over the toll bridge to Gulf Boulevard; turn left and sanctuary is seven blocks south.

JOHN'S PASS VILLAGE AND BOARDWALK, 12901 Gulf Blvd., Madeira Beach. Tel. 391-7373.

Named after Juan (John) Levique, a sea-turtle fisherman who lived here in the 19th century, this rustic Florida fishing village lies on the southern edge of Madeira Beach, where the waters of Boca Ciega Bay meet the Gulf. It is composed of a string of simple wooden structures topped by tin roofs, all resting on pilings 12 feet above sea level and connected by a 1,000-foot boardwalk. Most of the buildings have been converted into shops, art galleries, and restaurants.

The focal point is the large fishing pier and marina, where you can see the commercial and charter fishing boats unloading their daily catch, or sign up for a day's fishing trip on a party boat. Stroll the boardwalk and you're bound to find a good spot to watch the pelicans skimming the tops of the waves in search of fish or the dolphins playing in the tidal currents. This is also the home port of the *Europa Sun* cruise ship, the starting point for the Trolley Tours (see "Organized Tours and Cruises," below in this chapter), and the base for many other water-sports activities.

Admission: Free.

Open: Daily 9am–6pm or later for shops and activities, 7am–11pm for most restaurants. **Directions:** From downtown, take Central Avenue west via Treasure Island Causeway to Gulf Boulevard; turn right, go north for 20 blocks and cross over the bridge.

SUNSHINE SKYWAY BRIDGE, I-275 and U.S. 19, St. Petersburg. Tel. 823-8804.

Spanning the mouth of Tampa Bay, this 4.1-mile-long bridge connects Pinellas and Manatee counties and the city of St. Petersburg with the Bradenton/Sarasota area. Built at a cost of $244 million over a period of five years (1982–87), this is Florida's first suspension bridge, soaring 183 feet above the bay. The bridge's cables are painted yellow and illuminated at night. An older bridge, which still stands to the west, is being dismantled, with plans to make its approaches into Florida's longest fishing piers.

Toll: $1 each way.

Open: Daily, 24 hours.

2. MORE ATTRACTIONS

ST. PETERSBURG WATERFRONT HISTORICAL SOCIETY MUSEUM, 335 2nd Ave. NE, St. Petersburg. Tel. 894-1052.

Located on the approach to the Pier, this museum chronicles local and state history, with a series of exhibits ranging from the founding of the city to the first commercial flight and the famous St. Petersburg "green benches."

Admission: $2 for adults, $1.50 for seniors and students, 50¢ for children under age 12.

Open: Mon–Sat 10am–5pm, Sun 1–5pm. **Directions:** Downtown, east of Bayshore Drive and west of The Pier.

SUNKEN GARDENS, 1825 4th St. N., St. Petersburg. Tel. 896-3186.

One of the city's oldest attractions, this seven-acre tropical garden park dates back to 1935. It contains a vast array of 5,000 plants, flowers, and trees, including an orchid arbor, trails, walkways, and bridges. In addition, there is an aviary and over 500 rare birds, many of which perform in bird shows throughout the day. The complex also contains a huge gift shop and a wax museum depicting Biblical figures.

Admission: $6.95 for adults, $4 for children 3–11.

Open: Daily 9am–5:30pm. **Directions:** North of downtown, between 18th and 19th streets N.

YESTERDAY'S AIR FORCE MUSEUM, 16055 Fairchild Dr., Clearwater. Tel. 535-9007.

In a delightful location beside Old Tampa Bay and in the shadow of modern airplanes taking off from the adjacent airport, this indoor-outdoor museum features vintage military aircraft, from patrol planes and fighter-bombers to supersonic interceptors and a rescue helicopter, many dating from the World War II era. In addition, there are fire trucks and other vehicles, weapons, and artifacts from all branches of the armed forces.

Admission: $2 for adults, 50¢ for children under 16.

Open: Tues–Sat 10am–4pm, Sun 1–5pm. **Directions:** Off Route 686 between St. Petersburg–Clearwater Airport and the Boatyard Village shopping complex.

HAAS MUSEUM COMPLEX, 3511 2nd Ave. S., St. Petersburg. Tel. 327-1437.

Encompassing a full city block, this is a ten-building exhibit of 19th-century life in Florida, featuring a blacksmith shop, a barber shop, a railroad depot, a caboose, and a collection of model trains. In addition, there are the Lowe House, a sea captain's house built in 1888, one of the oldest homes in the county and a prime example of a board-and-batten construction; and the Grace Turner House, a Florida bungalow filled with antiques, small-scale furniture, and a collection of toys.

Admission: $2 for adults, $1.50 for seniors and students, 50¢ for children 6–11.

Open: Thurs–Sun 1–5pm. **Directions:** West of downtown, and one block west of U.S. 19, between 35th and 36th streets S.

HERITAGE PARK, 11909 125th St. N., Largo, Tel. 462-3474.

This 21-acre turn-of-the-century historical park features 17 of Pinellas County's oldest existing historic homes and buildings, "transplanted" to this pine-tree-shaded site north of St. Petersburg. The attractions include the oldest homestead in the county—the McMullen-Coachman log house—as well as a church, school, barn, store, bandstand, and train depot. There are periodic demonstrations of crafts such as rug-hooking, wool-spinning, flax-making, and weaving on a loom.

Admission: Donations are accepted.

Open: Tues–Sat 10am–4pm, Sun 1–4pm. **Directions:** North of downtown, off U.S. Alt. 19, between Walsingham Road and Ulmerton Road, east of Indian Rocks Beach.

CLEARWATER MARINE SCIENCE CENTER, 249 Windward Passage, Clearwater. Tel. 447-0980.

On an island in Clearwater Harbor, this facility is dedicated to the rescue and rehabilitation of marine mammals and sea turtles. The center also operates a turtle hatchery that releases more than 3,000 hatchlings each year in local waters. Visitors can view a 500-pound sea turtle and baby sea turtles, an Atlantic bottle-nosed dolphin, and a 210-gallon coral reef tank.

Admission: $2.75 for adults, $1.50 for children 3–11.

Open: Mon–Fri 9am–5pm, Sat 9am–4pm, Sun 11am–4pm. **Directions:** One mile east of Clearwater Beach on Island Estates; from the mainland, turn right at Island Way.

3. COOL FOR KIDS

GREAT EXPLORATIONS, 1120 4th St. S., St. Petersburg, Tel. 821-8885.

With a variety of "hands-on" exhibits, this museum welcomes visitors of all ages, but it is most appealing to children, especially on a rainy day. To name just a few of the activities, kids can explore a long, dark tunnel; shoot a game of laser pinball; paint a work of art with sunlight; play a melody with a sweep of the hand.

Admission: $3.75, $3 for seniors, free for children under 2.

Open: Mon–Sat 10am–5pm, Sun 1–5pm. **Directions:** South of downtown, one block west of the bayfront and the Dalí Museum.

BOYD HILL NATURE PARK, 1101 Country Club Way S., St. Petersburg. Tel. 893-7326.

Located at the south end of Lake Maggiore, this 216-acre city park has six scenic trails and boardwalks that meander through natural subtropical vegetation and native trees. Each loop averages 15 minutes of walking time, for a total of one and a half hours. Children are especially delighted to see birds, young reptiles, and other native species along the paths. There is also a library and nature center with exhibits, four aquariums, an observation beehive, and changing exhibits, as well as a picnic area and children's playground.

Admission: 75¢ for adults, 35¢ for children 17 and under.

Open: Daily 9am–5pm; till 8pm Tues and Fri Apr–Oct. **Directions:** Travel south on 9th St. S. to Country Club Way and bear right to entrance.

MOCCASIN LAKE NATURE PARK, 2750 Park Trail Lane, Clearwater. Tel. 462-6024.

This is a 51-acre wildlife preserve with a 5-acre lake, nature trails,

FROMMER'S COOL FOR KIDS

HOTELS

Days Inn Marina Beach Resort (see p. 47). With game room and water-sports rentals.

Don CeSar (see p. 52). Supervised children's activity programs, beachfront location, and water-sports rentals.

Innisbrook (see p. 70). Operates a summer golf institute for junior golfers; also has a supervised children's activity program, children's play area, game room, and pool.

Tradewinds (see p. 53). On the beach; operates full-time children's and teens' programs including barbecues and movies at night, plus paddle boats, bicycles, watersports, and life-size chess and checkers sets.

RESTAURANTS

Balloon Palace (see p. 88). Dozens of miniature hot-air balloons float across the ceiling, and the menu offers barbecued choices or finger foods, just right for small appetites.

Island House (see p. 100). An extensive menu just for kids, and a free balloon for each youngster who finishes dinner.

94th Aero Squadron (see p. 101). Old planes and World War I memorabilia fascinate kids of every age, as do the views of planes taking off from the adjacent airport.

an aviary, and exhibits on animals, plants, and energy sources. There is also an assortment of live native reptiles, fish, and aquatic reptiles. Solar energy provides the park's electrical power.

Admission: $1 for adults, 50¢ for children 3–12.

Open: Tues–Fri 9am–5pm, Sat–Sun 10am–6pm. **Directions:** Inland, northeast of Clearwater Beach; east of U.S. 19 and north of Gulf-to-Bay Boulevard.

4. ORGANIZED TOURS AND CRUISES

Take to the road, the sky, or the water to see the sights of the St. Petersburg area—and beyond.

LAND AND AIR TOURS

TROLLEY TOURS OF AMERICA, Hamlin's Landing, 401 2nd St. E., Suite 125, Indian Rocks Beach. Tel. 596-9776.

The closest thing you can get to a guided tour of the St. Petersburg area is "Lolly the Trolley." This colorful motorized trolley offers a continuous two-hour narrated trip around downtown and the beach strip, including the Pier, Dalí Museum, Sunken Gardens, other major sights, shopping malls, and hotels. You can stay on one trolley and do the whole tour at once, or get off at certain attractions and reboard a later trolley at no extra cost. Trolleys depart from John's Pass in Madeira Beach, but you can also commence a tour at any of the dozen stops along the route, including major St. Pete Beach hotels. If you're based in the Clearwater area, there is a shuttle service available to get you to John's Pass. Tickets can be purchased at hotels or from the drivers.

Prices: $16 for adults, $5 for children under 12.

Operates: Mon–Fri, departing John's Pass at 9am, 10am, 11am, noon, 1:30pm, and 2:30pm.

ELAN AIR INC., St. Petersburg–Clearwater Airport, Clearwater. Tel. 392-8686.

See the St. Petersburg area, including the Skyway Bridge and Suncoast Dome, from the air aboard a twin-engine plane. The most popular flight features the beach area at sunset, with free champagne. Cameras are permitted and reservations are required.

Prices: $100 per flight (for two to five people).

Open: Daily, schedule varies. **Directions:** North of St. Petersburg, off Ulmerton Road and Roosevelt Boulevard, in the Page AvJet Building of the airport.

WATER TOURS

One of the most enjoyable ways to see the sights of the St. Petersburg area is to board a boat and see the skyline and harborsides from the various bays and Gulf waters. There are a variety of boats, from paddlewheelers and old fishing vessels to pirate ships and pontoons, all of which take passengers for an hour or two, or longer.

Many offer lunch or dinner cruises, often with dancing and entertainment. Here are a few to whet your appetite.

THE *ADMIRAL* TOUR BOAT, Clearwater Beach Marina, Clearwater Beach. Tel. 462-2628 or toll free 800/444-4814.

Using an air-conditioned, 300-passenger, triple-decker craft, this company provides two options for seeing the sights of the Clearwater Harbor area—either an afternoon narrated sightseeing and bird-feeding cruise, or an evening dinner/dance cruise. The latter offers sit-down dinner (with an entrée choice of filet mignon, stuffed flounder, chicken Cordon Bleu, or sea bass), plus live music, and cocktail service (extra charge). In both cases, boarding is half an hour before departure time. Reservations are not taken for the sight-seeing cruise, but are required for the dinner cruise.

Fare: Daytime cruises $5.75 for adults, $3.50 for children 12 and under; evening dinner cruise $21.95.

Schedule: Year round Tues–Sat (and some Sun) 7pm–10pm; mid-Feb through Nov only; Tues–Fri 2–3:30pm. **Directions:** At the Clearwater Beach Marina, at the west end of Route 60.

ALBION CRUISES, 801 Pass-A-Grille Way, St. Petersburg Beach. Tel. 360-2263.

If you feel like escaping to a nearby unspoiled island south of St. Petersburg, here's the way. This company offers regular shuttle service to Shell Island on a 32-passenger pontoon-style boat. The ride takes 15 minutes and you can return when you wish, on the next shuttle or on the last one of the day. Once on the island, you can go shelling, swimming, fishing, or observe the local birds and wildlife. On some days, there is also a half-hour sunset cruise (by reservation only).

Fare: $10 for adults, $5 for children under 90 lbs (40.5 kg).

Schedule: Daily 10am, noon, 2pm, 4pm. **Directions:** Take the Pinellas Bayway to St. Petersburg Beach, turn left on Gulf Boulevard, and go south to Eighth Avenue at Pass-A-Grille.

CAPT. ANDERSON, St. Petersburg Beach Causeway, 3400 Pasadena Ave. S., St. Petersburg. Tel. 367-7804 or toll free 800/533-2388.

Docked between St. Petersburg and the beach area, this three-deck boat plies the waters of Boca Ciega Bay and the Gulf of Mexico. Cruises are operated at lunch and dinner times, with buffet meal service, as well as at midafternoon for dolphin-watching and bird-feeding. Mealtime cruises feature dance music by the Captain's Combo, as well as cocktail service (at an extra charge). Boarding for all trips is half an hour before departure and reservations are required for lunch and dinner cruises. On certain evenings, cruises with special themes, such as Gospel music, are offered; check in advance for exact schedules.

Fare: Cruise only, $5.25 for adults, $4.75 for seniors, $2.50 for children; lunch cruise, $11.60 for adults, $10.60 for seniors, $6.10 for children; dinner cruises, $19.95 for adults, $18.95 for seniors, $12.95 for children.

Schedule: Oct to mid-May, Tues–Sat lunch cruise 11am–1pm, dolphin/bird cruise 2–4pm; Wed, Fri–Sat dinner cruise 7–10pm. **Directions:** From downtown St. Pete, take Central Avenue west to St. Petersburg Beach Causeway, and follow signs.

CAPTAIN MEMO'S PIRATE CRUISE, Clearwater Beach Marina, Clearwater Beach, Tel. 446-2587.

This is a cruise that's particularly fun for those looking for a bit of "adventure" at sea. Decorated with all the trappings of an authentic pirate ship, the 49-passenger motorized sailboat *Sea Hogge* offers swashbuckling cruises, under the direction of fearless Captain Memo (Bill Wozencraft) and his all-female crew. The cruise goes along the

Intracoastal Waterway and into the Gulf of Mexico near Clearwater Beach, with frequent sightings of dolphins and maybe a few pirates along the way. The price includes complimentary beer, wine, or soft drinks, and champagne on the evening departure.

Fare: $23–$25 for adults, $17 for seniors and children 13–17, $10 for children 12 and under.

Schedule: Tues–Sat at 10am–noon, 2–4pm, and 5–7pm. **Directions:** In the Clearwater Beach Marina, at the west end of Route 60.

CITY OF SANDUSKY, 401 2nd Ave. NE., St. Petersburg. Tel. toll free 800/426-6286.

Based at the Vinoy Basin next to the Pier, this 110-foot, two-decked vessel offers some of the best views of the downtown St. Petersburg skyline. The boat takes its name from its home base of Sandusky, Ohio (where it returns every June). During the winter/spring season, it offers cruises of Tampa Bay as far south as the Sunshine Skyway Bridge. Facilities on board include a bar and snack bar. Saturday-night cruises include a dance band.

Fare: Cruise only $7.50; with lunch ($5.50 extra), dinner or Sun brunch ($10.50–$18.50 extra).

Schedule: Dec–May, Tues and Thurs–Fri 11:30am–1:30pm and 6:30–9:30pm; Wed and Sun 11:30am–1:30pm; Sat 11:30am–1:30pm and 7–10pm. **Directions:** Downtown, docked on the north side of the Pier complex.

CLEARWATER FERRY SERVICE, W. Drew Street, Clearwater. Tel. 442-7433.

Launched in 1990, this is a new catamaran boat service, offering a five-hour excursion from downtown Clearwater via the Intracoastal Waterway and Anclote River to Tarpon Springs, a town of predominantly Greek heritage that is famous for its sponge-diving industry. The trip includes lunch at a Greek restaurant overlooking the water, an escorted tour of the sponge docks, and ample time for shopping at the open-air markets. In addition, this company operates a regularly scheduled ferry service to Caladesi Island, a state park on a barrier island north of Clearwater Beach. Reservations are required for the Tarpon Springs excursion but not for the Caladesi Island ferry.

Fare: Cruise to Tarpon Springs with lunch $17.50, return trip by bus or boat $6; ferry to Caladesi Island, $6.95 round-trip.

Schedule: Tarpon Springs cruise Tues and Thurs 10am–3pm; Caladesi Island ferry daily, schedule varies. **Directions:** On the waterfront of downtown Clearwater, at the Drew Street Dock, just west of the offices of the Greater Clearwater Chamber of Commerce.

FLAMINGO CRUISES, Marine Tours, Inc., Clearwater Beach Marina, Clearwater Beach. Tel. 461-3113.

This 120-passenger vessel offers four different narrated sightseeing options in the Clearwater area—the Gulf of Mexico beaches, the inland waterways, the shoreline homes of Island Estates, or bird and dolphin areas. The boat has two decks, one of which is covered, and there is a snack bar on board; wine and cocktails are also sold.

Fare: $6–$7.50 for adults, $3.15 for children 4–12.

Schedule: Feb and Dec, Tues–Sun 2–4pm; Mar–Oct, Tues–Sat 10:30am–noon, 2–4pm, 5:30–7:30pm; Sun 5:30–7:30pm; Nov Tues–Sat 10:30am–noon and 2–4pm. **Closed:** Jan. **Directions:** In the Clearwater Beach Marina, at the west end of Route 60.

STARLITE PRINCESS, Hamlin's Landing, S.R. 688, Indian Rocks Beach. Tel. 595-1212.

Docked at Hamlin's Landing, a new condo/shopping development on the Intracoastal Waterway near Indian Rocks Beach, this authentic 106-foot, three-deck paddlewheeler offers four different types of cruises—sight-seeing only (with optional lunch), a luncheon/dance cruise, a dinner/dance cruise, and a full-day excursion to Tampa's Harbour Island (offered once a week). Most of the trips follow a scenic itinerary along inland waters, but the Tampa excursion also takes in parts of the Gulf of Mexico, Tampa Bay, and the Hillsborough River. Reservations are required for all cruises except the sight-seeing-only option. There is a snack bar on board, as well as optional cocktail service. Boarding is a half hour before departure.

Fare: Cruise only, $6.50 for adults, $4.50 for children 2–12; cruise with lunch, $12.75–$20.50; cruise with dinner, $26.45; all-day Tampa excursion with breakfast and lunch, $30.50 (optional transport back from Tampa is $6 per person).

Schedule: Cruise only (lunch optional), Tues, Fri–Sat noon–2pm; luncheon/dance cruise, Wed 11am–2pm; dinner/dance cruise, Tues–Wed, Fri–Sat, 7:30–10:30pm; all-day cruise to Tampa, Thurs 9am–5pm. **Directions:** North of St. Petersburg, at the west end of Route 688, at the Hamlin's Landing dock.

MINI-CRUISES

Whether you'd like to cruise for half a day or for a week, you'll find an option here.

EUROPA SUN, John's Pass, Gulf Blvd. at 129th Street, Madeira Beach. Tel. 393-5110 or toll free 800/688-PLAY.

Cruise by day or night in the waters of the Gulf of Mexico on board this 275-passenger, three-deck luxury ship. The facilities include first-class restaurants, live entertainment, casino gambling, cabaret shows, and dancing. Reservations required.

Fare: Day cruises $39.95; night cruises $39.95–$49.95; port charges and tax are extra.

Schedule: Mon 10am–4pm, 7pm–midnight; Tues 10am–4pm, 6–11pm; Thurs 11am–5pm, 6pm–midnight; Fri 11am–5pm, 7pm–1am; Sat 11am–5pm, 6pm–midnight. **Directions:** Docked at the John's Pass Marina, on the southern tip of Madeira Beach.

OCEAN SPIRIT, St. Petersburg Cruise Terminal, 250 8th Ave. S.E, St. Petersburg. Tel. toll free 800/338-3483.

This is the only extended-stay cruise trip sailing regularly from the St. Pete port. Operated by Ocean Quest International of New

Orleans, it is a modern 457-foot vessel, accommodating up to 320 passengers and offering such amenities as dining rooms and party lounges, a disco, a casino, sundecks, a swimming pool, and boutiques. Unlike other cruises, however, this one offers an "aquaventure," an itinerary geared for active sports enthusiasts. The ship, designed to serve as a mobile scuba-diving complex and water-sports resort, is equipped with sailboats, windsurfing boards, fishing craft, kayaks, snorkeling equipment, jet skis, and a teaching staff for each activity. The seven-night cruises go to the western Caribbean destinations of Cozumel, Belize, and the Bay Islands, all good diving spots.

Fare: $595–$1,795.

Schedule: Year round, departing each Sunday. **Directions:** Departs from Bayboro Harbor on Tampa Bay, south of the Pier and the Bayfront Center.

SEASCAPE, St. Petersburg Cruise Terminal, 351 8th Ave. S.E., St. Petersburg. Tel. toll free 800/432-0900.

A pioneer in the "cruise to nowhere" concept, this company operates mini-cruises in the Gulf of Mexico, on board the 1,105-passenger ship *Tropicana*. On weekends there is a choice of two 7-hour itineraries, departing either in the morning or evening, and during the rest of the week there is a 10-hour full-day cruise. The price includes buffet meals, Las Vegas–style floor shows, disco dancing, casino games, bingo, pool swimming, a kids' program, and skeet shooting. For the weekday cruises, complimentary motorcoach transport is provided to and from major hotels.

Fare: Day or evening mini-cruises $39 for adults and teens, $15 for children 11 and under; full-day cruise $69 for adults, $49 for teens 12–17, $15 for children under 12. Port charges and tax are extra.

Open: Fri–Sat 9am–5:30pm and 7pm–2:30am; Sun–Thurs 10am–8:30pm. **Directions:** Departs from Bayboro Harbor on Tampa Bay, south of the Pier and the Bayfront Center.

5. SPORTS AND RECREATION

SPECTATOR SPORTS

BASEBALL   Baseball and St. Petersburg have been linked for over 75 years. Al Lang, one of the city's early mayors, was an avid baseball fan and actively promoted St. Petersburg as a base for spring training. The St. Louis Browns were the first to come in 1914, and over the years they were followed by the Philadelphia Phillies, Boston Braves, New York Yankees, and New York Mets.

Currently, St. Petersburg is the winter home of the St. Louis Cardinals. Nearby Clearwater and Dunedin also serve as training grounds to two other major-league teams, the Philadelphia Phillies and the Toronto Blue Jays, respectively.

Up until 1990, Al Lang Stadium was the major baseball venue in downtown St. Petersburg. With the recent opening of the Florida Suncoast Dome, however, baseball will be bigger than ever in this city. Here is a rundown on the baseball scene at present:

FLORIDA SUNCOAST DOME, 1 Stadium Dr., St. Petersburg. Tel. 825-3100.

This is St. Petersburg's new centerpiece, a $110 million domed stadium with a seating capacity of 43,000 for baseball, as well as 37,400 for football, 28,900 for boxing, and 35,000 for basketball. As we go to press, this facility has just opened and is still searching for a major-league baseball team. In under a month, more than 22,000 season tickets have been reserved, with deposits, in anticipation of the inaugural year of regular-season major-league baseball in St. Pete. Exact schedules and prices will be announced when arrangements for a team are finalized.

Directions: Between 10th and 16th streets S., off 1st Avenue S. (exit 9 off I-275).

AL LANG STADIUM, 230 1st St. S., St. Petersburg. Tel. 893-7490.

This is the winter home of the St. Louis Cardinals, who hold their spring training here each February and March. The crack of the bat can also be heard at other times, with major-league exhibition games in the spring, followed by the St. Petersburg Cardinals, a class-A minor-league team (April through September), and the St. Petersburg Pelicans, part of the newly formed Senior Professional Baseball Association for former major-league players 35 and over (November through January).

Admission: $2.50–$6.

Open: Year round. **Directions:** Downtown, between the Pier and Bayfront Center.

JACK RUSSELL STADIUM, 800 Phillies Dr., Clearwater. Tel. 441-8638.

The Philadelphia Phillies play their winter training season at this 7,000-seat stadium, a short drive from Clearwater Beach.

Admission: $5–$6.

Open: Mid-Feb to Apr. **Directions:** North of St. Petersburg, less than a mile northeast of downtown Clearwater, and 3.5 miles west of U.S. 19, between Palmetto Street and Greenwood Avenue.

GRANT FIELD, 373 Douglas Ave., Dunedin. Tel. 733-9302.

This newly expanded field is the winter home of the Toronto Blue Jays.

Admission: $6–$7.

Open: Mid-Feb to Apr. **Directions:** Three miles north of Clearwater and 3.5 miles west of U.S. 19, just south of Main Street.

DOG RACING

DERBY LANE, 10490 Gandy Boulevard, St. Petersburg. Tel. 576-1359.

Founded in 1925, this is the world's oldest continually operating greyhound track, with indoor and outdoor seating, and standing areas. Facilities include restaurants and a cocktail lounge.

Admission: $1 for adults, $2.50 for Derby Club level; parking free for self-park, $3 for valet park.

Open: Jan–May, Mon–Sat 7:30pm; matinees Mon, Wed, Sat noon. **Directions:** North of downtown, half a mile east of 4th Street N.

FOOTBALL See Chapter 11, "What to See and Do in Tampa."

HORSE RACING See Chapter 11, "What to See and Do in Tampa."

JAI-ALAI See Chapter 11, "What to See and Do in Tampa."

RECREATION

With year-round sunshine and 28 miles of coastline along the Gulf of Mexico, the St. Petersburg area offers a wide choice of participatory sporting activities. To supply you with the latest happenings, the city operates a "Leisure Line" with recorded information on sports and recreational activities (tel. 893-7500). Here is a sampling of some of the things you can do:

BICYCLING With miles of flat terrain, St. Petersburg is ideal for biking. One of the prime routes is along the bayfront, and around Straub Park where there is a signposted biking trail. Other recommended areas include Fort DeSoto Park and Pass-A-Grille.

A county-wide system of bike trails is currently being developed. Check with the chamber of commerce for latest information at the time of your visit. Bikes can be rented from the following:

THE AUTUMN OLIVE BICYCLE RENTALS, 215 Central Ave., St. Petersburg. Tel. 822-4095.

A midcity rental station, it is ideal for downtown biking. This company operates a second branch at 522 Cleveland St., Clearwater (tel. 449-2479).

Price: $10 a day, $30 a week.

Open: Daily 9am–5pm. **Directions:** Downtown, at the Hotel Detroit (St. Petersburg International Youth Hostel), two blocks west of the bayfront.

CROSSROADS CYCLERY, 2036 Tyrone Blvd., St. Petersburg. Tel. 345-5401.

This company rents touring and racing bicycles. It also operates a location near the Pinellas Bayway at the Skyway Shopping Center, 6085 9th St. S., St. Petersburg (tel. 866-2225).

Price: From $10 a day.

Open: Mon–Sat 9am–8pm, Sun 11:30am–4:30pm. **Directions:** Northwest of downtown, in the Crossroads Shopping Center, at the intersection of 66th Street N. and 22nd Avenue N.

BEACH CYCLIST, 7517 Blind Pass Rd., St. Petersburg Beach. Tel. 367-5001.

In the beach area, this place offers several types of bikes, from a beach cruiser (allowed on the beaches at Treasure Island and Madeira Beach), to a selection of standard racing bikes.

Price: From $10 for 4 hours, $12 for 24 hours.

Open: Mon–Sat 10am–6pm, Sun 11am–4pm. **Directions:** On the northern tip of St. Pete Beach, off 75th Avenue and west of the St. Petersburg Beach Causeway.

FISHING With over 300 varieties of fish in Tampa Bay and Gulf of Mexico waters, fishing is a year-round sport in the St. Petersburg area.

Saltwater fishing is particularly popular along the Gulf shoreline, with catches ranging from grouper and snapper to trout, flounder, pompano, sea bass, tarpon, sailfish, snook, redfish, kingfish, and mackerel. Fishing can be done from the shore itself, as well as from piers, bridges, and boats. A popular option for visitors is to join a "party boat," a large seagoing craft that accommodates a number of customers for full- or half-day trips at a moderate per-person cost.

As of 1990, visitors are required to have a license for all saltwater fishing, from land or sea. The cost is $30 per year or $15 for a seven-day license. A stamp for taking crayfish (sometimes called Florida lobster) is an additional $2, as is a stamp for catching snook. Children under 16 are exempt from the fees.

The licenses are available at all county tax collectors' offices and at many bait-and-tackle shops, with a 50¢ and $1.50 surcharge, respectively. Most captains of charter fishing fleets have licensed vessels for saltwater fishing, so guests on those boats do not need a separate license. Always check in advance, as infractions carry a $500 fine.

The St. Petersburg area also offers freshwater fishing for sunfish, catfish, speckled perch, and bass. This too requires a license for nonresidents at a cost of $30 per year or $15 for seven days. For more information, call the Florida Game and Freshwater Fish Commission (tel. toll free 800/282-8002).

Here is a sampling of companies that cater to visitors:

DOUBLE EAGLE'S DEEP SEA FISHING BOATS, Clearwater Beach Marina, Clearwater Beach. Tel. 446-1653.

This company offers a change from the usual fishing boat, using two modern catamarans, 83 feet and 65 feet in length. The vessels go 20 to 25 miles offshore into the Gulf on four- or seven-hour day trips, with bait provided.

Fare: $18–$29 for adults; $16–$25 for children; $4 for tackle.

Schedule: Daily 8am–noon, 1–5pm, 9am–4pm. **Directions:** On the Clearwater Beach Marina, at the west end of Route 60.

CAPT. HUBBARD'S MARINA, 150 128th Ave., Madeira Beach. Tel. 393-1947 or 392-0167.

Known as a "fish famous" spot, this marina is the focal point of John's Pass, a huge recreational village perched on pilings where Boca Ciega Bay meets the Gulf. From here, you can try all types of fishing, from the dock and catwalks, or on party boats. Capt. Wilson Hubbard, who has been overseeing the operations since 1929, claims that John's Pass fishing boats catch more fish on nine out of ten days than any other boats on the Florida coast. It's not unusual for over 4,000 pounds of grouper to be landed in a day. Reservations are required for the longer trips.

Price: $20 half-day; $35 full-day; overnight $70 including the use of a bunk.

Schedule: Daily, half-day trips 8am–1pm and 1–6pm; full-day trips 8am–6pm; overnight trips Tues and Fri departing 8pm. **Directions:** Northwest of St. Petersburg, at the southern tip of Madeira Beach.

CAPTAIN KIDD, 801 Pass-A-Grille Way, St. Petersburg Beach. Tel. 360-2263.

Departing from the southern end of St. Petersburg Beach, this is a 63-foot twin-diesel-powered fishing vessel offering four- and six-hour fishing trips in the Gulf. On-board facilities include a snack bar and free fishing instruction for beginners; fish cleaning service is also available.

Fare: $21–$31 for adults, $19–$28 for seniors and children.

Schedule: Mon–Fri 8am–12:30pm, 1–5:30pm, Fri 6–10:30pm, Sat–Sun 8:30am–3pm. **Directions:** From downtown St. Petersburg, take the Pinellas Bayway to Gulf Boulevard, turn left and go south to 8th Avenue.

CAPT. DAVE SPAULDING'S QUEEN FLEET, Clearwater Beach Marina, Clearwater Beach. Tel. 446-7666.

One of the largest party-boat fishing fleets in the Clearwater area, this company offers trips of varying durations. Bait is furnished but rod rental is extra. Private charters for evenings are also available. Reservations are encouraged but not required.

Fare: $18 for half day, $29 for three-quarters day, $37 for full-day; $5 for rods.

Schedule: Daily 8am–noon, 1–5pm, 9am–4pm, 8am–5pm. **Directions:** On the eastern dock of the Clearwater Beach Marina, at the west end of Route 60.

REDINGTON LONG PIER, 17490 Gulf Blvd., Redington Shores. Tel. 391-9398.

Extending 1,021 feet into the Gulf of Mexico, this pier is a favorite with fishermen and sightseers alike. For the best fishing, according to the local authorities, come early in the evening, from about an hour before sunset until midnight, especially if the tide is incoming. Fishing is also recommended early in the morning, from before dawn until about daybreak, particularly if the tide is coming in. The pier offers a snack bar, rest rooms, rod rentals, bait, tackle, shelters and benches, and fish-cleaning facilities. If you are in the Clearwater area, you can also cast a line from Big Pier 60, off Gulfview Boulevard, Clearwater Beach (tel. 446-0060).

Price: Fishing charges, $4.50 for adults, $3.50 for children; rod rental, $3.75 plus $5 deposit; spectators or walk-ons, 50¢.

Open: Daily 24 hours. **Directions:** Off Gulf Boulevard at 175th Avenue.

GOLF   There are over 40 golf courses and schools in the St. Petersburg area. Many of these facilities welcome visitors. Here are a few suggestions:

AIRCO FLITE GOLF COURSE, 3650 Roosevelt Blvd., Clearwater. Tel. 573-4653.
This is an 18-hole, par-72 course, with driving range, clubhouse, restaurant, lounge, and snack bar. Lessons and golf-club rentals are also available. Bookings can be made up to six days in advance.
   Prices: $33 per person including cart.
   Open: Daily 7am–6pm. **Directions:** Adjacent to the St. Petersburg–Clearwater Airport and behind the Showboat Dinner Theater.

BARDMOOR COUNTRY CLUB, 8000 Bardmoor Blvd., Largo. Tel. 397-0483.
Often the venue of major tournaments, this semiprivate club offers two 18-hole courses, par-71 and -72, designed by Tom Fazio, plus a driving range, restaurant, lounge, and snack bar. Lessons and rental clubs are also available. The south course is open to the public.
   Prices: Greens fees $30 weekdays, $35 weekends, with cart.
   Open: Daily 7am–6pm. **Directions:** North of St. Petersburg, off Starkey Road, and south of Route 688.

CHI CHI RODRIGUES GOLF COURSE, 3030 McMullen-Booth Rd., Clearwater. Tel. 725-2945.
Newly opened in 1989, this is an 19-hole, par-69 course, with driving range, restaurant, lounge, and snack bar. Lessons and rental clubs are also available.
   Prices: $25 weekdays, $27 weekends, with cart.
   Open: Daily 7am–6pm. **Directions:** Northeast of Clearwater, and one-quarter mile north of Route 580.

FLORIDA GOLF SCHOOL, Belleview Biltmore Resort, 25 Belleview Blvd., Belleair/Clearwater. Tel. 441-4173 or toll free 800/464-3706.
Geared to players of all abilities, this school offers a program of three- and five-day courses in the sport, with class sizes of no more than four students per professional. Each day consists of five hours of lessons, video analysis, classroom theory sessions, and lunch.
   Prices: $430 for a three-day program, $735 for a five-day program; $699 and $1,155 with accommodations and all meals.
   Open: Year round. **Directions:** 1 mile south of downtown Clearwater, off Ft. Harrison Avenue U.S. Alt. 19.

INNISBROOK GOLF INSTITUTE, Innisbrook Resort, off Klosterman Rd., Tarpon Springs. Tel. 813/942-2000, ext. 5383 or toll free 800/456-2000.
Play on the Copperhead, Florida's top-rated course, as part of this program. A typical four-day/three-night program includes 12 hours of individual instruction, videotape analysis, on-course supervision, personal lockers for storing clubs, overnight

accommodations, play and greens fees on Innisbrook's three championship 18-hole courses, unlimited range balls, breakfast and lunch daily, cocktail reception, and all related service charges. A similar five-night regimen for junior golfers, aged 13–17, is also available in the summer. See Chapter 5, "St. Petersburg Accommodations," for more information on Innisbrook.

Prices: $780–$1,131 single, $660–$891 double for the four-day program; $750 for the five-night junior plan.

Open: Jan–June and Sept–Dec, Thurs–Sun and Sun–Wed; June–Aug for juniors. **Directions:** Between U.S. 19 and U.S. Alt. 19, five miles north of Clearwater.

LARGO MUNICIPAL GOLF COURSE, 12500 131st St., Largo. Tel. 587-6724.

A popular course with local residents, this is an 18-hole par-62 public course, within two miles of Indian Rocks Beach.

Prices: Green fees $9 before 2pm, $7 after 2pm.

Open: Daily 7am–6pm. **Directions:** North of St. Petersburg, four blocks north of Route 688.

MANGROVE BAY GOLF CLUB, 875 62nd Ave. NE, St. Petersburg. Tel. 893-7797.

One of the top 50 municipal golf courses in the U.S., this course hugs the inlets of Old Tampa Bay and offers 18-hole, par-72 play. Facilities include a driving range and snack bar; lessons and golf-club rentals are also available.

Prices: $15 with no cart, $23 with cart.

Open: Daily 6am–6pm. **Directions:** In the northeast corner of St. Petersburg, 1 mile east of 4th Street N.

SAILING Whether you want to perfect your sailing skills or learn from scratch, this area offers many opportunities to practice and participate. Clearwater, in particular, is a mecca for sailboat rides and rentals. Here are a few suggestions:

ANNAPOLIS SAILING SCHOOL, 6800 34th St. S., St. Petersburg. Tel. 813/867-8102 or toll free 800/237-0795.

Learn to sail or perfect your sailing skills at this branch of the famous Maryland-based school. Various courses are offered for two, five, seven, or nine days. Depending on the course you take, you'll overnight at the adjacent Days Inn Marina Beach Hotel or on board one of the cruising sloops.

Price: $185–$980 per person, depending on season and length of course.

Open: Daily year round. **Directions:** From downtown, take I-271 south to Pinellas Point Drive (exit 3); school is on the left.

PHOENIX, Dolphin Landings, 4737 Gulf Blvd., St. Petersburg Beach. Tel. 813/360-7411 or 367-4488.

Based on Boca Ciega Bay, this 41-foot sailing ketch offers trips to various Gulf of Mexico ports, including nearby natural barrier islands and Egmont Key. Most trips are from two to eight hours in duration and include complimentary soft drinks. Reservations are required.

Price: $20–$50 for adults, $10–$25 for children; reduced rates for some Tues–Thurs departures.

Schedule: Daily 8:30am and 12:30pm, but departures vary according to demand. **Directions:** Directly behind the Dolphin Village Shopping Center, between 47th and 48th avenues.

SOUTHERN ROMANCE, Clearwater Beach Marina, Clearwater Beach. Tel. 813/461-6148.

This is a 40-foot ocean racing/cruising yacht that takes a maximum of six passengers at a time for sailing in Clearwater Harbor and Gulf waters. Advance reservations suggested.

Price: $25 per person.

Schedule: Departures daily at 10am, 1:30pm, 4:30pm. **Directions:** On the Clearwater Beach Marina, at the west end of Route 60.

SUNCOAST SAILING CENTER, Clearwater Beach Marina, Clearwater Beach. Tel. 813/581-4662.

Sail aboard a 65-foot windjammer or a 38-foot racing yacht. You can be part of the crew or just relax for 2½ hours and enjoy the views of the Gulf waters. Rentals of small sloops and sailing lessons also available. Reservations required.

Price: $19.50–$22.50 for adults, half-price for children.

Schedule: Departures daily at 10am, 1:30pm, 4:30pm. **Directions:** In the Clearwater Beach Marina, at the west end of Route 60.

SWIMMING Edged by dozens of sugar-white sandy beaches, the St. Petersburg area is ideal for swimming, sunning, or just walking along the shore. There is never a fee for using a beach, but there are charges for metered parking, usually 25¢ for each half-hour. Most beaches have rest rooms, refreshment stands, and picnic areas.

Many of the hotels sit right on the beach, so you can just step outside the door and put your feet in the sand. In case your accommodations are not beachfront, or if you just want to sample a different beach or two each day, here is a run-down of prime swimming areas that offer public access:

✪ **St. Petersburg Beach:** The prime beach of St. Pete's Gulf Coast shores, it is 3 miles long, just west of Gulf Boulevard. Public access and parking areas include 46th Street (Belle Vista Beach), 68th Street (Upham Beach), and at Pass-A-Grille, on 8th Avenue.

✪ **Ft. DeSoto Park:** South of St. Petersburg, this string of islands offers three miles of beaches with shorelines fronting Tampa Bay as well as the Gulf of Mexico. There are also extensive picnic and camping facilities here, with no parking charges.

Treasure Island: North of St. Pete Beach, this small island has 45 dune walkovers and street ends, giving pedestrian access to Gulf beaches between 77th and 127th avenues, with some parking meters at 77th, 90th, 100th, 112th, 120th, and 126th avenues.

Madeira Beach: Sea oats and sand dunes add to the beach scene here, with 1.5 miles of natural beachfront off Gulf Boulevard, on the southern end of Sand Key Island. The best access and parking are at the Madeira Beach County Park, along 141st to 148th avenues, at Archibald Memorial Beach at 152nd Avenue, and near John's Pass at 129th Avenue.

Redington Beaches: A largely residential area, these Gulf beaches (Redington Beach, North Redington Beach, and Redington Shores) offer numerous public accesses but little parking except at the fishing pier at 175th Avenue at Redington Shores.

Indian Rocks Beach: Here are 3 miles of Gulf beaches, with street parking access between 15th and 27th avenues and 1st and 8th avenues. Parking is limited but free.

Sand Key Park: This is the area's largest and newest beach park, situated at the north tip of Sand Key Island. It offers a beachfront overlooking the Gulf of Mexico or the boating channel of Clearwater Pass.

✪ **Clearwater Beach:** Equally distant from St. Petersburg or Tampa (22 miles in either direction), this wide and sandy 4-mile stretch is the largest of all the beaches in the Tampa Bay area. The major points of access and parking (over 800 parking spaces) are along Gulfview Avenue at the south end of the island.

TENNIS   There are more than 200 private and public tennis courts in the St. Petersburg area. Many resorts, hotels, and motels have their own tennis courts on site and offer court time to guests on a complimentary or reduced-rate basis. In addition, here are a few other tennis facilities that welcome visitors.

TERRY ADDISON'S AUSTRALIAN TENNIS INSTITUTE, Innisbrook Resort, off Klosterman Road, Tarpon Springs. Tel. 813/942-2000, ext. 5142.

⭐   Under the direction of Australian Davis Cup player Terry Addison, this is a four-day, three-night program for tennis enthusiasts, with the pace geared to individual players, whether novice or advanced. The price includes 12 hours of on-court instruction, accommodations, breakfast and lunch daily, unlimited court time, slow-motion stop-action video analysis, instructional videotape for home use, tennis towel and T-shirt, and all related service charges. See Chapter 5, "St. Petersburg Accommodations," for more information about Innisbrook.

Prices: $555–$795 single, $435–$555 double.

Open: Year round. **Directions:** North of Clearwater, off U.S. 19, between Lake Tarpon Drive and Klosterman Road.

HURLEY PARK, Gulf Way at 15th Avenue, Pass-A-Grille, St. Petersburg Beach.

There is just one court here, opposite the beach, open on a first-come, first-play basis.

Price: Free.

Open: Daily, during daylight hours. **Directions:** Take Pinellas Bayway to Gulf Boulevard, turn left and go to 15th Avenue, then turn right.

McMULLEN PARK, 1000 Edenville Ave., Clearwater. Tel. 462-6144.

This inland facility offers 17 lighted courts, a pro shop, and locker room; lessons are also available. Reservations recommended.

Price: $2–$2.50 per hour per court.

Open: Mon–Fri 8am–10pm, Sat 8am–8pm, Sun 8am–7pm.
Directions: Southeast of Clearwater Beach, off U.S. 19, between Gulf-to-Bay Drive and Belleair Road.

RACQUET CLUB OF PARADISE ISLAND, 10315 Paradise Blvd., Treasure Island. Tel. 360-6062.

Surrounded by the waters of Boca Ciega Bay, this facility offers 20 courts, of which 16 are clay and 4 are hard; 6 are lighted. Lessons are available.

Price: $5 Mon–Fri, $7 Sat–Sun.

Open: Mon–Fri 8am–dark, Sat–Sun 8am–6pm. **Directions:** On Paradise Island, off the Treasure Island Causeway, between Treasure Island and the mainland.

ST. PETERSBURG TENNIS CENTER, 650 18th Ave. S., St. Petersburg. Tel. 894-4378.

This facility offers 15 tennis courts, as well as snack bar, locker rooms, and showers. Private lessons and clinics are available.

Price: $3–$5; after 4pm, $3.

Open: Daily 9am–dark. **Directions:** Just south of downtown, in Bartlett Park, five blocks from Lassing Park and Tampa Bay.

WATER SPORTS In addition to fishing, sailing, and swimming, the St. Pete area offers an abundance of other water-related activities. Just step on the beach or go near the bay and you'll see a myriad of inviting craft, from aquacycles to Aqua-Ray boats, catamarans to kayaks, pontoon or paddle boats to parasails, and wave-runners or windsurfers to water skis, just to mention a few. Here are a few good sources for renting equipment:

BEACH MOTOR SPORT RENTALS, Clearwater Beach Marina, Clearwater Beach. Tel. 446-5503.

If you can handle a boat yourself, this company rents crafts equipped with 50hp to 150hp motors. Sizes range from 16 to 20 feet, carrying three to seven persons. Eight-foot miniboats with 6hp engines, ideal for two people, can also be rented by the hour.

Price: $75–$130 half day, $130–$190 full day, miniboats $20 an hour.

Open: Daily 9am–5pm. **Directions:** On the Clearwater Beach Marina, at the west end of Route 60.

CAPT. FRANK'S WATERSPORTS, 6000 Gulf Blvd., St. Petersburg Beach. Tel. 345-4500.

Located on the beach behind the Sandpiper Hotel, this is a good spot to rent aquacycles, catamarans, kayaks. You'll find another Capt. Frank's behind the TradeWinds Hotel at 5500 Gulf Blvd.

Prices: $6–$10 for a half hour, $10–$20 an hour, depending on equipment.

Open: Daily 8am–6pm or later. **Directions:** West of downtown, in the middle of St. Pete Beach, off 60th Avenue.

CAPT. MIKE'S WATERSPORTS, 6300 Gulf Blvd., St. Petersburg Beach. Tel. 360-1998 or 367-2921.

Located on the beach behind the Colonial Gateway Inn, this company offers parasailing rides, wave runners, pontoon boats, fishing equipment, boat rentals, and water-ski rentals and lessons. "Early bird" reduced rates ($5 off) are available between 9 and 10am. Other locations are behind the Dolphin Beach Hotel at 4900 Gulf Blvd. and at Winston's Marina, 9540 Blind Pass Rd.

Prices: From $35 for parasailing, $20 for water-skiing; $35 for wave runners; $25 for lessons.

Open: Daily 8am–6pm or later. **Directions:** West of downtown, in the middle of St. Pete Beach, off 63rd Avenue.

INTERNATIONAL BOAT RENTAL, 17811 Gulf Blvd., Redington Shores. Tel. 391-6308.

Located on Boca Ciega Bay, this company rents craft for use on the Intracoastal Waterway, including 14-foot, 25hp boats, and 18-foot, 70hp boats, either for sight-seeing or fishing. Aqua-Ray boats and water-ski equipment are also available.

Price: $40 half day, $80 full day for smaller boats; $85 half day, $159 full day for larger boats.

Open: Daily 8am–5pm. **Directions:** From downtown St. Pete, take I-275 to Route 694 (exit 15) and go west to Gulf Boulevard; turn left and go 1 mile south to 179th Avenue.

PARASAIL ADVENTURES, 14505 Gulf Blvd., Madeira Beach. Tel. 397-1050.

A combination scenic aerial ride and boating adventure, parasailing is offered by this company at various beach locations. Launches are available with a choice of 300-foot rides or 600-foot rides. Reservations required.

Price: $35–$45 per ride.

Open: Daily 9am–5pm or later. **Directions:** From downtown St. Pete, take the Tom Stewart Causeway to Madeira Beach, turn left on Gulf Boulevard.

SAIL-A-DAY, 2300 Gulf Blvd., Indian Rocks Beach. Tel. 595-WIND.

This shop rents sailboards and sailboats for use on nearby Gulf beaches. Lessons, either four or eight hours in duration, are also available.

Price: $10–$12 an hour, $24–$28 for four hours, $30–$35 a day, $120–$140 a week. Lessons $40–$75.

Open: Daily 8:30am–6pm. **Directions:** Take Ulmerton Road (Rte. 688) west to Gulf Boulevard; turn right and go to 23rd Avenue.

SHERATON SAND KEY RESORT, 1160 Gulf Blvd., Clearwater Beach. Tel. 395-1611.

This is one of the largest water-sports centers on the entire beach strip, with rentals for glass-bottom paddle boats, Hobie Cats, windsurfers, and snorkeling equipment. Lessons are also available for windsurfing.

Price: $12–$25 per half hour or hour, depending on equipment rented; snorkeling gear $8.50 all day; windsurfing lessons $8.

Open: Daily 9am–6pm or later. **Directions:** At the northern tip of Sand Key Island, next to Sand Key Park.

WALKING TOUR —
DOWNTOWN ST. PETERSBURG

Start: Florida Suncoast Dome
Finish: The Pier
Time: Allow approximately two hours
Best Times: Weekends
Worst Times: Weekday morning or evening rush hours

FROM THE SUNCOAST DOME TO THE CARNEGIE LIBRARY Start your tour at the:

1. **Florida Suncoast Dome,** 1 Stadium Drive (between 10th and 16th streets, off 1st Avenue S.), the city's new stadium/showplace on 66 acres. You may wish to walk the grounds or just admire the huge slant-roofed dome from 1st Avenue S., a good picture-taking vantage point. Next, head one block north to Central Avenue and stop at the:

2. **Gas Plant Antique Arcade,** 1246 Central Avenue (between 12th and 13th streets N.). This four-story complex, housed in a former gas plant, is the largest antique mall on Florida's west coast, with more than 100 dealers displaying their wares.

   Continue along Central Avenue for five blocks to 7th Street N. This stretch still has some empty stores and a few pawn shops, although the advent of the Suncoast Dome is beginning to perk up the area. Stop to look at the:

3. **Green-Richman Arcade,** 689 Central Avenue. Built in 1923, this Mediterranean Revival–style shopping arcade displays a style of architecture that was popular in St. Pete in the 1920s. A forerunner of the modern shopping mall, this arcade once housed a major boom-era real estate firm.

   At 7th Street, head north and go two blocks to Arlington Avenue. Cross Arlington, turn right, and go one block to Mirror Lake Drive. On your left is the:

4. **Unitarian Universalist Church,** 719 Arlington Avenue, built in 1926. The design was inspired by the mission churches of the Spanish Colonial period. Turn left on Mirror Lake Drive and take time to admire:

5. **Mirror Lake,** the city's first source of drinking water. Landscaped in the early 1900s as a park with shady palm trees and benches, it soon became St. Pete's first lovers' lane. Today it is a tranquil spot to rest and enjoy the birdsong and reflections of the fine houses that surround the lake. Continue north three blocks,

passing the lake. On the southwest corner of Mirror Lake Drive and 3rd Avenue N. is:

6. **St. Petersburg Junior High School,** 296 Mirror Lake Drive, a Mediterranean Revival structure built in 1924. Cross 3rd Avenue, continuing east, and you will see two more Mediterranean Revival buildings:

7. **Mirror Lake Christian Church** (1926), and

8. **St. Petersburg Public High School,** 709 Mirror Lake Drive (1919). Continue east across 7th Street and the adjacent parking lot to the:

9. **St. Petersburg Shuffleboard Club** (1924), the largest shuffleboard club in the world. Walk through the grounds to 4th Avenue N. Turn right and see the:

10. **St. Petersburg Lawn Bowling Club,** 536 4th Avenue N. (1926), one of the oldest clubs for this sport in the country. Directly across the street is the:

11. **Coliseum Ballroom,** 535 4th Avenue N. (1924), one of the oldest continually operating big-band-era dance halls in the United States. Continue east on 4th Avenue N. to 5th Street N., turn right and continue south till you cross 3rd Avenue N. On your right is the:

12. **Carnegie Library,** 300 5th Street N. Dating back to 1915, this beaux arts structure was the city's first library building and was financed by a grant from the Carnegie Foundation.

REFUELING STOP The best place for refreshment in this area is the **13. Heritage Grille,** 234 3rd Avenue N., at the corner of 2nd Street, two blocks east of the Carnegie Library. The restaurant is housed in the Heritage, a restored inn that was originally known as the Martha Washington Hotel when built in the early 1920s. It is a bright and airy café, with a menu of light regional cuisine.

FROM ST. PETERSBURG CITY HALL TO STRAUB PARK

From the Carnegie Library, continue south on 5th Street, across Mirror Lake Drive (it now becomes 2nd Avenue N.). Make a left, crossing 5th Street, and on your right is:

14. **St. Petersburg City Hall,** 175 5th Street N. Built in 1939, this Mediterranean Revival structure was one of the last buildings of this style built in the city. Backtrack a few steps and make a right onto 2nd Avenue N., then turn right onto 4th Street to see:

15. **St. Peter's Cathedral,** 140 4th Street N., dating back to 1899 and one of the first Episcopal houses of worship in the city. On the opposite side of the street is the:

16. **Randolph Hotel,** 200 4th Street N., a good example of an art deco–style hotel in the downtown area. One-half block farther down 4th Street is:

17. **Williams Park,** dating back to 1888 and laid out as the city's main square when St. Petersburg was plotted. It is named after

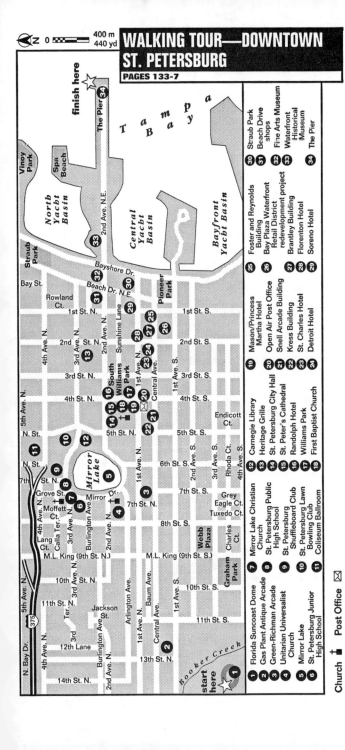

WALKING TOUR—DOWNTOWN ST. PETERSBURG

PAGES 133-7

400 m
440 yd

Tampa Bay

finish here

Vinoy Park

Spa Beach

North Yacht Basin

Straub Park

Central Yacht Basin

Bayfront Yacht Basin

Pioneer Park

Bayshore Dr.

Beach Dr. N.E.

Bay St.

Rowland Ct.

1st St. N.

1st St. S.

4th Ave. N.

2nd Ave. N.

3rd St. N.

2nd St. N.

Sunshine Lane

2nd Ave. S.

2nd St. S.

1st Ave. S.

South Williams Park

3rd St. N.

3rd St. S.

3rd Ave. N.

Central Ave.

5th Ave. N.

4th St. N.

4th St. S.

Endicott Ct.

N. St.

5th St. N.

5th St. S.

N. St.

7th

Mirror Lake

6th St. S.

2nd St. S.

3rd St. S.

Rhoda Ct.

4th Ave. S.

Grove St.

Mirror Dr.

7th St. N.

7th St. S.

Grey Eagle Ct.

Tuxedo Ct.

Moffett Ct.

Lang Ct.

Calla Ter.

4th Ave. N.

3rd Ave. N.

Burlington Ave.

2nd Ave. N.

8th St. S.

Webb Plaza

Charles Ct.

M.L. King (9th St. N.)

M.L. King (9th St. S.)

Graham Park

10th St. N.

3rd St. N.

1st Ave. N.

Baum Ave.

Arlington Ave.

Central Ave.

1st Ave. S.

10th St. S.

11th St. N.

Jackson St.

11th St. S.

Florida Suncoast Dome

12th Lane

13th St. N.

N. Bay Dr. N.

4th Ave. N.

Burlington Ave. N.

2nd Ave. N.

14th St. N.

Booker Creek

start here

375

5th St. N.

① Florida Suncoast Dome
② Gas Plant Antique Arcade
③ Green-Richman Arcade
④ Unitarian Universalist Church
⑤ Mirror Lake
⑥ St. Petersburg Junior High School
⑦ Mirror Lake Christian Church
⑧ St. Petersburg Public High School
⑨ St. Petersburg Shuffleboard Club
⑩ St. Petersburg Lawn Bowling Club
⑪ Coliseum Ballroom
⑫ Carnegie Library
⑬ Heritage Grille
⑭ St. Petersburg City Hall
⑮ St. Peter's Cathedral
⑯ Randolph Hotel
⑰ Williams Park
⑱ First Baptist Church
⑲ Mason/Princess Martha Hotel
⑳ Open Air Post Office
㉑ Snell Arcade Building
㉒ Kress Building
㉓ St. Charles Hotel
㉔ Detroit Hotel
㉕ Foster and Reynolds Building
㉖ Bay Plaza Waterfront Retail District redevelopment project
㉗ Brantley Building
㉘ Florenton Hotel
㉙ Soreno Hotel
㉚ Straub Park
㉛ Beach Drive shops
㉜ Fine Arts Museum
㉝ Waterfront Historical Museum
㉞ The Pier

Church ✝   Post Office ⊠

John Williams, one of the city's founders. Today it is a shady refuge in the midst of downtown and the site of frequent open-air band concerts. Across from the park is the neoclassical:

18. First Baptist Church, 136 4th Street N., dating back to 1924. (The structure is currently for sale, as the congregation is moving to new and larger quarters on Gandy Boulevard.) Next door is the:

19. Mason/Princess Martha Hotel, 401 1st Avenue N. Dating back to 1923–24, this neoclassical-style hotel was one of the largest built during the boom era. Cross 1st Avenue N. and you will see the:

20. Open Air Post Office, 400 1st Avenue N., dating back to 1917. The world's first open-air post office, it was built so that box holders could take advantage of St. Pete's mild climate. It is now partially enclosed. Cross the adjacent alley south to the:

21. Snell Arcade Building, 405 Central Avenue. Built in 1926 by real estate developer Perry Snell, it was designed primarily as an office building, but it also had an arcade of shops on the ground level and a rooftop restaurant on the third floor.

Now back on Central, there are a number of landmarks worth a look, including the glazed terra-cotta:

22. Kress Building, 475 Central Avenue, built in 1925–27 and originally a five-and-dime store, now renovated as offices. Continuing east, between 2nd and 3rd streets, is the:

23. St. Charles Hotel, 241-45 Central Avenue, dating back to 1903 and now the site of Jannus Landing, a small shopping/ entertainment complex. The city's first hotel, built in 1888, is the:

24. Detroit Hotel, 215 Central Avenue. Named after the hometown of John Williams, this vintage building is now a youth hostel. The:

25. Foster and Reynolds Building, 175 Central Avenue, dating to 1909, is typical of the early brick storefronts that originally lined Central Avenue, the city's main street. Across the street is Phase I of the:

26. Bay Plaza Waterfront Retail District, a new shopping and commercial development that will rejuvenate the streetscapes of downtown St. Pete. Target date for opening is 1991–92.

Leaving Central Avenue now, turn left onto 2nd Street and go north to the:

27. Brantley Building, 17 2nd Street N., a small frame structure that is reputed to be the oldest structure in the downtown area, Adjacent is the:

28. Florenton Hotel, 25 2nd Street N., which dates back to 1910 and is said to have been the city's first masonry hotel, now renovated into offices. Turn right onto 1st Avenue N. and walk two blocks east to the:

29. Soreno Hotel, 110 Beach Drive NE, a huge Mediterranean Revival–style building dating back to 1923–24. Although it has fallen into disuse now and faces an uncertain future, in its day it was touted as St. Pete's first "million-dollar hotel." Cross over Beach Drive at 1st Avenue NE and you are now at:

30. Straub Park, named in honor of William Straub, a local newspaper editor who led a campaign for public ownership of the city's waterfront in the early 1900s.

Walk one block north to 2nd Avenue NE. You are now in the heart of the city's bayfront district and have a number of options to complete your tour—visit some of the fashionable shops along the adjacent:

31. Beach Drive, stop at the:

32. Fine Arts Museum or:

33. Waterfront Historical Museum, both just steps away, or turn right and head to:

34. The Pier, the city's unique shopping/dining/entertainment complex on the water.

REFUELING STOP For something light, head to **The Pier,** where the choice includes Alessi's and a fast food court on the ground level, or Cha Cha Coconuts, known for its tropical drinks as well as basic American fare, on the rooftop. On the fourth floor, there is also a branch of the famous Spanish restaurant The Columbia.

---

6. SHOPPING

Souvenir shopping is big business in the St. Petersburg area—from postcards and local shell crafts to sea-scene art, beachwear, and tropical clothing, with shops spread throughout downtown and the beach strip.

For many years, the most famous department store in the area has been **Maas Brothers,** a company that has dominated downtown St. Pete (101 3rd St. N., tel. 895-7525) and the surrounding communities.

In 1991–92, plans call for the opening of the Bay Plaza Waterfront Retail District, a new upscale midtown shopping development in a Mediterranean-style open-air layout. Located just west of the Pier, it is expected that this new retail complex will greatly revitalize the downtown shopping scene. There is speculation that even Maas Brothers will move to this new site.

At the present time, however, some of the best shopping is near the beaches or residential areas, with many stores clustered in malls, markets, or themed shopping villages.

MALLS, MARKETS, AND SHOPPING CLUSTERS

BAY AREA OUTLET MALL, 15525 U.S. 19, Clearwater. Tel. 535-2337.

Known for selling well-known brand names at bargain prices, this is a huge 80-unit complex spread over four wings. Manufacturers represented range from Bally and Foot-Joy to Seiko, Monet, Revlon, Bass, Aileen, and Laura Ashley. Also on sale are records, ribbons, jewelry, toys, and affordable art.

Open: Mon-Sat 10am-9pm, Sun noon-6. **Directions:** At East Bay/Roosevelt Boulevard and U.S. 19.

BAYSIDE MARKET, 5501 Gulf Blvd., St. Petersburg Beach. Tel. 367-2784 or 367-4485.

A new development, this cluster of shops offers resort and tropical clothing, swimwear, hats, T-shirts, handpainted clothing, and nautical crafts, as well as a gourmet deli, art gallery, and a tour-booking kiosk. Plans also call for the rejuvenation and reopening of the wax museum that was on this site for many years.

Open: Daily 10am-9pm. **Directions:** Next to Silas Dent's restaurant and opposite the TradeWinds Resort, between 55th and 56th avenues.

BOATYARD VILLAGE, 16100 Fairchild Dr., Clearwater. Tel. 535-4678.

Overlooking the waters of Old Tampa Bay, this shopping complex is designed to re-create the atmosphere of a turn-of-the-century fishing village. Most of the buildings are made of aged wood and tin and a wooden boardwalk meanders around the entire site. In addition to restaurants, snack shops, a theater, and a small museum, there are over 20 shops selling everything from sportswear to designer clothes to handcrafted leather jewelry, ornamental glass, country crafts, shell art, nautical woodworks, musical toys, rare records, new and used books, and old-time candies.

Open: Mon-Thurs 10am-7pm, Fri-Sat 10am-9pm, Sun noon-6pm. **Directions:** Adjacent to the St. Petersburg-Clearwater Airport, off Route 686.

DOLPHIN VILLAGE, 4615 Gulf Blvd., St. Petersburg Beach. Tel. 367-3138.

Situated on Boca Ciega Bay, this is a large two-story art deco-style shopping center with a glass-enclosed elevator. There are over 50 stores, restaurants, and boutiques including a charter boat center, a grocery store, and beauty and barber salons, as well as shops specializing in shells, books, leatherwork, beach rentals, swimsuits, and imports.

Open: Daily 9am-6pm or later. **Directions:** In the middle of St. Pete Beach, at 46th Avenue.

GAS PLANT ANTIQUE ARCADE, 1246 Central Ave., St. Petersburg. Tel. 895-0368.

Housed in a former gas plant, this four-story complex is the largest antique mall on Florida's west coast. More than 100 dealers display their wares, from buttons to breakfronts, as well as a wide range of jewelry, toys, art glass, perfume bottles, Hummels, bronzes, quilts, and paintings.

Open: Mon–Sat 10am–5pm, Sun noon–5pm. **Directions:** Downtown, two blocks from Suncoast Dome.

JOHN'S PASS VILLAGE AND BOARDWALK, 12901 Gulf Blvd., Madeira Beach. Tel. 391-7373.

Situated on the water, this converted fisherman's village houses over 60 shops, selling everything from antiques and arts and crafts to beachwear, resort wear, sporting goods, woodwork, glasswork, and jewelry. There are also several art galleries, including the Bronze Lady, which is the largest single dealer in the world of works by Red Skelton, the comedian-artist. This shop stocks prints from his limited-edition canvas-transfer collection, plus his storybooks, collector plates, figurines, radio cassettes, drawings, pastels, and paintings.

Open: Daily 9am–6pm or later. **Directions:** North of St. Petersburg Beach, at the southern tip of Madeira Beach.

THE PIER, 800 2nd Ave. NE, St. Petersburg. Tel. 821-6164.

Ever since it was reopened in 1988, this has been the hub of shopping for the downtown area, with more than a dozen boutiques, eateries, and other attractions in a panoramic waterside setting. Most of the major shops are indoors on the ground level of the building, but there is also an outdoor marketplace with two rows of pavilions and carts lining the driveway that leads from the parking areas to the Pier entrance. Items on sale range from hats, clothing, and jewelry, to toys, country crafts, and artwork, as well as a fudge-and-candy shop and a flag-and-kite emporium.

The Pier also leads to Beach Drive, one of the most fashionable strolling and shopping streets in the downtown area, with a string of shops offering everything from contemporary art to nautical and imported gifts.

Open: Mon–Sat 10am–6pm or later, Sun 11am–6pm. **Directions:** Downtown, north of the Bayfront Center on Tampa Bay.

TYRONE SQUARE MALL, 6901 22nd Ave. N., St. Petersburg. Tel. 345-0126.

One of the oldest and largest air-conditioned malls in the area, with a six-theater movie complex, food court, tourist information desk, and 135 stores including Maas Brothers, Sears, Maison Blanche, and J. C. Penney. Other outlets include jewelry shops, fashion boutiques, sporting-goods stores, and booksellers, such as B. Dalton and Waldenbooks.

Open: Mon–Sat 10am–9pm, Sun noon–6pm. **Directions:** Northwest of downtown, at the intersection of Tyrone Boulevard and 66th Street N.

WAGON WHEEL FLEA MARKET, 7801 74th Ave. N., Pinellas Park. Tel. 544-5319.

The area's largest and most popular open-air market, offering curios, collectibles, and crafts of all kinds, with hundreds of stalls and vendors from near and far. A smaller gathering, the 49er Flea Market, also operates each weekend nearby at 10525 49th St. N., Pinellas Park (tel. 573-3367).

Open: Sat–Sun 8am–4pm. **Directions:** North of St. Petersburg, at the intersection of 78th Street N. and Park Boulevard (Rte. 694).

SHOPS AND STORES

ART

BACK IN THE WOODS GALLERY, 242 Beach Drive NE, St. Petersburg. Tel. 821-7999.

Across from Museum of Fine Arts and within view of the Pier, this shop specializes in limited-edition prints of wildlife art, as well as farm scenes, wildlife stationery, and other gift items.

Open: Tues–Fri 11am–5pm, Sat 11am–3pm. **Directions:** Downtown, between 2nd and 3rd avenues N., opposite Straub Park.

P. BUCKLEY MOSS, 190 4th Ave. NE, St. Petersburg. Tel. 894-2899.

This gallery/studio features the works of one of Florida's most individualistic artists, with a style combining abstraction and realism. She is best known for her portrayal of the Amish and Mennonite people. In addition to paintings, graphics, and offset lithographic reproductions, the gallery offers porcelain plates, figurines, and collector dolls.

Open: Year round Mon–Sat 10–5; Sept–Apr, Sun noon–5. **Directions:** Downtown, opposite Straub Park.

BEACHWEAR

SWIMSUIT OUTLET, 7116 Gulf Blvd., St. Petersburg Beach. Tel. 367-1545.

If you forgot your swimsuit or need a new one, this place is hard to beat. In addition to a large selection of swimwear, you'll find cover-ups, sportswear, sandals, shirts, T-shirts, jogging gear, and beach accessories at discount prices, with savings as great as 50% to 60%.

Other locations in the St. Pete area: Carter Plaza Municipal Drive, off Gulf Blvd., Madeira Beach; 19601 Gulf Blvd., Indian Shores; and 600 Mandalay Ave., Clearwater.

Open: Mon–Sat 10am–6pm, Sun 12:30–4:30pm. **Directions:** Four blocks south of the St. Pete Beach Causeway, between 71st and 72nd avenues.

BOOKS

HASLAM'S, 2025 Central Ave., St. Petersburg. Tel. 822-8616.

Although the St. Pete area has lots of book shops (including such chains as B. Dalton and Waldenbooks), this huge emporium claims to be Florida's largest, with over 300,000 books—new and used, hardcover and paperback. Founded in 1933, this family-run business is an attraction in itself, almost like a library, with plenty of bargains on every topic from antiques to zoology.

Open: Mon–Sat 9am–5:30pm, Fri to 9pm. **Directions:** Downtown, between 20th and 21st avenues N.

FOOD

YELLOW BANKS GROVES, 14423 Walsingham Rd., Largo. Tel. 595-5464.

Famous for its citrus products, the St. Pete area is home to dozens of groves and fruit stores, selling a variety of grapefruits, oranges, tangerines, and tangelos. This establishment is one of the oldest (over 35 years) and most reliable, both for on-the-spot shopping and for shipping fruit back home. You can buy freshly squeezed juice by the glass or container, and fruit by the piece or in bags. In addition, you'll find citrus-related and tropical products, such as grapefruit cherry marmalade, guava jelly, and jellied candies, as well as coconut patties, pecan log rolls, and shell-art souvenirs.

Open: Nov–May daily 8am–5pm. **Directions:** On Route 688, 1¼ miles east of Gulf Boulevard.

GIFTS AND CRAFTS

FLORIDA CRAFTSMEN GALLERY, 235 3rd St. S., St. Petersburg. Tel. 821-7391.

Founded in 1986, this is a showcase for the works of over 100 Florida artisans and craftspersons. Designed to appeal to serious collectors as well as those seeking moderately priced gifts, the items include both functional and whimsical creations in jewelry, ceramics, woodwork, fiberwork, glassware, paper creations, metalwork.

Open: Tues–Sat 10am–4pm. **Directions:** Downtown, at the corner of 3rd St. S. and 3rd Ave S.

GREEN TURTLE, 6707 Gulf Blvd., St. Petersburg Beach. Tel. 367-1578.

If you're looking for bargain souvenirs, it's hard to beat this place. Every item is priced under $2, including glasses, sponges, hats, suntan lotions, shell art, beach gear, jewelry, and cards.

Open: Daily 9am–6pm or later. **Directions:** At the upper end of St. Pete Beach, between 67th and 68th avenues.

THE IRISH SHILLELAGH/HOLLAND HOUSE, 520 Corey Ave., St. Petersburg Beach. Tel. 367-6907.

If you tire of shell art or sea scenes, here's a shop that brings a touch of old Europe to the beach. You'll find a wonderful assortment of imported Irish and Dutch crafts, from Waterford Crystal and Belleek China to Blue Delft China, as well as Irish fisherman's sweaters, heraldry products, and Claddagh jewelry.

Open: Mon–Sat 11am–5pm. **Directions:** Off the St. Pete Beach Causeway, between Gulf Boulevard and Coquina Way.

SUNSHINE GIFT SHOP, 330 5th St. N., St. Petersburg. Tel. 893-7101.

All of the items for sale at this shop are handmade by senior citizens of the area. The choices range from baby clothes and toys to shell crafts, sweaters, quilts, afghans, greeting cards, household items, beadwork, jewelry, ceramics, stained glass, woodwork, and ornaments.

Open: Mon–Fri, 9am–4:30pm and some weekends (call to check). **Directions:** Downtown, between 3rd and 4th avenues N.

JEWELRY

EVANDER PRESTON CONTEMPORARY JEWELRY, 106 8th Ave., St. Petersburg Beach. Tel. 367-7894.

If you're in the market for some one-of-a-kind jewelry, it's well worth a visit to this unique gallery/workshop, housed in a 75-year-old building on Pass-A-Grille. A celebrated character in the St. Pete area, the bearded Preston creates striking hand-hammered pieces that reflect European classic styles as well as 20th-century contemporary art. Among his most famous works is a tiny toy train, the *EP Express,* with an 18-karat gold electrically powered locomotive, platinum wheels, a one-half-carat diamond headlight, and cargo car that includes an emerald, a sapphire, and a ruby, plus gold nuggets. It took four months to make, and is often on display in the gallery here, a room with suede-covered walls, contemporary paintings and sculpture, and primitive African art. In addition to his pieces for men and women, the artist also creates jewelry items for dogs.

Open: Mon–Sat 10am–5:30pm. **Directions:** Take the Pinellas Bayway to Gulf Boulevard, turn left and go south to 8th Avenue, between Pass-A-Grille and Gulf ways.

7. EVENING ENTERTAINMENT

From Broadway shows and ballroom dancing to rock and roll, reggae, and dinner theater, the St. Petersburg area offers a varied selection of nighttime entertainment. And don't forget the option of an evening cruise on the bay or Gulf waters (see "Organized Tours and Cruises," above in this chapter).

The best way to keep abreast of what's on is to read the *St. Petersburg Times,* the city's award-winning daily newspaper. In particular, don't miss the Friday edition's "Weekend" supplement packed with information on theaters, shows, nightclubs, festivals, and all sorts of local activities.

Another excellent publication is *Tampa Bay Life,* a monthly magazine that covers all facets of the lively arts in the area. It is on sale at local newsstands. Unlike some cities, St. Petersburg does not have a central ticket booth for reduced-rate, same-day performances. If you can't make it to a particular box office, you can reserve tickets to shows at Ticketmaster outlets at the Bayfront Center, the Pier, and other locations in major shopping malls throughout the city, or by calling 813/287-8844.

THE PERFORMING ARTS
MAJOR CONCERT/PERFORMANCE HALLS

BAYFRONT CENTER, 400 1st St. S., St. Petersburg. Tel. 892-5767 or 892-5700 (recorded information).

This is the city's waterfront showplace, featuring the 8,400-seat Bayfront Arena and the 2,000-seat Mahaffey Theater. Between them, they host a variety of major concerts, Broadway shows, national touring companies, big-band festivals, ice shows, the circus, and sporting events. **Open:** Box office Mon–Fri 10am–6pm; curtain for evening events usually 7:30 or 8pm, for matinees 3 or 3:30pm. **Directions:** Downtown, south of the Pier between 4th and 5th avenues S.
Admission: $5–$40, depending on event.

FLORIDA SUNCOAST DOME, 1 Stadium Dr., St. Petersburg. Tel. 825-3100.

Built at a cost of $110 million, this giant arena opened in March of 1990 with a Kenny Rogers extravaganza including a cast of 5,000 performers, a laser show, and fireworks. The Dome has a capacity of 50,000 for concerts, although its primary purpose is to provide a home for a new baseball team. Other large-scale events are slated in the months ahead. **Open:** Evening performances usually start at 7:30pm, but schedule varies according to event. **Directions:** Downtown between 10th and 16th streets S., off 1st Avenue S. (exit 9 off of I-275).
Admission: $15–$30.

RUTH ECKERD HALL, Richard B. Baumgardner Center for the Performing Arts, 1111 McMullen-Booth Rd., Clearwater. Tel. 791-7400.
North of St. Petersburg, this 2,200-seat auditorium is the major venue for a varied program of Broadway shows, ballet, drama, symphonic works, popular music, jazz, and country music. The facility includes a café and a shop specializing in theatrical books, collector's music boxes, and other gifts pertaining to the performing arts. **Open:** Box office Mon–Sat 10am–9pm, Sun noon–5pm; curtain for evening performances is at 7:30 or 8pm, matinees Wed and Sat 2pm, Sun 1 or 3pm; gift-shop hours Mon–Sat 10am–3pm. **Directions:** East of Clearwater Beach, and one mile north of Route 60.
Admission: $10–$40, depending on the event.

THEATERS AND DINNER THEATERS

AMERICAN STAGE COMPANY, 211 3rd St. S., St. Petersburg. Tel. 822-8814.

This is St. Petersburg's resident professional theater, presenting contemporary dramas and comedies. In May, the company performs outdoors at Demens Landing on the waterfront. **Open:** Oct–June, box office Mon–Fri 9am–5pm and on weekends when a play is running; curtain time Wed–Fri 8pm, Sat 2pm and 8pm, Sun 7:30pm. **Directions:** Downtown, between 2nd and 3rd avenues S.

Prices: $16–$20.

BOATYARD VILLAGE THEATRE, 16100 Fairchild Dr., Clearwater. Tel. 536-8299.

This is a small theater in a shopping village, adjacent to the St. Petersburg–Clearwater Airport. It presents a range of plays from classics such as *A Streetcar Named Desire* to serious contemporary dramas. In addition, on some weekends there are late-night shows, usually contemporary works and sometimes offbeat productions. **Open:** Reservations by phone, pay at the door. Curtain for evening shows is at 8pm, matinees at 2pm; late-night series at 11:15pm. **Directions:** Off Route 686 (Roosevelt Boulevard).

Prices: $7–$8; with dinner, $16.

MYSTERY CAFE, 923 McMullen-Booth Rd., Clearwater. Tel. toll free 800/441-5885.

Murder is on the menu at this unique dinner theater, housed at the Kapok Tree restaurant. Mystery plays are presented and the actors serve as waiters, with continuous interaction between cast and audience adding to the suspense of the evening. Although the plays vary, in each case members of the audience are given a set of clues and play an active roll in solving a murder mystery. At the end of the evening, a "super sleuth" prize is awarded to the audience member who most cleverly deduces the solution. **Open:** Reservations by phone, Mon–Sat 9am–6pm; payment by credit card or check in advance by mail (no box-office sales). Performances Fri–Sat 7:30pm, Sun 1pm. **Directions:** East of Clearwater Beach, just under a mile north of Route 60.

Price: $27.

SHOWBOAT DINNER THEATRE, 3405 Ulmerton Rd., Clearwater. Tel. 573-3777.

Designed with a vintage showboat facade, this inland theater is located on a busy east-west thoroughfare north of downtown St. Petersburg. It presents a variety of Broadway comedies and musicals, with major stars, along with buffet meals. **Open:** Box office Mon–Tues 9am–6pm, Wed–Sat 9am–9pm. Performances Wed–Sat, dinner 7pm, curtain 8:15pm; Sun, dinner 5pm, curtain 6pm; Wed, Thurs, Sat matinees, lunch at noon, curtain 1:15pm. **Directions:** Off I-275, on Route 688, next to the St. Petersburg–Clearwater Airport.

Prices: Evenings $25–$29; matinees $21.

TIDES DINNER THEATER, 16720 Gulf Blvd., N. Redington Beach. Tel. 393-1870.
Billing itself as the only dinner theater on the beach strip, this facility presents classic Broadway musicals such as *The Pajama Game* with performances by the local Seminole Players. **Open:** Box office Mon–Fri 9am–1pm, or make reservations by phone. Performances Nov–Apr, Fri–Sat, cocktails 6pm, dinner 7pm, show 8:15pm; Sun cocktails 4pm, dinner 5pm, show 6:15pm. **Directions:** In the Bath Club complex on the beach, between 167th and 168th avenues.
Prices: $25 evening, $21 matinee.

THE CLUB AND MUSIC SCENE
NIGHTCLUBS/LOUNGES

BALI HAI, 5250 Gulf Blvd., St. Petersburg Beach. Tel. 360-1811.
Set atop the St. Petersburg Hilton Inn, this is a revolving rooftop lounge, featuring live music, mostly of the contemporary genre. It's a romantic spot, particularly at sunset time; Polynesian drinks are also available. **Open:** Tues–Sun 8:30pm–12:30am. **Directions:** In the center of St. Pete Beach, between 52nd and 53rd avenues.
Prices: Drinks $2–$4; no cover charge.

THE BANK LOUNGE, 11595 Gulf Blvd., Treasure Island. Tel. 360-2221.
Decorated with flags of all nations, this informal spot offers a variety of entertainment nightly, from live contemporary music on Tuesday and Thursday, to a talent show on Wednesday nights with audience participation and cash prizes. **Open:** Daily, 8pm–midnight. **Directions:** Eight blocks north of the Treasure Island Causeway.
Prices: Drinks $2–$4; no cover charge.

REFLECTIONS, 5500 Gulf Blvd., St. Petersburg Beach. Tel. 367-6461.
This is a relaxing piano lounge at the TradeWinds Resort, overlooking waterways, an outdoor deck, and a gazebo. In addition to cocktails, fine wines are available by the glass. **Open:** Daily 5pm–2am; entertainment starts at 9pm. **Directions:** In the heart of St. Pete Beach, between 55th and 56th avenues.
Prices: Drinks $2–$5; no cover charge.

SURF CLUB, 400 Mandalay Ave., Clearwater Beach. Tel. 461-3222.
In the Holiday Inn Surfside on the beach, this is one of the newer and trendier night spots, featuring a multilevel dance floor with the latest in lighting, state-of-the-art sound systems, and multiscreen videos. **Open:** Tues–Sat 8pm–2am. **Directions:** Take Route 60 west to the beach, turn right on Mandalay; hotel is at corner.
Prices: Drinks $2–$5; no cover charge.

THE WINE CELLAR, 17307 Gulf Blvd., N. Redington Beach. Tel. 393-3491.

Home of an award-winning restaurant, this elegant lounge on the beach strip is an attraction in itself. Easy-listening music, and sometimes jazz and blues, is featured by live combos. **Open:** Tues–Sat 4:30pm–1am. **Directions:** Northwest of downtown St. Pete, on the bay side of Gulf Boulevard between 173rd and 174th avenues.

Prices: Drinks $3–$6.

COMEDY CLUBS

COCONUTS COMEDY CLUB, 6110 Gulf Blvd., St. Petersburg Beach, Tel. 360-NUTS, 360-6887, or 360-4575.

One of the oldest and best-known comedy spots on the beach strip, this club features an ever-changing program of live stand-up comedy acts. Shows Tues–Thurs and Sun at 9:30pm, Fri–Sat at 9pm and 10:30pm. **Directions:** Next to the Sandpiper Beach Resort, between 61st and 62nd avenues.

Prices: $5–$6 cover charge.

COMEDY LINE, 401 2nd Ave. N., Indian Rocks Beach. Tel. 595-9484.

This club is on the second level of Hamlin's Landing, a new shopping/condo development less than half a mile from the beach. Shows Fri–Sat at 9pm and 10:30pm. **Directions:** On the Intracoastal Waterway, just off Route 688.

Prices: $6 cover charge.

CHAPPELOW'S LAUGH TRACKS, 11160 Gulf Blvd., Clearwater Beach. Tel. 595-1611.

In the rooftop lounge of the Sheraton Sand Key Resort, this live comedy show is followed by a DJ or a live band playing contemporary dance music. **Open:** Tues–Sat 8:45pm comedy show; 10pm–2am music. **Directions:** On the ninth floor of Sheraton Sand Key Resort, at the northern tip of Sand Key Island.

Prices: $2 cover charge on weekends.

RON BENNINGTON'S COMEDY SCENE, 401 U.S. 19, Clearwater. Tel. 791-4477.

Nationally known comedians perform at this popular club; dinner/show packages are available. Reservations suggested. **Open:** Tues–Thurs and Sun 8:30pm, Fri–Sat 8:30pm and 10:45pm. **Directions:** At the junction of U.S. 19 and Route 60, in the Rodeway Inn.

Prices: $5–$8 cover charge; dinner/show $16.95.

ROCK AND TOP 40

CHA CHA COCONUTS, 800 2nd Ave. NE, St. Petersburg. Tel. 822-6655.

Situated on the rooftop of the Pier, this spot offers live rock (and sometimes jazz or reggae) music, with tropical drinks and panoramic views of the St. Pete skyline. Additional locations at 1241 Gulf Blvd.,

Clearwater Beach (tel. 596-6040), and on Harbour Island, Tampa (see Chapter 11, "What to See and Do in Tampa"). **Open:** Fri 8pm–midnight, Sat 2pm–midnight, Sun 2–10pm, Wed 7–11pm. **Directions:** Downtown, on the fifth floor of the Pier.

Prices: Drinks $2.50–$4; no cover charge.

COCOMO'S, 200 Madonna Blvd., Tierra Verde. Tel. 867-8710

This new and lively spot, at the Tierra Verde Yacht and Tennis Resort, blends a sporting atmosphere with live contemporary music, either at its outdoor Checkered Flag pool bar or the indoor Winner's Circle Lounge. **Open:** Daily 5–11pm or later. **Directions:** Take Pinellas Bayway toward Fort DeSoto, and make the first right after the drawbridge.

Prices: Drinks $1.25–$3.95; no cover charge.

GIGGLES USA, 1520 4th St. N., St. Petersburg. Tel. 894-1183.

Offering a disco-style dance format with Top 40 music, this club caters to an over-20 clientele who prefer their drinks to be nonalcoholic. Free coffee and inexpensive snacks are available. **Open:** Wed–Sat 9pm–2am. **Directions:** Just north of downtown and three blocks south of Sunken Gardens, between 15th and 16th avenues N.

Prices: $4 cover charge.

GREENSTREETS, 20001 Gulf Blvd., Indian Shores. Tel. 596-1940.

This casual dockside spot sits on the Intracoastal Waterway in LaConcha Plaza. It offers recorded Top 40 music most nights, but also features live jazz and reggae on some weekends. Call for schedule. **Open:** Daily 9pm–1am. **Directions:** Take Route 688 to Gulf Boulevard, turn left and go 1 mile to 200th Avenue.

Prices: Drinks $2.95–$4.95; no cover charge.

KETCH 22, 9595 4th St. N., St. Petersburg. Tel. 577-4990.

This nautically themed lounge features live bands performing current top 40 music. **Open:** Daily 9pm–2am. **Directions:** North of downtown, between 95th and 96th Avenues N., opposite the Koger Executive Center and south of Gandy Boulevard.

Prices: Drinks $1.25–$4; no cover charge.

JAZZ/BLUES/REGGAE

THE HURRICANE LOUNGE, 807 Gulf Way, St. Petersburg Beach. Tel. 260-4875.

Recently named by *Tampa Bay Life* magazine as one of the three best places for jazz on either side of the bay, this beachside spot has a "long-term, unwavering commitment to jazz." **Open:** Fri–Sat 9:30pm–1:30am; Sun, Wed–Thurs 9am–1pm. **Directions:** Take Pinellas Bayway to Gulf Boulevard, turn left, go to 8th Avenue, then turn right to Gulf Way.

Prices: Drinks $2–$4; no cover charge.

RINGSIDE CAFE, 2742 4th St. N., St. Petersburg. Tel. 894-8465.

Housed in a renovated boxing gymnasium, this informal neighborhood café has a definite sports theme, but the music often focuses on live blues (and sometimes reggae). **Open:** Fri–Sat 10pm–2am. **Directions:** North of Sunken Gardens, between 27th and 28th avenues.

Prices: Drinks $2–$4; cover charge $2 or more.

SILAS DENT'S, 5501 Gulf Blvd., St. Petersburg Beach. Tel. 360-6961.

Although there is contemporary music on most nights at this rustic lounge, there is usually reggae on Sundays. **Open:** Mon–Sat 9pm–1am, Sun 9pm–midnight. **Directions:** In the middle of St. Pete Beach, opposite the TradeWinds Resort, between 55th and 56th avenues.

Prices: Drinks $2–$4; cover $1–$2.

BALLROOMS

COLISEUM BALLROOM, 535 4th Ave. N., St. Petersburg. Tel. 892-5202.

Dating back to 1924, this landmark Spanish-style building is an attraction in itself, and was featured in the motion picture *Cocoon*. With a 13,000-square-foot maple dance floor (one of the nation's largest), it's *the* place to go in downtown St. Pete for an evening of dancing to big-band music. Frequent concerts are also given by the Tampa Bay Symphony and other musical groups. No liquor is served, but you may bring your own. **Open:** Wed 8–11pm, Fri–Sat 8pm–midnight. **Directions:** Downtown, between 5th and 6th streets N., or exit 10 off of I-275.

Prices: $5–$10.

JOYLAND, 11225 U.S. 19, Clearwater. Tel. 573-1919.

This is the area's only country-and-western ballroom, featuring live bands and well-known performers. Free dance lessons are offered on Wednesday, Thursday, and Sunday nights. **Open:** Wed–Sun 7pm–1am. **Directions:** North of St. Petersburg, 1 mile south of Ulmerton Road (Rte. 688).

Prices: $5–$10.

THE BAR SCENE

HARP AND THISTLE PUB, 650 Corey Ave., St. Petersburg Beach. Tel. 360-4104.

You don't have to be Irish to love this little bit of the auld sod on the beach. It's a popular spot to hear authentic Irish folk music, as well as for sipping draft Guinness and other Irish brews. **Open:** Daily 9pm–1am or later. **Directions:** West of the St. Petersburg Causeway, between Coquina and Sunset Ways.

Price: Drinks $2–$5; occasional $2 cover charge.

HORSE AND JOCKEY, 1155 Pasadena Ave., South Pasadena. Tel. 345-4995.

For a taste of Old London, here's a typically British pub. You can try your hand at a game of darts, imbibe a few of the 11 British beers on tap, or come in the afternoon and sample a traditional "high tea"—with finger sandwiches, scones, sherry trifle, and a brimming pot of English tea (24-hour notice and reservations required). **Open:** Daily noon–midnight or later; high tea Mon–Fri 3–5pm. **Directions:** From downtown, take Central Avenue west and turn left on Pasadena Avenue.

Prices: Drinks $2–$5; $6.95 for high tea.

PAPA JOE'S BAR, 351 S. Gulfview Blvd., Clearwater Beach. Tel. 441-2548.

On the upper level of Seafood and Sunsets at Julie's restaurant, this cozy enclave is the ideal spot to watch the sunsets over Clearwater Beach. To add to the Key West atmosphere, there are ceiling fans, oldies music, and walls covered with vintage posters, pictures, and memorabilia. **Open:** Daily 5pm–10pm. **Directions:** Take Route 60 to the beach; turn left on Gulfview Boulevard.

Prices: Drinks $1.25–$3; no cover charge.

TIKI BAR AT THE FRIENDLY TAVERN, 18121 Gulf Blvd., Redington Shores. Tel. 393-4470.

Famous for its wide selection of imported beers, this informal indoor-outdoor spot is across the street from the beach and a favorite with the locals, who like to sit and watch the auto and pedestrian traffic go by. On Wednesday through Sunday nights, there are audience-participation shows at 9pm. **Open:** Daily 10am–2am. **Directions:** 1 mile south of the Park Boulevard Causeway (Rte. 694).

Prices: $1–$4; no cover charge.

CHAPTER 8

GETTING TO KNOW TAMPA

Just as Walt Disney World put Orlando on the tourism map, Busch Gardens is the main draw for most first-time visitors to Tampa. But after arriving, most travelers find there's a lot more to Tampa than the famous Anheuser-Busch theme park.

Sitting on the Hillsborough River and rimmed by Hillsborough Bay and Tampa Bay, Tampa is a city of many waterfront views and activities—a natural mecca for vacationers. This metropolis of nearly 300,000 people is also a major business hub on Florida's west coast. The base for many financial, manufacturing, shipping, agricultural, and high-tech industries, Tampa is the seventh largest port and one of the fast-growing cities in the U.S.

Like neighboring St. Petersburg, Tampa is both old and new. The Spanish architecture, Cuban foods, and flamenco music of Ybor City hark back to an earlier time, while the sleek mirrored-glass skyscrapers of the downtown district and the state-of-the-art workings of the airport have given Tampa a head start into the 21st century.

1. ORIENTATION

ARRIVING
BY AIR

Tampa International Airport, off Memorial Highway and Florida Route 60, Tampa (tel. 813/276-3400), situated 5 miles northwest of downtown Tampa, is the gateway for all scheduled domestic and international flights. See Chapter 4, "Getting to Know St. Petersburg," for a description of the airport's services.

GETTING INTO TOWN **Hillsborough Area Regional Transit Authority** (HARTline; tel. 254-HART) operates service between the airport and downtown on its no. 31 bus. This is not an airport express bus, but a local route that makes stops at the airport between the hours of 6am and 8:15pm. Look for the HARTline bus sign outside of each airline terminal; the fare is 75¢, and the ride takes 25 to 30 minutes.

Central Florida Transit (tel. 813/276-3730) operates van service between the airport and downtown hotels. No reservations are necessary; just proceed to the transport booth outside of each baggage-claim area. For early morning or late-night service, it is best to make a reservation in advance; otherwise vans make continuous pickups at least every half hour; the ride takes about 20 minutes. Fare is $10 for up to two passengers. For taxi service to downtown Tampa and its environs, **Yellow Cab Taxis** (tel. 253-0125) and United Cabs (tel. 253-2424) line up outside the baggage-claim areas 24 hours a day. Average fare from the airport to downtown Tampa is $10 to $12, and the trip takes about 15 minutes.

BY TRAIN

Amtrak trains from points north terminate at the Tampa Amtrak Station, 601 Nebraska Ave. N., Tampa (tel. 813/221-7600).

BY CAR

The Tampa area is linked to the interstate system and is accessible from I-275, I-75, I-4, U.S. 19, U.S. 41, U.S. 92, U.S. 301, and many state roads.

BY BUS

Greyhound Trailways buses from destinations around the United States arrive at the carrier's downtown depot at 610 Polk St., Tampa (tel. 813/229-2174).

TOURIST INFORMATION

For free brochures and helpful advice while you are in Tampa, plan to stop into the Visitor Information Center of the Tampa/Hillsborough Convention and Visitors Association (THCVA), 111 Madison St., Suite 110, Tampa, FL 33602-4706 (tel. 223-1111 or toll free 800/44-TAMPA). It's located downtown, on the ground level of the First Florida Tower building, at the corner of Ashley and Madison streets. Open Mon–Sat 9am–5pm. In addition, the THCVA also maintains unstaffed information/brochure carts on Harbour Island and at Ybor Square.

CITY LAYOUT

Tampa's downtown district is laid out according to a grid system. Kennedy Boulevard (Fla. Rte. 60), which cuts across the city in an east-west direction, is the main dividing line for north and south street addresses; and Florida Avenue is the dividing line for east and west street addresses. The two major arteries bringing traffic into the downtown area are I-275, which skirts the northern edge of the city, and the Crosstown Expressway, which extends along the southern rim.

Tampa

Amtrak Station ⑲
Ashley Street ⑰
Busch Boulevard ❹
Crosstown Expressway ⑬
Dale Mabry Highway ⑫
Florida Avenue ⑱
Fowler Avenue ❶
Gandy Boulevard ⑪
Greyhound / Trailways
 Depot ⑳
Kennedy Boulevard ⑲
Peter O. Knight
 Airport ㉓
Tampa International
 Airport ❻
Westshore Boulevard ❾

NEIGHBORHOODS:
Busch Gardens ❸
Carrollwood ❺
Courtney Campbell
 Causeway ❽
Davis Islands ㉒
Downtown ⑯
East Tampa ❼
Harbour Island ㉑
Hyde Park ⑮
Temple Terrace ❷
West Shore ⑩
West Tampa ⑭
Ybor City ㉔

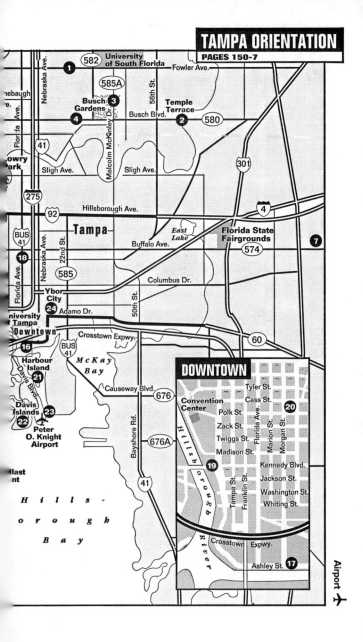

University
of South Florida
582
Fowler Ave.
Nebraska Ave.
1
585A
56th St.
Busch
Gardens
3
Temple
Terrace
Busch Blvd.
Malcolm McKinley Dr.
580
2
4
41
owry
ark
Sligh Ave.
Sligh Ave.
hebaugh
e.
Florida Ave.
301
275
92
Hillsborough Ave.
4
Tampa
East
Lake
Florida State
Fairgrounds
BUS
41
Buffalo Ave.
574
7
18
22nd St.
Nebraska Ave.
Florida Ave.
585
Columbus Dr.
50th St.
Ybor
City
24
Adamo Dr.
niversity
f Tampa
60
Downtown
Crosstown Expwy.
16
BUS
41
McKay
Bay
Harbour
Island
21
Davis Blvd.
Causeway Blvd.
Bayshore Rd.
676
Davis
Islands
23
22
Peter
O. Knight
Airport
676A

DOWNTOWN

Tyler St.
Convention
Center
Cass St.
Polk St.
20
Zack St.
Twiggs St.
Madison St.
Florida Ave.
Marion St.
Morgan St.
19
Kennedy Blvd.
Tampa St.
Franklin St.
Jackson St.
Washington St.
Whiting St.

Hillsborough River

Crosstown Expwy.

Ashley St.
17

41

H i l l s -

o r o u g h

B a y

last
nt

Airport ✈

? DID YOU KNOW . . . ?

- No chewing gum is on sale anywhere at Tampa Airport—because all floors are fully carpeted throughout.
- Teddy Roosevelt was headquartered at the Tampa Bay Hotel while training his Rough Riders for service in the Spanish-American War (1898).
- John F. Kennedy Boulevard (Fla. Rte. 60), formerly Lafayette Street, was renamed after the 35th U.S. president because he rode down this thoroughfare the day before his assassination in Dallas.
- More than three million cigars a day are still produced in Tampa, which was once considered the "Cigar Capital of the World."
- Busch Gardens is home to the largest captive breeding herd of elephants in the world.

All of the streets in the central core of the city are one-way, with the exception of Franklin Street which has been transformed into one continuous pedestrian mall. From the southern tip of Franklin, you can also board the People Mover, an elevated tram to Harbour Island.

One of the streets of most interest to visitors is Ashley Street, a wide thoroughfare that runs along the west corridor of the city close to the Hillsborough River. Ashley Street is the location of the Tampa Bay Performing Arts Center, the Tampa Public Library, Tampa Museum, the new $130 million Tampa Convention Center, and the Visitor Information Office of the Tampa/Hillsborough Convention and Visitors Association, as well as major banks and businesses.

One-way streets are not quite as prevalent in other parts of Tampa, although certain sections, such as Ybor City and parts of Hyde Park, have a predominance of one-way traffic.

Since the streets in Tampa's downtown district all have names instead of numbers, there's no simple way to find an address as there is in St. Petersburg. The Tampa/Hillsborough Convention and Visitors Association can supply you with a basic map of major streets; the best way to master the layout of streets is to get the map and walk or drive around a bit.

The streets of Ybor City are numbered, which makes getting around that area comparatively easy, but in most other areas—including Hyde Park, Busch Gardens, and West Shore—streets are named, not numbered. Most of the locals will gladly give directions, however, based on the address's proximity to a familiar point of reference: "five blocks east of Busch Gardens," for example, or "2 miles west of the airport." In many cases, directions will start with the exit of I-275 that is closest to the place you are trying to reach. If you use I-275 as a focal point, chances are you'll be able to find almost any address.

NEIGHBORHOODS IN BRIEF

Downtown is the core of Tampa, a compact business and financial hub. There are dazzling bank buildings at every turn, from

Citizens, and Chase, to Empire, First Florida, First National, First Union, Florida Federal, Freedom, NCNB, Southeast, and Sun.

Although there are a few hotels, there is very little midtown residential housing, not even the apartment complexes or condominiums you might expect to see along the river. Most of the skyscrapers are new, and indeed much of downtown Tampa has been built in the past 20 years. No doubt, more housing will spring up in the downtown area in the next few years, but, for the moment, the streets tend to be relatively quiet at night and on weekends, except around the hotels or the Performing Arts Center.

Harbour Island   South of the downtown business district and linked by an elevated People Mover to the mainland, this is the city's new waterfront playground, sort of a small-scale version of Baltimore's Inner Harbor. Surrounded by water, it is home to the luxurious Wyndham Hotel, dozens of fine shops, restaurants, and nightclubs, and all sorts of riverfront activities, from gondola rides to paddle boats. There is also a marina for private craft, several blocks of condominiums, and an athletic club. The island was built 85 years ago on reclaimed land, and from 1909 to 1972 it was used to transfer cargo from ships to waiting railroad cars. It was transformed to its present glamorous state in 1985.

Hyde Park   Just west of downtown, it's the city's classiest residential neighborhood, sort of the Beverly Hills of Tampa. Its development was spurred a century ago when Henry Plant built his spectacular Tampa Bay Hotel (now the University of Tampa) on the west bank of the Hillsborough River in 1891. Hyde Park rapidly drew prominent citizens who built homes south of the hotel, often with views of Hillsborough Bay. Many of these homes remain today, and are part of a National Register Historic District reflecting a host of architectural styles—from colonial and federal revival, to neoclassical, Italian Renaissance, Gothic Revival, Tudor Revival, Queen Anne, Mediterranean Revival, American Foursquare, and pure Victorian.

In the center of the district is Old Hyde Park Village, an upscale shopping development designed to retain all the original charm of the neighborhood. On the southern edge of Hyde Park is palmtree-lined Bayshore Boulevard, rimming Hillsborough Bay with the longest continuous sidewalk in the world. Between the Hyde Park area and Harbour Island is yet another residential district, known collectively as Davis Islands; to the south of Hyde Park are more fine residential clusters (such as Palma Ceia and Sunset Park) and the MacDill Air Force Base.

The West Shore   West of Hyde Park, this the most southwesterly part of the city, approaching Old Tampa Bay. Roughly speaking, it runs from Tampa International Airport southward, particularly along Westshore Boulevard. The success of the airport has been a prime factor in developing this neighborhood into a commercial and financial hub. Huge office towers, banking centers, and commercially oriented hotels have sprung up along this corridor, making it a prime

WHAT'S SPECIAL ABOUT TAMPA

Architectural Highlights
- ☐ The Hyde Park National Register Historic District, a showcase of American architecture from colonial to Victorian.
- ☐ The Columbia Restaurant, Ybor City (1905), with hand-painted tiles, stained-glass windows, and other antique accoutrements.

Museums
- ☐ The Henry B. Plant Museum, once part of a landmark hotel, now a showcase of antiques and old Tampa grandeur.
- ☐ Ybor City State Museum, for a look at the development of Tampa's Latin Quarter.

Events/Festivals
- ☐ Gasparilla Festival, Tampa's traditional annual frolic, with modern-day pirates, parades, concerts, and more.
- ☐ Florida State Fair, a two-week fest of the best in Florida and Tampa.

For the Kids
- ☐ Busch Gardens, for up-close views of 3,000 animals in natural settings, and thrilling rides and activities.

- ☐ Museum of Science and Industry, for a look at a simulated space-shuttle operation, ham radio center, and weather station.
- ☐ Lowry Park Zoo, a 24-acre parklike facility of animals in their natural settings including an aviary, wildlife center, habitat for nocturnal animals, and a manatee hospital.

Activities
- ☐ Viewing the Tampa skyline from an authentic gondola, as it floats along the channels and under the bridges of Tampa Bay and the Hillsborough River.
- ☐ Running, walking, or driving along the world's longest continuous sidewalk on Bayshore Boulevard.
- ☐ Exploring Harbour Island's indoor and outdoor activities.

Shopping
- ☐ Old Hyde Park Village, Tampa's "Rodeo Drive."
- ☐ Alessi Farmers Market, for the best of Florida's produce and gourmet foods.

place to stay as well as to do business. The Dale Mabry Highway, a busy commercial strip offering a string of restaurants and night spots (and home to the Tampa Stadium), also rims this area.

Courtney Campbell Causeway A small strip, running west of the airport, where Kennedy Boulevard (Fla. Rte. 60) crosses Old Tampa Bay and continues over to the Gulf Beaches. It is not really a neighborhood, per se, but it is a popular place for visitors, with a cluster of fine hotels, many waterfront restaurants, a beach, and water-sports centers. The International Shrine Headquarters is also here.

The Busch Gardens Area Surrounding the theme park of the same name north of downtown. Busch Boulevard, which runs from east to west, is a busy commercial strip just south of the Busch Gardens entrance. It is lined with motels, restaurants, and other enterprises. The major road running north of Busch Gardens is Fowler Avenue, an equally commercialized strip that is also home to the University of South Florida–Tampa campus. Surrounding residential neighborhoods of note include Carrollwood and Temple Terrace.

Ybor City East of downtown, this is Tampa's Latin Quarter, an enclave founded more than 100 years ago when Don Vincent Ybor (pronounced "Eee-bor") settled here and started a cigar factory. Ybor City eventually became "the cigar capital of the world," and thousands of Cuban cigar workers poured into this corner of Tampa. Although the factory has since been converted into a shopping complex (Ybor Square), many vestiges of Ybor City's heyday remain, including the landmark Columbia restaurant, famous for its Spanish cuisine and flamenco dancing, and several ethnic mutual-aid societies such as the Cuban Club, the Spanish Club, and the Italian Club. In recent years, local artists have also set up studios in many of the buildings, adding a bohemian charm and ambience to the area.

East Tampa A mostly residential area, has a popular focal point where I-4 meets I-75. As might be expected, various commercial enterprises have sprung up here, including a huge bingo parlor on the site of the Seminole Native American Reservation. This is also the home of the Florida State Fairgrounds, venue for major annual events and fairs. From I-4, many visitors also head further east to neighboring destinations such as Plant City (spring training grounds of the Cincinnati Reds), or set out for Walt Disney World and other Orlando-area attractions, just over an hour away.

MAPS

The Tampa/Hillsborough Convention and Visitors Association is a good source for up-to-date maps of the Tampa area. The newsstands and gift shops at Tampa International Airport and the bookstores in and around the city also carry current maps, but the best general map store in the region is across the bay—Rand McNally Commercial Maps, 4278 28th St. N., St. Petersburg, FL 33714 (tel. 813/525-0879). They also sell maps by mail, in case you want to study one before you arrive.

2. GETTING AROUND

BY PUBLIC TRANSPORTATION
BY BUS

Hillsborough Area Regional Transit/HARTline (tel. 254-HART) provides regularly scheduled bus service on more than 50 routes between downtown Tampa and the suburbs. The service is geared mainly to commuters, although visitors staying at downtown hotels certainly can use a bus to get to the airport or major shopping centers. It would not be practical, however, to depend totally on bus service to reach most attractions, hotels, and restaurants.

Fares are 75¢ for local service, $1 for express routes; correct change is required. If you'd like to try a bus, ask for a complimentary "visitor courtesy pass," good for one free ride, from the Tampa/Hillsborough Convention and Visitors Association.

Many buses start or finish their route downtown at the new Marion Street Transit Parkway, between Tyler and Whiting streets. It provides well-lit open-air terminal facilities, including 40-foot-long shelters with copper roofs, informational kiosk, benches, newsstands, and 24-hour security.

BY TRAM

The **People Mover** is a motorized tram on elevated tracks connecting downtown Tampa with Harbour Island. It operates from the third level of the Ft. Brooke Parking Garage, on Whiting Street between Franklin and Florida streets. Travel time is 90 seconds, and service is continuous Monday through Saturday from 7am to 2am and Sunday 8am to 11pm. Fare is 25¢ each way and exact change is required.

BY TAXI

Taxis in Tampa do not normally cruise the streets for fares, but they do line up at public loading places, such as hotels, the performing arts center, and bus and train depots. If you need a taxi, it is best to ask at your hotel or call either **Yellow Cab** (tel. 253-0125) or **United Cab** (tel. 251-3525). Both companies also provide vans for small groups or families.

BY CAR

The Tampa/Hillsborough County area encompasses over 1,000 square miles of land, crossed by three major highways, I-275, I-4, and the Crosstown Expressway. Nearly every attraction is within five miles of I-275 (which runs in a north-south direction) or I-4 (which goes east-west), neither of which charges any tolls. The Crosstown Expressway stretches from Gandy Boulevard east through downtown to the suburb of Brandon and costs from 50¢ for shorter distances to $1.25 to drive its entire length (exact change required). Most locals use I-275 as their thoroughfare of choice, and most directions are given with I-275 as the major point of reference.

RENTALS

Although the downtown area can be easily walked, it is virtually impossible to see the major sights and enjoy the best restaurants of Tampa without a car. Most visitors step off a plane and pick up a car right at the airport for use thoughout their stay.

Five major firms are represented on the grounds of Tampa International Airport: Avis (tel. 813/276-3500), Budget (tel. 813/877-6051), Dollar (tel. 813/276-3640), Hertz (tel. 813/874-3232), and National (tel. 813/276-3782). Most of these companies also maintain offices downtown and in other parts of Tampa.

In addition, many smaller firms and local companies have premises just outside of the airport along the corridor that includes Westshore Boulevard, Spruce Street, and Cypress Street. These firms, which provide van pickups to and from the airport and often post the most competitive rates, include Alamo (tel. 813/289-4323), A-Plus (tel. 813/289-4301), Auto Host (tel. 813/289-4848), Exchange (tel. 813/289-1686), General (tel. 813/289-4029), Lindo's (tel. 813/872-8967), Payless (tel. 813/289-6554), Superior (tel. 813/289-8129), Thrifty (tel. 813/289-4006), USA (tel. 813/286-7770), and Value (tel. 813/289-8870).

Note: Under a new Florida law, rental-car agencies are required to charge drivers 50¢ per car per day (or part of a day) to help finance drug education for young people and for law enforcement. This rule applies to all rentals up to a maximum of 30 days.

PARKING

Because so many of the locals use their own cars to get to work or for sojourns downtown, Tampa has plenty of parking. You have a choice of enclosed garages, attended and metered lots, or metered on-street parking. Average parking charges in garages are 60¢ to $1 per hour, $3.60 to $5.50 per day; in lots, 30¢ to $1 per hour, $2.50 to $3.50 per day; and at street meters, 50¢ to $1 per hour. The majority of meters take quarters only, although some accept dimes and nickels. It's wise to carry quarters, if you plan to use metered parking. Meter rules are enforced Monday through Friday from 8am to 5pm. Fines for parking violations range from $7 to $100, depending on the infraction.

The City of Tampa publishes a handy leaflet with the latest parking locations and prices. To obtain the leaflet or to ask a question about parking in the city, contact the Parking Office, 107 N. Franklin St., Tampa (tel. 223-8177).

If you drive over to Harbour Island, covered parking under the shops is free for the first two hours and $1 for each additional hour, up to a daily maximum of $5.

DRIVING RULES

The speed limit in residential or business districts is 30 mph. Right turns at red lights are legal, after a full stop except when a sign indicates otherwise. Pedestrians at crosswalks have the right of way; automobiles must yield to them. Seat belts are mandatory for front-seat passengers; children five or younger must be in protective seats.

 TAMPA

Area Code   813.

Airports   See "Orientation: Arriving," above in this chapter.

Auto Rentals   See "Getting Around," above in this chapter.

Baby-sitters   With a few hours' advance notice, most hotels can arrange for baby-sitters. Otherwise, call the Baby Sitter's Agency Bureau and Registry (tel. 681-2002).

Buses   See "Getting Around," above in this chapter.

Business Hours   See "Fast Facts—St. Petersburg" in Chapter 4.

Car Rentals   See "Getting Around," above in this chapter.

Climate   See "When to Go" in Chapter 2 and chart in Appendix.

Currency and Exchange   See Chapter 3, "For the Foreign Traveler."

Dentist   For information about dentists in the area, call **Hillsborough Dental Referral Services** (tel. 886-9040).

Doctor   Most hotels have a doctor on call; if not, contact the Doctor Referral Service of the **Hillsborough County Medical Association** (tel. 253-0471) or the 24-hour Ask-A-Nurse/Physician Referral Service of **St. Joseph's Hospital** (tel. 870-4444). There are **Doctor's Walk-in Clinics** at 2810 W. Buffalo Ave., Tampa (tel. 877-8450) and 13210 N. 30th St., Tampa (tel. 977-2777).

Documents Required   See Chapter 3, "For the Foreign Traveler."

Driving Rules   See "Getting Around," above in this chapter.

Drugstores   **Eckerd Drugs** is one of the leading pharmacy groups in the area, with over 35 stores throughout downtown and the suburbs, including a 24-hour branch at 11613 N. Nebraska Ave. (tel. 978-0775). Other chains with a large presence in the area include **Rite-Aid** and **Walgreens.** Consult the yellow pages under "Pharmacies" for complete listings.

Embassies/Consulates   See Chapter 3, "For the Foreign Traveler."

Emergencies   Dial 911 (free at pay phones).

Eyeglasses   Many national chains operate in the Tampa area, including **LensCrafters, Pearle Vision Center,** and **Sterling Optical.** Consult the yellow pages under "Optical Goods: Retail" for the nearest branch.

Hairdressers/Barbers   Hair-care businesses for men and women are plentiful, with some of the best shops located in department stores such as J. C. Penney or Montgomery Ward, and at the various shopping malls. Chains with several locations include **Fantastic Sam's, HairCrafters, ManTrap,** and **SuperCuts.** Consult the yellow pages under "Barbers," "Beauty Salons," and "Hair Styling" for the numbers of the locations nearest to you.

Holidays   See "When to Go" in Chapter 2, and also Chapter 3, "For the Foreign Traveler."

Hospitals   **Doctors Hospital of Tampa,** 4801 N. Howard Ave., Tampa (tel. 879-1550); **St. Joseph's Hospital,** 3001 W. Buffalo Ave., Tampa (tel. 870-4000); **Shriners Hospital for Crippled Children,** 12502 N. Pine Dr., Tampa (tel. 972-2250); **Tampa General Hospital,** Davis Islands (tel. 251-7000); and **University Community Hospital,** 3100 E. Fletcher Ave., Tampa (tel. 971-6000).

Information   See "Orientation: Tourist Information," above in this chapter.

Laundry/Dry Cleaning   Most hotels supply same-day laundry and dry cleaning service. Two local chains, each with at least a half-dozen locations spread throughout the Tampa area, include **Pioneer** (tel. 253-3323) and **Spotless** (tel. 236-5541).

Luggage Storage/Lockers   Tampa International Airport has coin-operated public lockers for luggage storage.

Libraries   The main branch of the Tampa Public Library is downtown at 900 N. Ashley St., Tampa (tel. 223-8945), with a north branch at 8916 North Blvd., Tampa (tel. 932-7594).

Liquor Laws   For general information, see "Fast Facts—St. Petersburg," in Chapter 4. In Tampa, most lounges serve alcohol until 3am.

Lost Property   If an article is lost or found at a hotel, restaurant, shop, or attraction, contact the management; if lost or found in public areas, contact the police.

Mail   Main post office is at Tampa Airport, 5201 W. Spruce St. (tel. 877-0635). Open daily 24 hours.

Maps   See "Orientation," above in this chapter.

Money   See Chapter 3, "For the Foreign Traveler."

Newspapers/Magazines   The *Tampa Tribune* is the daily newspaper; the best periodical covering the area is *Tampa Bay Life,* a monthly magazine.

Photographic Needs   **Eckerd Express Photo Services** offers one-hour processing at over half a dozen convenient Tampa locations, including the Henderson Boulevard Shopping Center (tel. 879-2020) and the Hillsboro Plaza Shopping Center (tel. 875-8665). For equipment repairs, try the **Camera Barn,** 100 E. Hillsborough Ave., Tampa (tel. 238-7777) or the **Camera Repair Service Center,** 2316 N. Dale Mabry Highway, Tampa (tel. 876-7099).

Police   See "Emergencies," above. To report lost or stolen goods, call 223-1515.

Radio/TV   See "Fast Facts—St. Petersburg," in Chapter 4.

Religious Services   There are hundreds of houses of worship in the Tampa area; inquire at the front desk of your hotel or consult the yellow pages under "Churches," "Religious Organizations," and "Synagogues."

Rest Rooms   All hotels, restaurants, attractions, and shopping centers have rest rooms available for customers. Most public or government buildings also have visitor restrooms.

Safety   Be mindful of money and valuables in public places; do not leave wallets or purses unattended on the beach; lock car doors and trunks at all times.

Shoe Repairs   Two handy downtown locations are **Florida Shoe Hospital,** 406 E. Zack St., Tampa (tel. 223-1020), and **Palace Shoe Repair,** 905 N. Tampa St., Tampa (tel. 223-5886).

Taxes   Airport, $6 departure tax for international flights; hotel, 10%; restaurant, 6%; sales, 6%.

Taxis   See "Getting Around," above in this chapter.

Time Zone   Eastern. For more information, see Chapter 3, "For the Foreign Traveler."

Tipping   See "Fast Facts—St. Petersburg," in Chapter 4.

Transit Information   Dial 254-HART.

Weather   Dial 622-1212.

TAMPA ACCOMMODATIONS

This city's greatest hotel, the legendary Tampa Bay Hotel, was opened a century ago, in 1891. The creation of railroad magnate Henry B. Plant, the 511-room hotel was the first large fully electrified building in Tampa. It was also the most extravagant, costing an astonishing (for those days) $2 million.

Set on the western shore of the Hillsborough River, the Tampa Bay Hotel was modeled after the Alhambra Palace in Spain. It was 1,200 feet long, topped by 13 silver minarets, and filled with priceless art and impeccable furnishings. A trendsetter in every way, the hotel had a casino, heated indoor swimming pool, golf course, and racetrack, as well as two ballrooms, a grand salon, two writing and reading rooms, solarium, billiard room, hair salon, and gentleman's bar. Rickshas were used to carry guests through the tropical gardens and long hallways. The guest list was a veritable who's who of the times—from Teddy Roosevelt and William Jennings Bryan to Babe Ruth, John Drew, and Anna Pavlova.

Sadly, this great landmark—the social center of Tampa—ceased to operate as a hotel in 1927. And there hasn't been anything like it since.

Today Tampa is a city of relatively new hotels, all built in the last 25 years or so, and most within the last decade. The architecture is decidedly modern, and the skyline is sleek.

Unlike many other cities, the downtown sector of Tampa is not full of hotels—banks outnumber hotels by at least two-to-one. This may change dramatically with the opening of Tampa's new convention center, but for the time being, the downtown hotels are limited mostly to a handful of familiar chain names.

The greatest concentration of Tampa's hotels is west of downtown, near Tampa International Airport. These properties are within a mile or two of the airport and its adjacent business corridor, primarily along Westshore Boulevard and the Courtney Campbell Causeway. Like their downtown cousins, these hotels cater to a largely commercial clientele, at least during the week.

**FROMMER'S SMART
TRAVELER—HOTELS**

VALUE-CONSCIOUS TRAVELERS SHOULD TAKE
ADVANTAGE OF THE FOLLOWING:

1. Off-season discounts May–December
2. Discounts sometimes available (to seniors, travel-club members, etc.)
3. Special weekend rates at hotels downtown or along a business corridor
4. Reduced-rate packages at hotels near Busch Gardens

QUESTIONS TO ASK IF YOU'RE ON A BUDGET

1. Is there a parking charge? In Tampa, many downtown hotels charge $4–$6 a night, although others, particularly in the Busch Gardens and Courtney Campbell Causeway area, provide free parking.
2. Is the 10% hotel tax included in the price quoted?
3. Is Continental breakfast included in the price quoted?
4. Is there a surcharge on local and long distance calls? At some hotels, local telephone calls are free.
5. Is there a discount for cash payment?

The third-largest cluster of lodgings is found north of downtown in the Busch Gardens area. These hotels and motels are geared more to vacationers and families.

The high season for prices is January through April, but rates do not vary as dramatically here as they do along the beaches surrounding St. Petersburg. The prices of Tampa's larger business-oriented hotels—downtown and west of the city—are pretty much the same throughout the year. The big price breaks come on weekends—all year long—when rates drop as much as 50%. A room or suite that costs $149 on weeknights can be as low as $69 on weekends.

The only exception is the Busch Gardens area, where hotels and motels are just as busy, if not busier, on weekends as on weekdays. By and large, rates do not dip on weekends, and they can be slightly higher at holiday weekends or during special events.

This is balanced, however, by the fact that overall rates in the Busch Gardens area tend to be at least 30% to 40% lower than at hotels in other parts of the city. Services are more limited at these properties and you won't get water views, but, if you want the lowest rates, this is where you'll find them. Many of the motels here also offer two- and three-day packages that include admission tickets to Busch Gardens.

The rates that we cite below give you the broad spectrum of the regular weekday rates. When you call, be sure to inquire about weekend rates and inclusive packages. These change with the seasons, but can often be real bargains.

In addition, at all times of the year you'll pay an extra 10% tax on the price of a room—6% for Florida state tax and 4% for city and resort tax, otherwise known as "bed tax" or "occupancy tax." Tipping is normally at your own discretion for daily maid service, valet parking, concierge arrangements, etc., unless otherwise specified.

The following price categories for Tampa area hotels are based on per-night, double-occupancy rates:

Very Expensive	Over $175
Expensive	$125–$175
Moderate	$65–$125
Inexpensive	Under $65

Reservations are a must in the high season and strongly recommended at other times. Tampa hotels are often booked up with meetings and groups at all times of the year, so it's never wise to leave anything to chance. You can shop around before you go—and compare prices—by using the toll-free reservations numbers provided by most hotels.

1. DOWNTOWN/HARBOUR ISLAND

EXPENSIVE

HYATT REGENCY TAMPA, 211 N. Tampa St., Tampa, FL 33602. Tel. 813/225-1234 or toll free 800/233-1234. Fax 813/223-4353. 519 rooms. A/C TV TEL **Directions:** On the corner of Tampa and Jackson streets.

$ Rates: $95–$125 single, $110–$140 double; Regency Club $135 single, $150 double. AE, CB, DC, DISC, MC, V. **Parking:** Valet parking $5.50, self-parking $4.50.

Standing out on the city skyline, with a striking mirrored facade, this 17-story tower is situated in the heart of downtown at Tampa City Center, adjacent to the Franklin Street Pedestrian Mall and the People Mover monorail station, and within three blocks of the new convention center. Currently Tampa's largest hotel, it is popular with convention and meeting groups. The interior is dominated by an eight-story atrium lobby with a two-story cascading waterfall, lots of foliage, and a resident macaw.

Guest rooms have a contemporary decor with light woods and coastal colors, and many units on the upper floors have bay or river views. The top two levels are devoted to Regency Club rooms, with added luxuries, concierge desk, and complimentary breakfast and cocktails.

Dining/Entertainment: Award-winning Florida-style cuisine is featured at Saltwaters Bar and Grille (see Chapter 10, "Tampa Dining") on the lobby level. Lighter meals are on tap at Pralines, a café with indoor and outdoor patio seating overlooking the mall area. For libations with piano music, take the escalator to Breeze's Lounge on the second floor of the atrium.

Services: Airport courtesy shuttle, 24-hour room service, concierge desk, valet laundry service.

Facilities: Outdoor heated swimming pool, whirlpool, health club, meeting rooms, car-rental and airline desks.

WYNDHAM HARBOUR ISLAND HOTEL, 725 S. Harbour Island Blvd., Harbour Island, Tampa, FL 33602. Tel. 813/229-5000 or toll free 800/822-4200. Fax 813/229-5322. 280 rooms, 20 suites. A/C MINIBAR TV TEL   **Directions:** Take the Franklin Street Bridge or People Mover to Harbour Island.

$ Rates: $109–$139 single, $119–$149 double, $190–$650 suites. AE, CB, DC, MC, V.   **Parking:** $5.

If location is everything, then this 12-story luxury property has a distinct advantage—it is just a minute or two from the bustle of the business district, yet it sits tranquilly on Harbour Island, surrounded by the channels linking the Hillsborough River and Hillsborough Bay. Easily accessible from downtown, it is likewise connected to the shops and waterside activities of the Harbour Island complex. It also offers its customers all the perks of living on the island, including guest privileges at the Harbour Island Athletic Club and use of 20 tennis courts, 5 racquetball courts, and 2 squash courts (a $10 basic fee per adult applies, plus hourly court fees).

The spacious guest rooms, all of which have views of the water, are furnished in dark woods and floral fabrics, and each has a well-lit marble-trimmed bathroom, executive desk, and work area. Suites, many of which have corner locations, also have wet bars.

Dining/Entertainment: Watch the yachts drift by as you dine at the Harbour View Room (see Chapter 10, "Tampa Dining"), or enjoy your favorite drink in the Bar, a clubby room with equally good views, both located on the lobby level. Snacks and tropical drinks are available throughout the day at the Pool Bar, accessible from the third floor.

Services: Courtesy airport shuttle, room service, concierge desk, secretarial services, notary public, turndown service, valet laundry service.

Facilities: Outdoor heated swimming pool and deck, 50 boat slips, meeting rooms, newsstand/gift shop.

MODERATE

HOLIDAY INN–ASHLEY PLAZA, 111 W. Fortune St., Tampa, FL 33602. Tel. 813/223-1351 or toll free 800/ HOLIDAY. Fax 813/221-2000. 322 rooms. A/C TV TEL   **Directions:** Just off I-275 (exit 25), at the corner of Ashley and Fortune streets.

$ Rates: $61–$91 single, $61–$101 double; executive level $86–$91 single, $91–$101 double. AE, CB, DC, DISC, MC, V. **Parking:** Free.

Perched along the Hillsborough River, this modern 14-story hotel is next to the Tampa Bay Performing Arts Center and is also within walking distance of most of the city's top attractions, including the Tampa Museum and the Franklin Street Pedestrian Mall. Guest rooms are spacious, with dark wood furnishings, rose or aqua-toned fabrics, and full-length wall mirrors. Most rooms on upper floors have views of the river. The top floor has 24 executive-style rooms with concierge, complimentary breakfast, and added amenities.

Dining/Entertainment: The lobby level offers three choices: The Backstage Restaurant, for moderately priced beef, seafood, and pasta dishes in a theatrical setting; the Deli for light fare; and the Encore lounge for drinks and occasional live music.

Services: Airport courtesy shuttle, room service, valet laundry service.

Facilities: Outdoor heated swimming pool, whirlpool, fitness room, meeting rooms, coin-operated laundry, gift shop, and car-rental desk.

RIVERSIDE HOTEL–TAMPA, 200 Ashley Dr., Tampa, FL 33602. Tel. 813/223-2222 or toll free 800/288-2676. Fax 813/273-0839. 265 rooms. A/C MINIBAR TV TEL   **Directions:** Between Jackson and Washington streets.

$ Rates: $99–$129 single, $115–$145 double. AE, CB, DC, MC, V.   **Parking:** Valet, $5.50.

Ideally located on the Hillsborough River and within two blocks of the new convention center, this six-story property was formerly the Tampa Hilton. Purchased in late 1989 by Helnan International, the entire hotel was renovated and revamped in 1989–90 at a cost of $6 million.

The refurbished guest rooms have a contemporary decor with dark woods and pastel tones; most units have private balconies with river views. Modern bathrooms have little extras, such as a makeup mirror, hair dryer, and phone.

Dining/Entertainment: Overlooking the river, the Mermaid is the main restaurant, serving contemporary American cuisine, with indoor and outdoor seating. Other venues, also with water views, are the Coffee Shop and the Lobby Bar, for light fare or a drink.

Services: Airport courtesy shuttle, room service, valet cleaning service (weekdays).

Facilities: Heated outdoor swimming pool, exercise room, gift shop, car-rental desk, meeting rooms.

INEXPENSIVE

DAYS INN–DOWNTOWN TAMPA, 515 E. Cass St., Tampa, FL 33602. Tel. 813/229-6431 or toll free 800/325-2525; toll free in Fla. 800/533-1317. Fax 813/228-7534. 180 rooms. A/C TV TEL   **Directions:** At the corner of Cass and Marion streets.

$ Rates: $32–$55 single, $36–$59 double. AE, DC, DISC, MC, V. **Parking:** Enclosed, free of charge.

If you want to stay downtown on a limited budget, this is the best choice, although it is not in a thriving part of the city. As long as you don't mind walking past a few boarded-up buildings, this eight-story hotel is situated within five blocks of the Tampa Bay Performing Arts Center and two blocks from the Franklin Street Mall. It is also next to the Greyhound bus station and the Marion Street Transitway, making it an ideal location if you're using public transport to get around. Guest rooms offer the usual amenities, and dining/ entertainment is limited to the Bayport lounge on the lobby level and the Bayport restaurant on the second floor. Guest facilities include an outdoor swimming pool on the second-floor level.

2. AIRPORT/WEST SHORE

EXPENSIVE

EMBASSY SUITES HOTEL, 4400 W. Cypress St., Tampa, FL 33607. Tel. 813/873-8675 or toll free 800/EMBASSY. Fax 813/879-7196. 263 suites. A/C MINIBAR TV TEL **Directions:** 1 mile from Tampa Airport, at Cypress Street and Westshore Boulevard.

$ Rates (including full breakfast and evening cocktail party): $119– $149 single, $129–$159 double. AE, CB, DC, MC, V. **Parking:** Free, outdoors.

With an exterior of salmon-toned Spanish-style architecture, this eight-story building adds an old-world charm to a busy corridor of modern glass-and-concrete structures. The interior includes a plant-filled atrium with cascading waterfalls and a tropical garden court-yard.

The guest units are suites with separate bedrooms and living areas, contemporary furniture, muted color schemes, and wet bar. Most have sofa beds, microwave ovens, coffeemakers, and private patios or balconies.

Dining/Entertainment: Regional dishes and local seafoods are the specialties at the Swan Court Café and Lounge, adjacent to the greenery-filled atrium.

Services: Airport courtesy shuttle, room service, valet laundry service.

Facilities: Indoor swimming pool, sauna, steam room, gift shop, meeting rooms.

GUEST QUARTERS HOTEL, 555 N. Westshore Blvd., Tampa, FL 33609. Tel. 813/875-1555 or toll free 800/424-2900. Fax 813/286-2038. 221 suites. A/C TV TEL **Directions:** Less than two miles from Tampa Airport, between Route 60 and I-275 (exit 21).

$ Rates (including continental breakfast and evening cocktail reception): $89–$125 single, $119–$145 double. AE, CB, DC, DISC, MC, V. **Parking:** $4.

This 16-story property stands out in the Westshore business district with a striking facade of white stucco and glass. The interior is equally appealing, with arched corridors and walls decorated with Florida seabird art. Each guest unit offers a separate bedroom and living area with contemporary pastel-toned furnishings and a fully equipped kitchen.

Dining/Entertainment: An art deco theme prevails at the Bay Café, a bright and brassy eatery and lounge on the second level. Outdoor dining is available at the Pavilion, overlooking fountains, a three-tier waterfall, and the pool.

Services: Airport courtesy shuttle, concierge desk, valet laundry service.

Facilities: Heated outdoor swimming pool, sundeck, saunas, whirlpool, exercise room, library, newsstand/gift shop, meeting rooms.

OMNI TAMPA HOTEL AT WESTSHORE, 700 N. Westshore Blvd., Tampa, FL 33609. Tel. 813/289-8200 or toll free 800/THE-OMNI. Fax 813/289-8200, ext. 6917. 278 rooms. A/C TV TEL **Directions:** 1 mile from Tampa Airport, between Cypress Street and Route 60.

$ Rates: $125–$140 single, $140–$175 double; $140 single, $165 double on Omni Club level. AE, CB, DC, MC, V. **Parking:** Free, outdoors.

A favorite hotel with traveling executives, this 11-story property is part of Austin Center South, a mixed-use business complex. Formerly the Howard Johnson Plaza-Hotel, it became an Omni in late 1989 and embarked on a $3 million renovation. The tapestry-filled lobby sets the tone of the "new look."

Guest rooms, accessible by computer-card keys, are decorated in rich dark tones of green, contrasted with pale grays and light oak, with mirrored closet doors and executive desks. Spacious bathrooms offer every amenity, including hair dryers. The entire 11th floor is the Omni Club, with private lounge, concierge, and added equipment such as a second telephone in the bathroom.

Dining/Entertainment: Seasons, the lobby-level restaurant noted for its American regional cuisine and local seafood, is traditional in style, with a decor rich in mahogany and fine tapestries; the adjacent lounge offers relaxing piano music each evening.

Services: Airport courtesy shuttle, room service, valet laundry service.

Facilities: Heated outdoor swimming pool, whirlpool, two saunas, fitness equipment, meeting rooms.

SHERATON GRAND HOTEL, 4860 W. Kennedy Blvd., Tampa, FL 33609. Tel. 813/286-4400 or toll free 800/325-3535. Fax 813/286-4053. 325 rooms, 23 suites. A/C TV TEL **Directions:** 2 miles from the airport, at the intersection of Route 60 and Westshore Boulevard.

Tampa

Best Western Safari Inn Resort 27
Days Inn-Busch Gardens 28
Days Inn-Downtown Tampa 5
Days Inn-Rocky Point 22
Econo Lodge at Busch Gardens 29
Embassy Suites Hotel 6
Embassy Suites-USF / Busch Gardens 23
Guest Quarters Hotel 7
Hampton Inn 15
Holiday Inn-Ashley Plaza 3
Holiday Inn-Busch Gardens 24
Holiday Inn-West Shore 12
Holiday Inn-Stadium / Airport Area 11
Hyatt Regency Tampa 1
Hyatt Regency West Shore 17
John Henry's Sleep Rite Inn 30
La Quinta-Airport 16
Omni Tampa Hotel at Westshore 8
Pickett Suite Hotel 18
Quality Suites-Busch Gardens 25
Radisson Bay Harbor Inn 19
Ramada Hotel North 26
Red Roof Inn 31
Residece Inn by Marriott 20
Riverside Hotel-Tampa 4
Saddlebrook 33
Sailport Resort 21
Sheraton Grand Hotel 9
Sheraton Tampa East 34
Sleep Inn 32
Tampa Airport Marriott 10
Tampa Hilton at Metro Center 13
Tampa Marriott Westshore 14
Wyndham Harbour Island Hotel 2

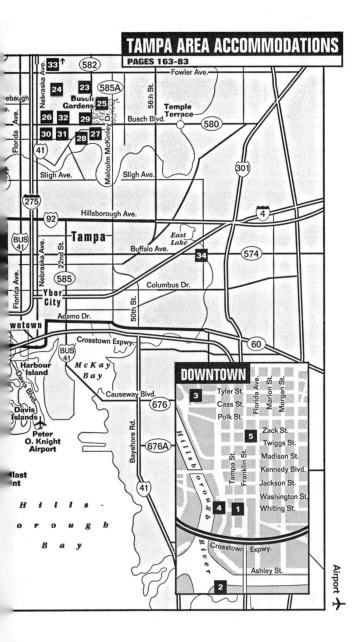

TAMPA AREA ACCOMMODATIONS

PAGES 163-83

Fowler Ave.

33

582

24   23   585A

Busch
Gardens   25

26   32   29

Temple
Terrace

Busch Blvd.   580

30   31

28   27

41

Sligh Ave.   Sligh Ave.

301

275

92   Hillsborough Ave.   4

BUS
41   **Tampa**

Buffalo Ave.   East
Lake   574

34

585   **Ybor
City**   Columbus Dr.

Adamo Dr.

wntown   Crosstown Expwy.

BUS
41   *McKay
Bay*

**Harbour
Island**

**Davis
Islands**   Causeway Blvd.
676

**Peter
O. Knight
Airport**   Bayshore Rd.

676A

**llast
int**   41

Hills-

o r o u g h

B a y

DOWNTOWN

3   Tyler St.

Cass St.

Polk St.

5   Zack St.

Twiggs St.

Madison St.

Kennedy Blvd.

Jackson St.

Washington St.

4   1   Whiting St.

Crosstown   Expwy.

2   Ashley St.

Airport ✈

$ Rates: $94–$104 single. $135–$145 double, $175–$425 suites. AE, CB, DC, MC, V. **Parking:** Free; valet parking $4.

★ Formerly the Lincoln Hotel–Westshore, this contemporary-style 11-story property is part of Urban Center, a financial office complex in the heart of the Westshore business district and across from the Westshore Plaza Shopping Mall. In addition to its steady business clientele, it attracts vacationers who enjoy the panoramic views from the three glass elevators, and the bright and airy atriums filled with indoor greenery and cascading fountains.

The guest rooms are equally attractive, with soft pink-and-gray color schemes, traditional dark wood furnishings, writing desks, easy chairs, full-length mirrors, built-in armoires, roomy closets, and marble-finished bathrooms. Rooms on the upper floors have distant views of Old Tampa Bay.

Dining/Entertainment: For Continental recipes and fresh Florida seafood, try J. Fitzgerald's on the lobby level. Other public areas include the Atrium Lobby Lounge, where there is piano music each evening, and the Courtyard Café for light meals in an indoor/outdoor setting.

Services: 24-hour room service, courtesy airport shuttle, concierge desk, valet laundry service.

Facilities: Outdoor heated swimming pool, meeting rooms, car-rental desk, gift shops, travel agency, florist, two banks, news/tobacco shop, rooms equipped for the disabled.

TAMPA AIRPORT MARRIOTT, Tampa International Airport, Tampa, FL 33607. Tel. 813/879-5151 or toll free 800/228-9290. Fax 813/873-0945. 296 rooms. A/C TV TEL **Directions:** Follow signs for "hotel" at airport; hotel is connected to departure terminals by an indoor walkway.
$ Rates: $100–$150 single or double; $155–$165 for concierge level. AE, CB, DC, DISC, MC, V. **Parking:** Valet $7; self-parking $4.

Wedged between the terminals, this is the only on-site hotel at Tampa's busy airport and a good specimen for those who thrive on the excitement of overnighting near the jetways. Guest rooms are well soundproofed, decorated in contemporary style with dark woods and fabrics of beige, pink, or raspberry tones. The sixth floor is the concierge level with larger executive-style rooms that include wet bars and added amenities.

Dining/Entertainment: An express elevator takes you to the 7th floor and CK's, the hotel's revolving rooftop restaurant and lounge, a popular attraction for those in transit and locals alike (see Chapter 10, "Tampa Dining"); on the lobby level there is the Garden Café for light fare and the Flight Room for cocktails and large-screen TV.

Services: Concierge, baby-sitting service, valet laundry service.

Facilities: Outdoor heated swimming pool, health club, gift shop, airline desk, car-rental desk, meeting rooms, and rooms equipped for disabled guests.

MODERATE

HOLIDAY INN–STADIUM/AIRPORT AREA, 4732 N. Dale Mabry Highway, Tampa, FL 33614. Tel. 813/877-6061
or toll free 800/331-5291; in Fla. toll free 800/952-1222. Fax 813/876-1531. 312 rooms. A/C TV TEL **Directions:** West of the airport, on U.S. 92 (Dale Mabry Highway), between Buffalo and Hillsborough avenues.

$ Rates: $53–$82 single, $55–$88 double. AE, CB, DC, DISC, MC, V. **Parking:** Free.

When Tampa Stadium hosts a major event, this place (just two blocks north of the stadium) really hops. Otherwise it is a basic one- and two-story motel on a busy commercial corridor close to the airport. Rooms have standard furnishings and some kitchenettes are available.

Dining/Entertainment: Ristorante Mama Mia, with a decor reminiscent of an Italian village and piazza, is a favorite in its own right with Tampa diners; other outlets include the Casbah lounge and a fast-food café.

Services: Airport courtesy shuttle, room service, baby-sitting service.

Facilities: Outdoor heated swimming pool, meeting rooms.

HOLIDAY INN–WEST SHORE, 4500 Cypress St., Tampa, FL 33607. Tel. 813/879-4800 or toll free 800/HOLIDAY. Fax 813/873-1832. 488 rooms. A/C TV TEL **Directions:** 1 mile from Tampa Airport, between Westshore Boulevard and Lois Avenue.

$ Rates: $66–$102 single, $76–$112 double. AE, CB, DC, DISC, MC, V. **Parking:** Free.

Outside of the downtown area, this is Tampa's largest hotel. Like its neighbors along the Westshore corridor, it caters primarily to business traffic and is a favorite for convention and meeting groups. It is built in a rectangular configuration with three six-story wings and one 10-story wing, all surrounding a central courtyard area with outdoor pool and gardens. The guest rooms, many of which have balconies, are as varied as the architecture. The decor primarily features dark wood furnishings and fabrics of pink, raspberry, and lavender tones, or beachy beige combinations. Most rooms overlook either the inner courtyard or nearby roadways, but units on the upper floors tower over nearby buildings and provide distant views of the bay.

Dining/Entertainment: The Cypress Café offers American cuisine, Wellington's Lounge has a large-screen TV for sports and entertainment, and the Gazebo Bar features tropical drinks by the pool.

Services: Airport courtesy shuttle, concierge desk, baby-sitting service, room service, valet laundry service.

Facilities: Outdoor heated swimming pool, Jacuzzi, fitness center with sauna and whirlpool, meeting rooms, gift shop, newsstand.

TAMPA HILTON AT METROCENTER, 2225 N. Lois Ave., Tampa, FL 33607. Tel. 813/877-6688 or toll free 800/ HILTONS. Fax 813/879-3264. 240 rooms. A/C TV TEL
Directions: 1 mile from the airport, at the corner of Boy Scout Boulevard and Lois Avenue.

$ Rates: $105 single, $115 double; $120–$130 for concierge level. AE, CB, DC, DISC, MC, V. **Parking:** Free.

Situated in a commercial corridor between the airport and downtown, this 12-story property has an inviting skylit lobby of cherry and lime tones, and is often a focal point for the local business clientele. Guest rooms are contemporary, with light beige walls and carpets contrasting with deeper tones of red or navy fabrics. Bathrooms have a separate vanity area. The top two floors feature concierge-style rooms with balconies. The entire eighth floor is designated for nonsmokers.

Dining/Entertainment: The main restaurant, Hemingway's, has a Key West atmosphere with ceiling fans, tropical plants, and appropriate background music. The Bay Breeze Lobby Bar overlooks the pool, where there is also a snack bar and gazebo.

Services: Airport courtesy shuttle, baby-sitting service, room service, valet laundry service.

Facilities: Outdoor heated swimming pool, hot tub, tennis court, gift shop, meeting rooms, rooms equipped for the disabled.

TAMPA MARRIOTT WESTSHORE, 1001 N. Westshore Blvd., Tampa, FL 33607. Tel. 813/287-2555 or toll free 800/228-9290. Fax 813/289-5464. 312 rooms. A/C TV TEL
Directions: 1 mile from the airport, at the corner of Spruce Street and Westshore Boulevard.

$ Rates: $100–$145 single or double; $145 on concierge level. AE, CB, DC, DISC, MC, V. **Parking:** Free.

Popular with a business clientele, this busy 14-story hotel greets guests with a contemporary skylit lobby. Bedrooms are well-maintained, with dark wood furnishings, full-length wall mirrors, and fabrics of dusty rose or aqua. The top floor is the concierge level, with larger layouts and enhanced amenities.

Dining/Entertainment: Kastan's Sea Grill Restaurant is noted for seafood, and Champions Sports Bar is a popular gathering place each evening, with over a dozen TVs for monitoring sports events and a DJ for contemporary dance music.

Services: Airport courtesy shuttle, valet laundry service.

Facilities: Heated indoor/outdoor swimming pool, health club, sauna, whirlpool, game room, gift shop, meeting rooms, rooms equipped for disabled guests.

INEXPENSIVE

HAMPTON INN, 4817 West Laurel St., Tampa, FL 33607. Tel. 813/878-0778 or toll free 800/HAMPTON. Fax 813/287-0882. 134 rooms. A/C TV TEL **Directions:** 1 mile from Tampa Airport, south of Spruce Street, and directly off Westshore Boulevard.

$ Rates (including continental breakfast and in-room local phone calls): $41–$53 single, $46–$53 double. **Parking:** Free.

Opened in the fall of 1988, this six-story property offers very good value in an otherwise high-priced airport/business corridor. Guest rooms are decorated with dark woods set off by pink, peach, and beige tones. Some units offer king-size beds and extra work areas, and a full 50% of the rooms are designated for nonsmoking guests. Services and facilities are limited, but there is an outdoor heated swimming pool, meeting room, and a courtesy shuttle to the airport.

LA QUINTA–AIRPORT, 4730 W. Spruce St., Tampa, FL 33607. Tel. 813/287-0440 or toll free **800/531-5900.** Fax 813/286-7399. 122 rooms. A/C TV TEL **Directions:** Just outside of Tampa Airport exit, between O'Brien Street and Westshore Boulevard.

$ Rates: $50–$55 single, $55–$60 double. AE, CB, DC, DISC, MC, V. **Parking:** Free.

Equally convenient to the airport and the Westshore business district, this two-story hacienda-style motel offers a homey alternative to the many sleek high-rise properties in this area. Guest rooms, which surround a central courtyard, are decorated in a Southwestern motif, with light woods, Pueblo art, and fabric tones of muted green, amber, and brown, while bathrooms are well lit with separate vanity areas. Public areas include a living room–style lobby with fireplace and a sundeck with sombrero-shaped umbrellas. There is a complimentary airport shuttle and an adjacent 24-hour restaurant.

3. COURTNEY CAMPBELL CAUSEWAY AREA

VERY EXPENSIVE

HYATT REGENCY WESTSHORE, 6200 Courtney Campbell Causeway, Tampa, FL 33607. Tel. 813/874-1234 or toll free **800/233-1234.** Fax 813/870-9168. 445 rooms. A/C TV TEL **Directions:** Just over 1 mile west of Tampa Airport, adjacent to Bayport Plaza Business Complex.

$ Rates: $150 single, $170 double; $175 single, $195 double on Regency Club level. AE, CB, DC, DISC, MC, V. **Parking:** Free; valet $5.50.

Overlooking Old Tampa Bay, this imposing 14-story property is nestled on a 35-acre nature preserve, convenient to the airport and downtown and yet sequestered in a world of its own. The lobby provides a warm welcome, with a blend of arches and columns, hand-painted murals, and imported marble flooring.

Seashore colors and light woods dominate the decor of the guest rooms, most of which provide expansive views of the bay and of evening sunsets. The Regency Club level on the 12th floor offers 44 rooms with extra amenities and services such as a complimentary limousine transfer to the Tampa business district.

Dining/Entertainment: On the 14th floor is Armani's, a rooftop Italian restaurant known for its fine food and views, and behind the main hotel a 250-foot boardwalk leads to Oystercatchers, a Key West–style seafood eatery with indoor and outdoor seating overlooking the bay (see Chapter 10, "Tampa Dining," for more information about both). On the lobby level, there is Petey Brown's Café and the Bistro Bar.

Services: Airport courtesy shuttle, 24-hour room service, concierge desk, baby-sitting service, valet laundry service.

Facilities: Two outdoor heated swimming pools, two lighted tennis courts, whirlpool, saunas, health club, nature walks and jogging trails, meeting rooms.

EXPENSIVE

GUEST QUARTERS SUITE HOTEL ON TAMPA BAY, 3050 N. Rocky Point Drive West, Tampa, FL 33607. Tel. 813/888-8800 or toll free 800/742-5388. Fax 813/888-8743. 203 suites. A/C MINIBAR TV TEL. **Directions:** 2 miles west of Tampa Airport, opposite International Shrine Headquarters.

$ Rates: $125 single, $145 double (including buffet breakfast). AE, CB, DC, DISC, MC, V. **Parking:** Free, outdoor.

One of the newest hotels along this strip overlooking Old Tampa Bay, this seven-story property has a unique facade in the shape of a trapezoid. The futuristic theme is carried into the lobby, which has a spacious three-story atrium.

Each guest unit is a suite, with separate bedroom and living room/dining area. Rooms have wide windows with views of the bay, dark woods, beige and pastel-toned fabrics, comfortable reclining chairs and ottomans, and little extras such as a mini-TV in the bathroom, full-length mirrored door, coffee/teamaker, and hair dryer.

Dining/Entertainment: The Galerie Restaurant and Lounge overlooks the bay and the pool area.

Services: Airport courtesy shuttle, nightly turndown service, room service, concierge desk, baby-sitting service, valet laundry service.

Facilities: Heated outdoor swimming pool, whirlpool, sauna, sun deck, exercise room, library, business center with computer access, meeting rooms.

MODERATE

RADISSON BAY HARBOR INN, 7700 Courtney Campbell Causeway, Tampa, FL 33607. Tel. 813/281-8900 or toll free 800/333-3333. Fax 813/281-0189. 260 rooms. A/C TV TEL **Directions:** 2 miles west of Tampa Airport; hotel is between the International Shrine Headquarters building and Ben T. Davis Beach.

$ Rates: $89–$129 single or double. AE, CB, DC, MC, V. **Parking:** Free.

One of the few hotels fronting Old Tampa Bay that actually has a sandy beach of its own, this six-story property was constructed to give all rooms a view of the water. To make the most of the views, each room also has a balcony or patio. Guest room decor, which uses mostly pastel-toned fabrics, reflects art deco influences, with rounded furnishings and shell-shaped chairs.

Dining/Entertainment: Views of the water and the beach are prime attractions at the lobby-level Yankee Trader Restaurant and Lounge.

Services: Airport courtesy shuttle, valet laundry service.

Facilities: Heated outdoor swimming pool, two lighted tennis courts, meeting rooms, hair salons for men and women, gift shop, car-rental desk.

RESIDENCE INN BY MARRIOTT, 3075 Rocky Point Dr., Tampa, FL 33607. Tel. 813/281-5677 or toll free 800/331-3131. Fax 813/281-5677. 176 rooms. A/C TV TEL **Directions:** 2 miles west of Tampa Airport, off the main road behind Days Inn; well signposted.

$ Rates (including continental breakfast and evening hospitality cocktail hour Mon–Fri): $89 single, $109 double. AE, DC, MC, V. **Parking:** Free.

For families or for long-term individual stays, this townhouse-style property offers great value. Set back from the main road, it overlooks the bay amid a well-landscaped community-style setting with its own fishing pier/boat dock. Each unit is a suite with bedroom, living area, and fully equipped kitchen, including microwave oven, coffeemaker, and dishwasher. Layouts include one-level studio suites or two-story penthouse suites; the larger units have two bedrooms, two bathrooms, and two televisions; many have fireplaces.

Services: Airport courtesy shuttle, baby-sitting service, grocery-shopping service, valet laundry service.

Facilities: Heated outdoor swimming pool, Jacuzzi, court for racket sports, rentals for water sports, complimentary pass to nearby health and racquet club, meeting rooms.

SAILPORT RESORT, 2506 Rocky Point Dr., Tampa, FL 33607. Tel. 813/886-9599 or toll free 800/255-9599. Fax 813/882-9510. 237 suites. A/C MINIBAR TV TEL **Directions:** 2 miles west of the airport, off the main road, just behind the International Shrine Headquarters.

$ Rates (including continental breakfast and newspapers in the lobby): $89–$129 single or double. AE, DC, MC, V. **Parking:** Free.

Overlooking Old Tampa Bay, this three-story property offers large suites that are really more like one- or two-bedroom apartments than hotel rooms. Each unit has a fully equipped kitchen and a living room with a queen-size sofa bed and a stereo system. Each bedroom has a queen-size bed. Other homey touches include some rattan furniture, seascape art, built-in bunk beds in the hallway, linen closets, and a medicine chest in the bathroom. There are no dining outlets, and check-in is confined to a small office rather than a formal lobby; but basic hotel functions, such as daily maid service and valet laundry service, are provided.

Facilities: Heated outdoor swimming pool, lighted tennis court, fishing pier, barbecue grills, meeting rooms, grocery/sundries store.

INEXPENSIVE

DAYS INN—ROCKY POINT, 7627 Courtney Campbell Causeway, Tampa, FL 33607. Tel. 813/281-0000 or toll free 800/325-2525; toll free in Fla. 800/332-6688. Fax 813/281-1067. 152 rooms. A/C TV TEL   **Directions:** 2 miles west of Tampa Airport, off Rocky Point Drive.

$ Rates: $54–$75 single or double.   **Parking:** Free.

Set back from the main road, this motel-style property has a lovely waterfront setting on Old Tampa Bay, but no beach. The layout encompasses six two-story wings surrounding an outdoor swimming pool with landscaped courtyard, so the bedrooms offer either bayview or poolside views. The units have a cheery decor of pink and green tones, and basic light wood furniture.

Dining/Entertainment: Off the lobby is the Paradise Café and Coral Lounge.

Facilities: Heated outdoor swimming pool, two tennis courts, shuffleboard court, horseshoes, badminton, volleyball court, children's playground, rentals for paddle boats, coin-operated guest laundry, meeting rooms.

4. BUSCH GARDENS AREA

MODERATE

EMBASSY SUITES HOTEL—USF/BUSCH GARDENS, 11310 N. 30th St., Tampa, FL 33612. Tel. 813/971-7690 or toll free 800/EMBASSY. Fax 813/972-5525. 129 suites. A/C MINIBAR TV TEL   **Directions:** Take I-275 north to Fowler Avenue (exit 34); go east for 1½ miles to 30th Street, turn right, cross over railroad tracks; hotel is on right.

$ Rates (including full breakfast and evening cocktail party): $69–$109 single or double. AE, CB, DC, DISC, MC, V.   **Parking:** Free.

Situated 1 mile north of Busch Gardens, this three-story all-suite property has a Southern mansion ambience, highlighted by well-landscaped grounds, wrought-iron trim, veranda-style outdoor corridors with hanging plants, and a central courtyard with shady palms and outdoor pool.

Each guest unit has a separate bedroom and living room with dining area/work space, wet bar, coffeemaker, and sofa bed. The color scheme blends light wood furnishings with refreshing peach and lime tones.

Services: Courtesy shuttle service to Busch Gardens, valet laundry service.

Facilities: Outdoor heated swimming pool, Jacuzzi, meeting rooms, suites designed for disabled guests.

HOLIDAY INN–BUSCH GARDENS, 2701 E. Fowler Ave. Tampa, FL 33612. Tel. 813/971-4710 or toll free 800/ HOLIDAY. Fax 813/977-0155. 395 rooms. A/C TV TEL **Directions:** Take I-275 north to Fowler Avenue (exit 34); go east on Fowler for just over 1 mile; hotel is on right.
$ Rates: $69–$74 single, $77–$84 double. AE, CB, DC, DISC, MC, V. **Parking:** Free.

The largest hotel in the area, this sprawling two-story complex is one mile north of Busch Gardens, and opposite the University of South Florida campus. The main focus here is a central outdoor courtyard with swimming pool, extensive tropical gardens, mini-waterfalls, rock gardens, gazebo, and wooden footbridges.

Guest rooms, most of which face the courtyard, are outfitted with light woods and touches of brass; color schemes vary from mauve and pink to a trio of blue, gray, and aqua.

Dining/Entertainment: Café Monterey overlooks the leafy foliage of the central courtyard; other outlets include an ice cream parlor, pool bar, and a two-story nightspot, Club Sydney's.

Services: Complimentary transport to Busch Gardens, airport courtesy shuttle, baby-sitting service, room service, valet laundry service.

Facilities: Outdoor heated swimming pool, health club, meeting rooms.

QUALITY SUITES–BUSCH GARDENS, 3001 University Center Dr., Tampa, FL 33612. Tel. 813/971-8930 or toll free 800/228-5151. Fax 813/971-8935. 150 suites. A/C TV TEL **Directions:** Take I-275 north to Busch Boulevard (exit 33); travel east on Busch for 1½ miles to 30th Street, turn left and drive ½ mile north, and hotel is on right off Bougainvillea Avenue.
$ Rates (including full breakfast and evening cocktail reception): $70–$98 single or double. AE, DC, DISC, MC, V. **Parking:** Free.

S Opened in the summer of 1989, this hacienda-style all-suite hotel sits directly behind the Busch Gardens property, although the entrance to the theme park is four blocks away. Besides its proximity to the area's major attraction, it has become a fast favorite with both business travelers and families because of its great value.

Each guest unit has a separate bedroom with built-in armoire, luggage rack, and well-lit mirrored vanity area, and a living/dining room with sofa bed, wet bar, coffeemaker, microwave oven, stereo/ VCR unit, and a phone system with voice-message and computer-hookup capabilities. The decor relies heavily on rounded art deco-style furnishings, with bright shades of pink, raspberry, or green.

Services: 24-hour gift shop/food store, VCR rentals, valet laundry service.

Facilities: Outdoor heated swimming pool, Jacuzzi, meeting rooms, coin-operated laundry, suites designed for disabled travelers.

RAMADA HOTEL NORTH, 820 E. Busch Blvd., Tampa, FL 33612. Tel. 813/933-4011 or toll free 800/228-2828. Fax 813/932-1784. 255 rooms. A/C TV TEL **Directions:** Take I-275 north to Busch Boulevard (exit 33); turn left at exit ramp light; hotel is on left.

$ Rates: $55–$75 single, $65–$80 double. AE, CB, DC, DISC, MC, V. **Parking:** Free.

Situated two miles west of Busch Gardens on the main thoroughfare, this two- and four-story hotel attracts a brisk business trade as well as theme-park attendees. The lobby leads to an enclosed skylit atrium-style courtyard with fountains, benches, streetlights, shops, cafés, bars, pool, and other sporting activities. Guest rooms, which surround the courtyard, offer standard furnishings, enlivened by eye-catching fabrics of red and orange tones.

Dining/Entertainment: The Connection Restaurant, off the lobby, features seafood dishes; the Lounge offers live entertainment Tuesday through Saturday; and the atrium offers a café, lounge, and coffee shop.

Services: Courtesy transport to Busch Gardens, concierge desk, secretarial services, valet laundry service.

Facilities: Indoor and outdoor heated swimming pools, two Jacuzzis, sauna, four lighted tennis courts, tennis pro shop, exercise room, game room, coin-operated laundry, gift shop, meeting rooms.

INEXPENSIVE

BEST WESTERN SAFARI INN RESORT, 4139 E. Busch Blvd., Tampa, FL 33617. Tel. 813/988-9191 or toll free 800/528-1234. Fax 813/988-9195. 99 rooms. A/C TV TEL **Directions:** Take I-275 north to Busch Boulevard (exit 33); go east on Busch for just over 2 miles; hotel is on right.

$ Rates: $35–$45 single, $40–$50 double. AE, CB, DC, MC, V. **Parking:** Free.

Situated almost directly across from the entrance of Busch Gardens, this two-story motel is a favorite with families. Built in 1973 and formerly an independent property, it has been flying the Best Western banner since late 1989. The guest rooms, most of which have private balconies or patios, offer standard furnishings in light woods, with wildlife prints on the walls, and bedspreads made of jungle patterns and colors. Most units have two double beds; 10 rooms are larger, with deluxe appointments including king-size bed, wet bar, and refrigerator.

Services: Complimentary shuttle to Busch Gardens and baby-sitting service.

Facilities: Outdoor heated swimming pool, Jacuzzi, saunas, video game room, meeting rooms.

DAYS INN–BUSCH GARDENS, 2901 E. Busch Blvd., Tampa, FL 33612. Tel. 813/933-6471 or toll free 800/325-2525. 179 rooms. A/C TV TEL **Directions:** Take I-275 north to Busch Boulevard (exit 33); go east on Busch for just over 1½ miles; hotel is on right at 30th Street.

$ Rates: $32–$59 single, $37–$64 double. AE, DC, MC, V. **Parking:** Free.

Within walking distance of Busch Gardens, this sprawling two-story motel is popular with families. Although the registration office is just off the main thoroughfare, most of the guest rooms are set back in a more quiet environment surrounding an outdoor swimming pool. Rooms offer standard furnishings, mostly with two double beds. There are no dining outlets on the premises, but a full-service restaurant is adjacent. In addition to the pool, on-site facilities include a children's playground, game room, gift shop, and coin-operated laundry.

ECONO LODGE AT BUSCH GARDENS, 9202 N. 30th St., Tampa, FL 33612. Tel. 813/935-7855 or toll free 800/446-6900. Fax 813/932-0350. 148 rooms, 12 suites. A/C TV TEL **Directions:** Take I-275 north to Busch Boulevard (exit 33); go east on Busch for 1½ miles, then left at 30th Street; hotel is on left.

$ Rates: $24.95–$34.95 single, $29.95–$49.95 double, suites from $70. AE, CB, DC, DISC, MC, V. **Parking:** Free.

Across the street from the west side of the Busch Gardens property, this three-story motel with an attractive mirrored facade is one of the closest to the giant theme park. Guest rooms offer standard amenities, with a few extra touches such as ceiling fans and separate vanity areas. The decor is eclectic, with some green and brown jungle-style tones and other bright purple and pink patterns, designed to delight visiting families. Facilities on the premises include a 24-hour fast-food restaurant, outdoor heated swimming pool in a tropical garden setting, game room, and an all-purpose shop.

JOHN HENRY'S SLEEP RITE INN, 1701 E. Busch Blvd., Tampa, FL 33612. Tel. 813/933-7681; Fax 813/935-3301. 240 rooms. **Directions:** Take I-275 north to Busch Boulevard (exit 33); go east on Busch for about ¾ mile; hotel is on right.

$ Rates: $24–$30 single, $28–$36 double. AE, CB, DC, DISC, MC, V. **Parking:** Free.

Formerly a Best Western, this two- and three-story motel is laid out with a central courtyard, about a mile west of Busch Gardens. Rooms are standard, mostly with two double beds or one king-size bed, small tiled bathroom with separate vanity area, and a decor of dark woods, blue and green tones, and wildlife art from Busch Gardens on the walls. This property is popular with families for its price level and also because it has a number of connecting units. Facilities include an outdoor swimming pool and a café/lounge designed in a railroad car motif.

RED ROOF INN, 2307 E. Busch Blvd., Tampa, FL 33612.
Tel. 813/932-0073 or toll free 800/THE ROOF. Fax 813/933-5689. 108 rooms. A/C TV TEL **Directions:** Take I-275 north to Busch Boulevard (exit 33), go east on Busch just over 1 mile; hotel is on right.

$ Rates (including complimentary coffee and unlimited local phone calls): $33.95–$44.95 single, $39.95–$50.95 double. AE, CB, DC, DISC, MC, V. **Parking:** Free.

A half-mile west of Busch Gardens, this two-story property is set back from the road in a grassy, well-landscaped setting. The layout consists of two adjacent wings with an outdoor pool and whirlpool in the center. The guest units, outfitted with bright checkered fabrics and standard furnishings, represent good value for the area.

SLEEP INN, 2106 E. Busch Blvd., Tampa, Fl 33612. Tel.
813/931-3313. 50 units. A/C TV TEL **Directions:** Take I-275 north to Busch Boulevard (exit 33), go east on Busch for 1 mile; hotel is on left.

$ Rates: $31–$43 single, $36–$48 double, $40–$53 for efficiencies. AE, DISC, MC, V. **Parking:** Free.

In spite of its name, this relatively new three-story motor inn is not part of the Quality Inn–owned Sleep Inn chain, but an independent property. Situated about half a mile west of Busch Gardens, it offers a choice of accommodations. Most rooms are standard doubles, and some have only a shower instead of a full bath. In addition, there are larger rooms with king-size beds and full baths; and over a third of the units are also outfitted with small kitchenettes. Facilities are limited, but there is an outdoor heated swimming pool.

5. EAST OF TAMPA

VERY EXPENSIVE/EXPENSIVE

SADDLEBROOK, 100 Saddlebrook Way, Wesley Chapel,
FL 34249. Tel. 813/973-1111 or toll free 800/237-7519; toll free in Fla. 800/282-4654. Fax 813/793-4504. 502 units. AC MINIBAR TV TEL **Directions:** Take I-275 to I-75; go north to exit 58; then travel 1½ miles east on County Road 54 to Saddlebrook entrance.

$ Rates: $140–$240 single or double. AE, CB, DC, MC, V. **Parking:** Free.

Situated on 480 acres of inland woodlands, this secluded resort is 25 miles northeast of Tampa Airport. A haven for sports enthusiasts, it is the home of two Arnold Palmer–designed golf courses and the Harry Hopman international tennis school.

Guest rooms are spread throughout the property in a layout of over 20 two-story villas, each with patios or balconies. Three types of accommodation are available: 123 standard hotel rooms, 154 one-bedroom condos, and 225 two-bedroom condo suites. Each unit is furnished in a homey, contemporary style, with dark woods, floral fabrics, and plants. All suites have fully equipped kitchens.

Dining/Entertainment: Restaurants include the large-scale Cypress Room and the smaller Gourmet Room. The Little Club offers casual dining in a tropical atmosphere, and the Little Club Patio serves outdoor breakfasts and lunches, while the Snack Shack serves poolside refreshments. Cocktails and nightly entertainment are provided in the Polo Lounge or the Little Club Lounge.

Services: Airport shuttle service ($15), room service, supervised children's program.

Facilities: Two 18-hole golf courses, 37 tennis courts, outdoor heated swimming pool with lifeguard, exercise room and fitness center, jogging trails, bicycle rental, massage therapy, meeting rooms, package store, gift shop, barber, beauty shop.

MODERATE

SHERATON TAMPA EAST, 7401 E. Hillsborough Ave., Tampa, FL 33610. Tel. 813/626-0999 or toll free 800/325-3535. Fax 813/626-0999, ext. 246. 156 rooms. A/C TV TEL
Directions: Take I-275 north to I-4; take I-4 east to Orient Road (exit 5); hotel is on right.
$ Rates: $60–$75 single, $70–$85 double. AE, CB, DC, MC, V.
Parking: Free.

Ten minutes from downtown, this three-story property is situated in a palm-tree–shaded setting, close to the State Fair Grounds and Seminole Bingo. It also makes an ideal base if you are planning day trips to Walt Disney World and other Orlando-area attractions, just an hour away. Guest rooms, many of which surround a central courtyard and pool area, are contemporary in decor, with dark woods, pastel tones, and wildlife art. Most units have balconies or patios.

Dining/Entertainment: The lobby area has a lounge bar with an informal atmosphere; or follow a covered walkway to an adjacent building and the Cypress Landing Restaurant and Lounge.

Services: Airport courtesy shuttle, room service, valet, laundry service, secretarial services.

Facilities: Outdoor heated swimming pool, health club, meeting rooms, gift shop.

TAMPA DINING

From the landmark Columbia with its flamenco dancing to the flamboyant and pricey Bern's Steak House, Tampa offers a wide variety of fine restaurants. The menu choices range from typical American fare to regional Southern dishes or Cajun/Creole cooking, as well as the cuisines of Spain, France, Italy, Germany, Mexico, and the Orient.

And, like neighboring St. Petersburg, the Tampa area is outstanding for seafood —fresh from Tampa Bay, nearby Gulf waters, and beyond. The port of Tampa is home to one of the state of Florida's largest shrimp-boat fleets. Other local favorites include grouper, pompano, snapper, stone crabs, rock shrimp, and crawfish. Fresher fish is hard to find anywhere.

Above all, from the channels surrounding Harbour Island to the shores of Tampa Bay, this city is known for its waterfront dining, from romantic rooftop settings to rustic beachside decks. Even Tampa Airport, so widely acclaimed as a transportation hub, has a great rooftop restaurant in its own right, the revolving CK's, with ever-changing views of nearby waters and the city skyline.

See Chapter 6, "St. Petersburg Dining," for general guidelines on reservations, tipping policies, alcoholic beverages, price ranges, and "early-bird" dining. Note, however, that the tax charged at Tampa restaurants is only 6%, not 7%.

1. DOWNTOWN/HARBOUR ISLAND

EXPENSIVE

HARBOUR VIEW ROOM, 725 S. Harbor Island Blvd., Harbour Island. Tel. 229-5001.
 Cuisine: AMERICAN. **Reservations:** Recommended. **Directions:** On the main lobby level of the Wyndham Harbour Island Hotel.

$ Prices: Entrées $5.95–$12.95 lunch, $12.95–$24.95 dinner. AE, CB, DC, MC, V.
Open: Mon–Sat 11:30am–2:30pm and 6–11 pm, Sun 10:30am–2:30pm and 6–10pm.

With wide-windowed views of the waterways surrounding Harbour Island, subdued lighting, and classical music playing in the background, this romantic hotel eatery is an attraction in itself. Sit back, relax, watch the yachts glide by, and enjoy local seafoods and specialties such as Mandarin grilled sirloin steak, herb-grilled lamb chops, coconut chicken breast with apricot chutney, or veal loin on lemon-pepper pasta, as well as prime ribs roasted with rock salt and cut to order. Lunch offers these items plus burgers, sandwiches, salads, designer omelets, and pizzas. The wine list is extensive and so are the bottle prices, $15 to $150.

rg's DOWNTOWN, One City Center, 110 N. Franklin St. Tel. 229-5536.

Cuisine: AMERICAN **Reservations:** Suggested. **Directions:** In the Tampa City Center Esplanande, between the Hyatt Regency Hotel and the Fort Brooke Parking Garage.
$ Prices: Entrées $3.50–$7.95 lunch, $14.95–$23.95 dinner. AE, CB, DC, MC, V.
Open: Mon–Thurs 11:30am–2pm and 5:30–10pm, Fri 11:30am–2pm and 5:30–11pm, Sat 5:30–11pm.

Overlooking waterfalls, fountains, trees, and flowers, this trendy downtown restaurant is the perfect place for people-watching—tucked beside Franklin Street's pedestrian mall, with both outdoor and indoor seating. Lunch items include soups and sandwiches as well as interesting dishes like smoked-salmon pasta salad and specialty pizzas. Dinner is more elaborate, with such choices as Maine lobster ravioli, mixed seafood grill, char-broiled shrimp, rack of lamb, and Southwestern grilled chicken.

A sister restaurant, rg's North, is located in the Carrollwood residential area of Tampa at 3807 Northdale Blvd., off Dale Mabry Highway (tel. 963-2356). It maintains the same hours, and also serves Sunday 5:30–9pm.

SALTWATERS BAR AND GRILLE, 2 City Center. Tel. 225-1234.

Cuisine: AMERICAN/SEAFOOD. **Reservations:** Recommended. **Directions:** On the lobby level of the Hyatt Regency Hotel, corner of Tampa and Jackson streets.
$ Prices: Entrées $6.50–$12.50 lunch, $14.50–$18.50 dinner. AE, CB, DC, MC, V.
Open: Mon–Fri 11:30am–4pm and 6–10:30pm, Sat 6–10:30pm.

Surrounded by an atrium filled with leafy plants and cascading waterfalls, this relaxing oasis seems far from the bustle of the Tampa business district, yet it is only steps away. The imaginative cuisine merits attention in its own right, and has recently won plaudits from the prestigious Chaîne des Rôtisseurs.

Specialty dishes include Florida lobster and flounder fricassee; saffron angel-hair pasta with lobster; pompano with citrus butter; loin of lamb in sweet-potato crust and roasted garlic sauce; and a signature mixed grill with lamb chop, tenderloin steak, and prawn and grouper sausage in bourbon mushroom sauce. Lunch offerings include these items plus lighter choices such as salads, burgers, and sandwiches.

MODERATE

THE COLUMBIA, 601 S. Harbor Island Blvd., Harbour Island. Tel. 229-2992.
   Cuisine: SPANISH.   **Reservations:** Recommended.   **Directions:** On the middle level of the Market Complex on Harbour Island.
$ Prices: Entrées $4.95–$8.95 lunch, $10.95–$16.95 dinner.
   Open: Daily 11am–11pm.

Opened in 1985, this is the downtown version of the famous Ybor City landmark. Here you get expansive views of the harbor instead of the Old Tampa ambience, antique accoutrements, and flamenco dancing. It's worth sampling both venues for the contrast. For a description of the cuisine, see the entry under "Ybor City," below in this chapter.

PARKER'S LIGHTHOUSE, 601 S. Harbour Island Blvd., Harbour Island. Tel. 229-3474.
   Cuisine: SEAFOOD.   **Reservations:** Suggested for dinner.
   Directions: On the upper level of the Market complex at Harbour Island.
$ Prices: Entrées: $5.95–$10.95 lunch, $10.95–$17.95 dinner, AE, MC, V.
   Open: Mon–Thurs 11:30am–2:30pm and 5:30–10pm, Fri–Sat 11:30am–2:30pm and 5:30–10:30pm, Sun 10:30pm–1:30pm and 4:30–9pm.

Overlooking the channels of the Hillsborough River and the Tampa skyline, this bright and airy restaurant is a favorite for outdoor dining, but you can also sit indoors with the benefit of full air conditioning and enjoy the views through floor-to-ceiling windows. If you are fond of fish, this place is a must.

Choose from an ever-changing selection that ranges from shark to swordfish, snapper to salmon, sheepshead to Spanish mackerel, or yellowfin tuna to trout. Then decide how you'd like it prepared—sautéed, baked, broiled, or blackened, and with a choice of seasoned butters (from ginger-lime to chive-parsley or pine nut). No pre-cooking here! The menu also includes lobsters, steaks, pastas, and chicken. Be sure to try the bacon-cheddar biscuits served at dinner. It's a fun place to watch the boats go by, and the service is enthusiastic. Lunch items range from sandwiches, pastas, and salads to smaller portions of mesquite-grilled seafoods; the lower-level lounge also serves burgers and sandwiches throughout the day and evening.

FROMMER'S SMART TRAVELER—RESTAURANTS

QUESTIONS TO ASK IF YOU ARE ON A BUDGET

1. Do you serve an "early bird" dinner? If so, what are the prices and the hours of service?
2. Is the service charge included in the bill's total?
3. Is the 6% state tax included in the total?
4. Do you have any specials today? What are the prices?
5. [If you're traveling with kids] Is there a children's menu?

INEXPENSIVE

CHA CHA COCONUTS, 601 S. Harbour Island Blvd., Harbour Island. Tel. 223-3101.
   Cuisine: AMERICAN. **Reservations:** Not necessary. **Directions:** On the middle level of the Market complex on Harbour Island.
$ Prices: $3.95–$7.95. AE, DC, MC, V.
   Open: Mon–Thurs 11am–10pm, Fri–Sat 11am–midnight, Sun noon–9pm.

Billed as a tropical bar and grill, this informal waterfront spot with indoor and outdoor seating is ideal for lunch or a light meal. The view is entrancing, and live music is often on tap. For details on the cuisine, see Chapter 6, "St. Petersburg Dining: Downtown."

2. HYDE PARK/BAYSHORE BOULEVARD

VERY EXPENSIVE

BERN'S STEAK HOUSE, 1208 S. Howard Ave. Tel. 251-2421.
   Cuisine: AMERICAN. **Reservations:** Highly recommended. **Directions:** West of downtown, at the corner of Marjory Avenue.
$ Prices: Entrées $13.90–$30.16, desserts $2–$10. AE, CB, DC, MC, V.

Open: Daily 5–11pm; dessert room open until 1am.

⭐ No visit to Tampa is complete without dinner at Bern Laxer's one-of-a-kind restaurant, an attraction in itself. Many people make reservations weeks in advance. Started on a small scale in 1953, and still totally unpretentious on the outside, it has grown into a two-story seven-room Tampa institution.

Above all, it is a temple of beef, where the motto is "Art in steaks." You order a prime, well-aged steak according to the thickness and weight you prefer, and then it is cut and broiled over charcoal to your exact desire. If beef is not your fancy, lamb, veal, chicken, and fish are also available. Depending on the season, most vegetables served at Bern's are grown in the restaurant's own organic garden, and the freshest of other ingredients—from creamery butter to coffee beans—are also the norm. All entrées come with onion soup, salad, baked potato, garlic toast, and onion rings. If you'd like a bottle of wine with your meal, you're bound to find a favorite—the phone-book–size wine list offers more than 7,000 selections.

Desserts are yet another event, served upstairs in a unique room with piano bar and dance floor, plus over 40 plush booths built from wine casks, each featuring a TV set and a telephone for placing personal music requests. Choose from over 40 desserts, including bitter chocolate pate, pistachio cake, bourbon bread pudding, banana cheese pie, and cappuccino parfait, plus cream drinks and "sipping desserts" made with liqueurs, sweet wines, and ports by the glass. It is possible to reserve a booth for dessert only, but preference is given to those who dine. (*Note:* Smoking is prohibited in the main dining rooms).

EXPENSIVE

SELENA'S, 1623 Snow Ave. Tel. 251-2116.

> **Cuisine:** CAJUN/ITALIAN. **Reservations:** Recommended. **Directions:** West of downtown, in the Old Hyde Park Village shopping complex.
>
> **$ Prices:** Entrées $4.95–$10.95 lunch, $8.95–$21.95 dinner. AE, CB, DC, MC, V.
>
> **Open:** Mon 11am–10pm, Tues–Thurs 11am–11pm, Fri–Sat 11am–midnight, Sun 11am–2:30pm and 4:30–9pm.

Step inside this charming restaurant and it feels like New Orleans, whether you sit in the plant-filled Patio Room, the eclectic Antique Room, or the elegant Queen Anne Room, decked out with fireplace, chandeliers, linens, and lace. Open the menu and you'll see an interesting blend of Cajun and Italian dishes, reflecting the owners' family backgrounds. Local seafoods, especially grouper and shrimp, top the menu at dinner, with much of it served Creole-style or blackened, as well as broiled and fried. Choices also include pastas, chicken, steaks, and veal. Desserts range from chocolate-mousse cake and Key lime pie to Cajun country bread pudding. Lunch items also include gumbos, salads, po-boy sandwiches, Italian sausages, casseroles, and quiches. In the evenings, jazz enlivens the atmosphere, as musical groups perform upstairs in a 200-seat lounge.

MODERATE

LE BORDEAUX, 1502 S. Howard Ave. Tel. 254-4387.

Cuisine: FRENCH. **Reservations:** Only accepted for parties of six or more. **Directions:** West of downtown, one block north of Bayshore Boulevard.

$ **Prices:** Entrées $7.95–$14.95. MC, V.

Open: Mon–Thurs 5:30–10pm, Fri–Sat 5:30–11pm, Sun 5:30–9:30pm **Closed:** August.

Located in a residential neighborhood, this bungalow/bistro is a real find, with first-rate French food at very affordable prices. The domain of French-born chef/owner Gordon Davis and partner Colette Hatch, it offers a homey ambience, with a choice of two dining rooms. The menu changes nightly and is usually confined to 10 entrée choices or less, but you can count on homemade pâtés and pastries. Specials often include salmon en croûte, papillote of halibut, veal with wild mushrooms, and filet of beef au roquefort. Beer and wine only.

THE COLONNADE, 3401 Bayshore Blvd. Tel. 839-7558.

Cuisine: AMERICAN/SEAFOOD. **Reservations:** Not accepted, except for large parties. **Directions:** West of downtown, between Julia Street and El Prado Boulevard.

$ **Prices:** Entrées: $4.95–$8.95 lunch, $7.95–$16.95 dinner. AE, DC, MC, V.

Open: Sun–Thurs 11am–10pm, Fri–Sat 11am–11pm.

Nestled in a palm-shaded residential neighborhood overlooking Tampa Bay, this is one of the city's loveliest dining spots, with an appealing wood-and-glass decor. Established in 1935, it has grown from a drive-in soda stop to a 300-seat local institution. Popularity has its price, however, and sometimes lines at this no-reservations restaurant can be a bit discouraging. Most folks console themselves by sipping a frozen drink in the adjacent lounge.

Seafood, caught by the restaurant's own fishing fleet, is the big draw here, but prime ribs, steaks, and chicken are also available. Specialties include group in lemon butter, crab-stuffed flounder, broiled Gulf mullet, wild Florida alligator, Cajun catfish, broiled Florida lobster, and a half-dozen varieties of shrimp dishes (from batter-dipped or crabmeat-stuffed to pecan-fried or scampi-style). Combination platters are also popular, such as the "Captain's" assortment of grouper, oysters, shrimp, scallops, clam strips, and half of a stuffed lobster.

INEXPENSIVE

CACTUS CLUB, 1601 Snow Ave. Tel. 251-4089.

Cuisine: MEXICAN/AMERICAN SOUTHWEST. **Reservations:** Not necessary. **Directions:** West of downtown, in the Old Hyde Park Village shopping complex.

Arigato Japanese
  Steakhouse (32)
Armani's (25)
Bern's Steak House (8)
Cactus Club (12)
Café by the Bay (13)
Café Creole and Oyster Bar (15)
The Castaway (27)
Cha Cha Coconuts (7)
CK's (26)
The Colonnade (11)
The Columbia, Harbour
  Island (5)
The Columbia, Ybor City (14)
Crabby Tom's (20)
Crawdaddy's (30)
Donatello (18)
Fat Jacque's Cajun Café (19)
Harbour View Room (1)
Hooter's (21)
Lauro Ristorante (2)
Le Bordeaux (10)
Lucy Ho's Bamboo Garden (33)
Mel's Hot Dogs (35)
Outback Steakhouse (22)
Oystercatchers (28)
Parker's Lighthouse (6)
r.g.'s Downtown (3)
Rough Riders (16)
Rumpelmayer's Restaurant (34)
Rusty Pelican (29)
Saltwaters Bar and Grille (4)
Selena's (9)
Shells, Dale Mabry Hwy. (23)
Shells 30th St. (36)
Silver Ring (17)
Tampa Bay Brewing
  Company (24)
Whiskey Joe's (31)

Nebraska Ave.

(33) University of South Florida

Fowler Ave.

(36) (582)

ebaugh

(41)

Busch Gardens

56th St.

Temple Terrace

(35) (34) Busch Blvd.

(580)

Malcolm McKinley Dr.

Florida Ave.

Sligh Ave.

Sligh Ave.

(301)

(275)

Hillsborough Ave.

(92)

(4)

Tampa

East Lake

22nd St.

Nebraska Ave.

Buffalo Ave.

(574)

(BUS 41)

(585)

Columbus Dr.

Florida Ave.

50th St.

Ybor City Adamo Dr.

town

(15) (14)

(60) (16)(17)

BUS 41

McKay Bay

(60)

Harbour Island

Davis Blvd.

Causeway Blvd.

(676)

Davis Islands

Peter O. Knight Airport

Bayshore Rd.

(676A)

last int

(41)

Hills-

o r o u g h

B a y

DOWNTOWN

Tyler St.

Cass St.

Florida Ave.

Marion St.

Morgan St.

Polk St.

Zack St.

Tampa St.

Franklin St.

Twiggs St.

Madison St.

Kennedy Blvd.

(4) (3) Jackson St.

Washington St.

(2) Whiting St.

Crosstown Expwy.

Ashley St.

H i l l s b o r o u g h

R i v e r

Crosstown Expwy.

(5) (7)

(5) (1)

Airport ✈

$ Prices: Entrées $4.95–$6.95 lunch, $5.95–$11.95 dinner. AE, CB, DC, MC, V.
Open: Mon–Sat 11:30am–midnight, Sun noon–midnight.

Big and brassy, yet casual and comfortable, this sometimes noisy café radiates southwestern pizzazz in the heart of old Tampa. It's an ideal spot to go if you're in the mood for fajitas, tacos, enchiladas, chili, hickory-smoked baby back ribs, Texas-style pizzas, blackened chicken, or guacamole/green chili burgers.

CAFE BY THE BAY, 1350 S. Howard Ave. Tel. 251-6659.
Cuisine: AMERICAN. **Reservations:** Not necessary. **Directions:** West of downtown, between Mississippi and Southview avenues.
$ Prices: $2.95–$6.95 for most dishes. Cash only.
Open: Mon–Fri 7:30am–2pm, Sat–Sun 8am–3pm.

The name may be a little misleading, since there are no water views, but the location is within walking distance of Bayshore Boulevard. It's also close to the Old Hyde Park Village complex, so it makes a good pre- or post-shopping refreshment stop. Early morning fare includes waffles and empanadas (hand-filled pastry shells), as well as omelets of all types. Lunch items range from salads and sandwiches (the Cuban sandwich is one of Tampa's best) to burgers and unusual sandwiches such as the guacamole Reuben, and snow crab on pumpernickel. Beer and wine only.

3. YBOR CITY

MODERATE

THE COLUMBIA, 2117 7th Ave. E., Ybor City. Tel. 248-4961.
Cuisine: SPANISH. **Reservations:** Recommended. **Directions:** East of downtown, between 21st and 22nd streets.
$ Prices: Entrées $4.95–$8.95 lunch, and $10.95–$16.95 at dinner. AE, CB, DC, MC, V.
Open: Daily 11am–11pm.

This is the Columbia that everyone hears so much about, the original of the genre, dating back to 1905. Occupying a full city block, it is Tampa's largest restaurant, with 1,660 seats in a dozen different dining rooms on three floors. The rooms vary from the airy and palatial to the intimate and dimly lit; the original café on the ground floor today has a wall full of old newspaper clippings and memorabilia telling the story of the Columbia through four generations of ownership. Throughout, the decor is full of hand-painted tiles, elaborate wrought-iron chandeliers, dark woods, rich red fabrics, and stained-glass windows.

Specialties include red snapper Alicante (baked in a casserole with sweet Spanish onions and green peppers, and topped with almonds, eggplant, and shrimp), filet mignon Columbia (a filet wrapped in bacon, with mushrooms, ham, onions, and green peppers in tomato and Burgundy sauce), traditional chicken and yellow rice, and three types of spicy paellas, either seafood, all-meat, or a combination of both. There are over a dozen other choices, some less exotic, such as silver pompano en papillote, if you prefer to go easy on the spices; lobster is also available at higher prices. All entrées come with traditional Cuban bread and heaping portions of the legendary "Original 1905 Salad"—lettuce, tomato, smoked ham, Swiss and Romano cheeses, olives, and lots more, with a house garlic dressing. At lunchtime, this salad is offered as an entrée, as are mini-paellas, Cuban sandwiches, burgers, soups, omelets, and an assortment of tempting tapas. If you have a choice, though, come for dinner: Besides the legendary food, you'll also get a flamenco show (8:30pm Mon–Sat).

CAFE CREOLE AND OYSTER BAR, 1330 9th Ave., Ybor City. Tel. 247-6283.
   Cuisine: CAJUN/CREOLE. **Reservations:** Suggested on weekdays and required on weekends. **Directions:** East of downtown, between 13th and 14th streets.
$ Prices: Entrées $4.95–$7.95 lunch, $6.95–$12.95 dinner. AE, CB, DC, MC, V.
   Open: Mon–Tues 11:30am–10pm, Wed–Thurs 11:30am–11pm, Fri–Sat 11:30am–midnight.

The setting of this restaurant tells quite a tale about Ybor City history. The building, dating back to 1896, was originally known as El Pasaje, and was famous as the home of the Cherokee Club, a gentleman's hotel and private club with a casino, restaurant, and bar. Artisans were brought from Spain and Cuba to create spectacular stained-glass windows, wrought-iron balconies, Spanish murals, and marble bathrooms. Among the prominent guests were Theodore Roosevelt, Grover Cleveland, and many of Florida's governors. During the Depression, the building was used variously as a political club, low-rent hotel, and WPA school of music, art, and dance. It was placed on the National Register of Historic Places in 1973, and new owners, the D'Avanza family from New Orleans, restored it in the 1980s as the Café Creole, complete with Louisiana-style cuisine and indoor-outdoor seating.

Specialties include Creole and Cajun dishes, such as red beans and rice with andouille sausage, blackened catfish, seafood gumbo, grouper Bienville, crawfish étouffé, and jambalaya. The oyster bar also offers Bayou country oysters from New Orleans served a half-dozen ways. At lunch, you can also order po-boy sandwiches and salads. On most days, there is outdoor dining in an adjacent courtyard.

ROUGH RIDERS, 1901 13th St., Ybor City. Tel. 248-2756.
   Cuisine: AMERICAN. **Reservations:** Not necessary.
   Directions: Located on the third floor of Ybor Square, at 8th Avenue and 13th Street.
$ Prices: Entrées $3.95–$12.95 lunch or dinner. AE, MC, V.
   Open: Mon–Thurs 11:30am–midnight, Fri–Sat 11:30am–2am, Sun noon–6pm.

One of a half-dozen eateries in the Ybor Square shopping complex, this informal spot commemorates the 1898 visit of Teddy Roosevelt and his band of "Rough Riders" to Ybor City during the Spanish-American War. The theme is reflected in the pictures on the walls and the names of the items on the menu. Don't expect gourmet cuisine, but you will get good hearty fare—burgers, steaks, prime ribs, and sandwiches.

INEXPENSIVE

SILVER RING, 1831 E. 7th Ave., Ybor City. Tel. 248-2549.
   Cuisine: SPANISH/AMERICAN. **Reservations:** Not needed.
   Directions: East of downtown, between 18th and 19th streets.
$ Prices: $2.25–$3.95. No credit cards.
   Open: Mon–Sat 6:30am–5pm.

Operating since 1947, this is now an Ybor City tradition, sort of an informal museum of life in this corner of Tampa. The walls are lined with old pictures, vintage radios, a 1950s jukebox, fishing rods, deer heads, and globes. Most of all, it is *the* place to come for a genuine Cuban sandwich—smoked ham, roast pork, Genoa salami, Swiss cheese, pickles, salad dressing, mustard, lettuce, and tomato on Cuban bread. At least 400 a day are sold here, and up to 800 on Friday and Saturday. Other items on the menu include Spanish bean soup, deviled crab, and other types of sandwiches. You can also buy some good locally made cigars.

4. AIRPORT/WEST SHORE

VERY EXPENSIVE

DONATELLO, 232 N. Dale Mabry Highway. Tel. 875-6660.
   Cuisine: NORTHERN ITALIAN. **Reservations:** Recommended. **Directions:** South of the airport, two blocks north of Kennedy Boulevard (Fla. Rte. 60).
$ Prices: Entrées $11.95–$12.95 lunch, $15.95–$24.95 dinner. AE, CB, DC, MC, V.
   Open: Mon–Fri noon–3pm, 6–11pm, Sat–Sun 6–11pm.

With stucco arches, Italian tile work, and peach-colored linens, this romantic restaurant has a Mediterranean atmosphere, artfully enhanced by soft individual table lighting and an attentive tuxedoed waiting staff.

The menu is similar at lunch and dinner, with slightly larger portions and more choices in the evening. Specialties include linguine with Maine lobster; breast of duck with Curaçao and orange sauce; veal "Dolce Vita," with ham, mushrooms, and truffles; salmon Stromboli, with asparagus, shrimp, and creamy white-wine sauce; and osso bucco alla milanese. All pastas and desserts are made on the premises. As a graceful final touch, each female diner is presented with a long-stemmed red rose. Valet parking.

MODERATE

CRABBY TOM'S OLD TIME OYSTER BAR AND SEAFOOD RESTAURANT, 3120 W. Hillsborough Ave. Tel. 870-1652.

Cuisine: SEAFOOD. **Reservations:** Not accepted, except for parties of 10 or more. **Directions:** Northwest of the airport, between Dale Mabry Highway and Armenia Avenue.

$ Prices: Entrées $4.95–$15.95 lunch or dinner. No credit cards. **Open:** Mon–Thurs 11am–10pm, Fri–Sat 11am–11pm, Sun 4–9pm.

As its name suggests, this informal eatery is affiliated with Crabby Bill's of Indian Rocks Beach in the St. Pete area. Like its counterpart, this spot lacks waterside views and an impressive decor, but it puts major emphasis on the "crab" in Crabby. Sit back, relax, and crack open a pile of mild or spicy steamed blue crabs, stone crab claws, Alaska snow crab claws, or king crab legs.

If you tire of crab, there's always a lobster from the 140-gallon tank, or an array of other seafood, from grouper, flounder, and catfish to shrimp, scallops, smelts, and smoked mullet, as well as clams and oysters on the half-shell, or a "seafood feast" that presents a sampling of almost everything. Chicken, pasta, and barbecued ribs are also on the menu, but this is really a place for seafood-lovers, with at least a half dozen daily or weekly maritime specials, usually announced by handmade signs on the walls. As long as you don't mind a noisy down-on-the-dock atmosphere, picnic-table seating, and paper placemat/menus, the prices are hard to beat anywhere. Wine and beer available.

FAT JACQUE'S CAJUN CAFE, 3605 W. Hillsborough Ave. Tel. 874-8657.

Cuisine: CAJUN/CREOLE. **Reservations:** Suggested. **Directions:** North of the airport, cross east over Dale Mabry Highway; restaurant is on the left in the Greenhouse Shopping Center.

$ Prices: Entrées $4.95–$13.95 lunch or dinner. AE, MC, V.

Open: Mon–Thurs 11am–midnight, Fri–Sat 11am–1am, Sun 10am–11pm.

Located beside a busy commercial intersection, this little oasis exudes a New Orleans ambience much like that of its St. Petersburg counterpart. See Chapter 6, "St. Petersburg Dining: North of Downtown," for a description of the decor and the cuisine.

OUTBACK STEAKHOUSE, 3304 Henderson Blvd. Tel. 875-4329.
    Cuisine: AUSTRALIAN/AMERICAN. **Reservations:** Not accepted. **Directions:** South of the airport, east of Dale Mabry Highway, between Swann Avenue and Azeele Street.
$ Prices: Entrées $6.95–$15.95. AE, DC, MC, V.
    Open: Mon–Thurs 11:30am–10:30pm, Fri 11:30am–11:30pm, Sat 4:30–11:30pm

For a description of the cuisine at this Aussie-style restaurant, see the entry in Chapter 6, "St. Petersburg Dining: North of Downtown." A second Tampa branch is located north of the airport in the Carrollwood section of the city at 11620 N. Dale Mabry Highway (tel. 969-4329), open Sunday to Thursday from 4:30 to 10:30pm and Friday and Saturday from 4:30 to 11:30pm.

INEXPENSIVE

HOOTERS, 4215 W. Hillsborough Ave. Tel. 885-3916.
    Cuisine: AMERICAN. **Reservations:** Not accepted. **Directions:** North of the airport, between Westshore Boulevard and Dale Mabry Highway.
$ Prices: Entrées $2.95–$12.95 lunch or dinner. AE, MC, V.
    Open: Mon–Fri 11am–midnight, Sat 11am–1am, Sun noon–10pm.

Though it's located far from the beach, a year-round beach-party atmosphere prevails at this typically Tampa Bay eatery. For a description of the decor and the menu, see the entry for the original Hooters across the bay in Clearwater (Chapter 10, "St. Petersburg Dining: Nearby Dining"). Beer and wine served.

SHELLS, 202 S. Dale Mabry Highway. Tel. 875-3467.
    Cuisine: SEAFOOD. **Reservations:** Not accepted. **Directions:** South of the airport, and two blocks south of Kennedy Boulevard, on left.
$ Prices: Entrées $4.95–$12.95. No credit cards.
    Open: Sun–Thurs 5–10pm, Fri–Sat 5–11pm.

In the Tampa Bay area, Shells is a local institution, known for fresh seafood at low prices. Founded in 1985, this restaurant has since been cloned in over twenty other locations in Florida and as far away as Georgia and midtown Manhattan. This inconspicuous spot is the original, the one that set the standards for the others—simple seafood menu, no frills, no reservations, no credit cards, and, above all, no strain on the budget. You'll probably have to wait at least a half hour to be seated, and then you'll eat at picnic-style tables and use paper and plastic utensils, but the food is worth it.

The menu features hefty portions of Alaskan king crab legs and claws, Dungeness crab clusters, snow crab, scallops, shrimp, grouper, cod, and pasta combinations such as shrimp with cheese tortellini. More elaborate dishes range from shrimp thermidor to seafood Newburg. Nightly specials include Maine lobsters or baby-lobster pasta (on Tuesdays). There are a few beef and chicken choices. Beer and wine available.

Other locations in the Tampa area: 14380 N. Dale Mabry Hwy. (tel. 968-6686) north of the airport, with a full bar; and 11010 N. 30th St. (tel. 977-8456), in the Busch Gardens area, serving beer and wine.

TAMPA BAY BREWING COMPANY, 10330 N. Dale Mabry Highway. Tel. 264-6669.
    Cuisine: AMERICAN. **Reservations:** Not required.
    Directions: North of the airport, past the Busch Boulevard interchange; restaurant is on left after Linebaugh Avenue in the Promenade Plaza Shopping Center.
$ Prices: Entrées $4.95–$10.95. MC, V.
    Open: Mon–Sat 11am–midnight or later, Sun 1pm–midnight.

The first of its kind in the Tampa Bay area, this relatively new brew pub/restaurant makes four different types of beer on the premises (pilsner, red ale, porter, and a "beer of the month"), using imported barley and hops from Europe. It's a lively and noisy spot, popular with a yuppie clientele. The simple menu offers food that goes well with such hearty brews, including half-pound burgers, steaks, fish and chips, chicken wings, chili, and an assortment of sandwiches. This spot is equally convenient to the Busch Gardens area, which lies about two miles to the east.

5. COURTNEY CAMPBELL CAUSEWAY AREA

EXPENSIVE

ARMANI'S, 6200 Courtney Campbell Causeway. Tel. 874-1234.
    Cuisine: NORTHERN ITALIAN. **Reservations:** Strongly recommended. **Directions:** Follow Route 60, west of the airport, to Hyatt Regency Westshore Hotel; restaurant is on 14th floor.
$ Prices: Entrées $10.95–$22.95. AE, CB, DC, MC, V.
    Open: Mon–Thurs 5–10pm, Fri–Sat 5–11pm.

Overlooking Old Tampa Bay, this romantic rooftop restaurant is a favorite with the locals as well as hotel guests. Most of the windows face west, making it an ideal place to watch sunsets while savoring fine cuisine with impeccable service.

Tableside preparation of dishes is a specialty here: try the piquant Caesar salad. Veal selections are particularly notable, such as scaloppine with mushroom cream cognac and black and white truffle sauce, or veal chop with Frangelico cognac, black walnuts, and cream. Other specialties include wide egg pasta with basil, crabmeat, and white (or fresh tomato) sauce; Black Angus filet mignon with three peppercorns; and filet of Norwegian salmon and sole poached over tomato cream. The antipasto bar and the wine list are extensive and all pastas are made on the premises. Free or valet parking.

CK's, Tampa Airport Marriott. Tel. 879-5178.
Cuisine: CONTINENTAL/AMERICAN. **Reservations:** Recommended. **Directions:** Follow "Hotel" signs at airport; take express elevator to eighth floor.

$ Prices: Entrées $5.95–$11.95 lunch, $13.95–$26.95 dinner. AE, CB, DC, MC, V.
Open: Mon–Sat 11:30am–2:30pm and 5–11pm, Sun 10:30am–2:30pm and 5–10pm.

In the heart of the airport, this is the only revolving rooftop restaurant in Tampa. Every table offers an ever-changing view spanning the adjacent jetways and more distant vistas of Tampa Bay and the city skyline.

The extensive dinner menu ranges from local seafoods to prime ribs, steaks, and chateaubriand. Specialties include veal Lemuel (sautéed with lobster, white asparagus, and hollandaise sauce) and Dover sole meunière. If you and your dining partner are extra hungry, try CK's sampler for two (veal Lemuel, French-cut lamb chops, deep-water tiger prawns, and petite swordfish steak). Lunch items include soups, salads, burgers, omelets, seafood, and steaks.

MODERATE

THE CASTAWAY, 7720 Courtney Campbell Causeway. Tel. 281-0770.
Cuisine: AMERICAN/POLYNESIAN/SEAFOOD. **Reservations:** Accepted for dinner, with seating at the first available table at the time requested. **Directions:** Follow Route 60 west of the airport; restaurant is visible on left after Rocky Point Drive.

$ Prices: Entrées $4.95–$7.95 lunch, $11.95–$21.95 dinner. AE, CB, DC, MC, V.
Open: Mon–Thurs 11am–3pm and 5–10pm, Fri 11am–3pm and 5–11pm, Sat noon–3pm and 5–11pm, Sun noon–3pm and 4–10pm.

Situated just east of the Ben T. Davis Municipal Beach, the Castaway bills itself as Tampa's only beachfront restaurant. The building rests on stilts over the waters of Old Tampa Bay, making the views hard to equal, especially at sunset time.

The menu is a blend of seafaring specials with a Polynesian

influence. Choices at dinner range from seafood tempura, stir-fry dishes, and Oriental curries, to mahimahi macadamia, coconut shrimp, sea pearls (scallops and vegetables in oyster sauce) and jumbo rock lobster tails, as well as an exotic presentation of a daily special "whole fish for one or two." Nonseafood selections include almond chicken, baby back ribs, and steaks. Salads, sandwiches, burgers, and seafood platters are available at lunch, but many people head for the weekday buffet, offering a huge variety of hot and cold dishes for $6.95.

CRAWDADDY'S, 2500 Rocky Point Dr. Tel. 281-0407.

Cuisine: REGIONAL/SEAFOOD.   **Reservations:** Suggested.
Directions: Follow Route 60 west of the airport to Courtney Campbell Causeway; turn left at Rocky Point Drive.
$ Prices: Entrées $3.95–$7.95 lunch, $10.95–$17.95 dinner. AE, CB, DC, MC, V.
Open: Mon–Thurs 11am–3pm and 4:30–11pm, Fri–Sat 11am–3pm and 4:30pm–midnight, Sun 4–10pm.

Situated on Old Tampa Bay in the same cul-de-sac as the Rusty Pelican, this more informal spot is named after Beauregard "Crawdaddy" Belvedere, a Roaring Twenties tycoon. He owned a fish camp on this site that attracted guests from near and far for dining and entertainment. The decor here has not changed much since those days—there are seven dining rooms, spread over three levels, all bedecked with Victorian furnishings, books, pictures, and collectables, and all sharing wide-windowed views of the bay.

The "down-home"–style menu ranges from beer-battered shrimp-and-fish camp fry (shrimp, scallops, and fresh fish, deep fried in corn crisp and almond coating, with jalapeño hush puppies) to surf-and-turf, prime ribs, and steaks. Lunch fare includes soups, salads, sandwiches, burgers, pastas, and seafood. Stir-fry dishes, raw-bar selections, and jambalayas are also featured at both lunch and dinner.

OYSTERCATCHERS, 6200 Courtney Campbell Causeway. Tel. 281-9116.

Cuisine: SEAFOOD. **Reservations:** Suggested. **Directions:** Follow Route 60 west of the airport to the Hyatt Regency Westshore Hotel; restaurant is behind hotel on the water.
$ Prices: Entrées $6.95–$11.95 lunch, $12.95–$19.95 dinner. AE, CB, DC, MC, V.
Open: Mon–Thurs 11:30am–2:30pm, 6–10:30pm; Fri 11:30am–2:30pm, 6–11pm; Sat 6–11pm, Sun 10am–2:30pm, 6–10:30pm

Nestled on the edge of a 35-acre nature preserve overlooking Old Tampa Bay, this restaurant is housed in a free-standing Key West–style building, connected by a 250-foot boardwalk to the Hyatt Regency Westshore complex. The atmosphere is casual, with indoor and outdoor seating and a decor of light blue and green sea tones, white patio-style furniture, and wide windows that give every table a view of the water.

The lunch menu offers salads, seafoods, steaks, and specialty dishes such as black-bean chili, hibachi chicken, lobster pita, and Everglades alligator scaloppine. Dinner choices focus primarily on "catch-of-the-day" seafoods, prepared in a variety of ways, from mesquite-grilled to blackened, sautéed, or poached. Local favorites include rock shrimp in snail butter and parchment-baked red snapper. There's also a variety of steaks, plus rack of lamb, and duck.

RUSTY PELICAN, 2425 Rocky Point Dr. Tel. 281-1943.
　　Cuisine: CONTINENTAL/SEAFOOD. **Reservations:** Suggested. **Directions:** Follow Route 60 west of the airport to Courtney Campbell Causeway; turn left at Rocky Point Drive.
$ Prices: Lunch buffet $5.95; entrées $12.95–$19.95 at dinner. AE, CB, DC, MC, V.
　　Open: Mon–Fri 11am–3pm and 5–11pm, Sat 5–11pm, Sun 11am–3pm and 5–10pm.

Situated on Old Tampa Bay at the south end of Rocky Point Drive, this is the top spot in a cluster of three restaurants that also includes Crawdaddy's and Whiskey Joe's. The decor, which features two huge stone fireplaces, ceiling-high potted trees, fine crystal, and pastel-toned linens, is enhanced by views of the water in a relaxing and romantic setting. As at all of the restaurants along this strip, the sunset hour is prime time here.

The innovative menu features a wide variety of seafood, from shellfish thermidor and cioppino to salmon en papillote, rainbow trout stuffed with Alaskan crab, grouper milanese, red snapper Floridian (with orange and grapefruit segments in a pool of Burgundy and citrus sauce), shrimp-and-lobster brochette, scallops Mornay, and specialty dishes such as surf-and-turf royale (double-cut lamb chop with rock lobster tail), filet mignon Oscar, and chicken dijonnaise. On weekdays, lunch is served buffet-style. Valet parking available.

INEXPENSIVE

WHISKEY JOE'S, 2500 Rocky Point Dr. Tel. 281-0577.
　　Cuisine: REGIONAL/AMERICAN. **Reservations:** Accepted only for parties of 10 or more. **Directions:** Follow Route 60 west of the airport to Courtney Campbell Causeway; turn left at Rocky Point Drive.
$ Prices: Entrées $3.95–$10.95 lunch or dinner. AE, CB, DC, MC, V.
　　Open: Mon–Thurs 11am–11pm, Fri–Sat 11am–midnight, Sun 1–11pm.

Adjacent to Crawdaddy's, this casual spot looks like an old shack on the outside, and isn't much better within, but that's part of its appeal. Peanut shells clutter the floor, the piped-in music can be a bit loud, and the menu is limited, but a relaxed, "let's-have-fun" atmosphere prevails. It does offer a choice of indoor or outdoor seating overlooking Old Tampa Bay. Favorite items on the menu include conch chowder, beer-cheese soup, burgers, peel-and-eat shrimp, conch fritters, Buffalo wings, mesquite-broiled fish, and barbecued baby back ribs.

6. BUSCH GARDENS AREA

MODERATE

ARIGATO JAPANESE STEAKHOUSE, 13755 N. Dale Mabry Highway. Tel. 960-5050.
Cuisine: JAPANESE. **Reservations:** Suggested on weekends. **Directions:** Northwest of Busch Gardens, in the Carrollwood section, one block north of Fletcher Avenue.
$ Prices: Entrées $7.95–$16.95. AE, MC, V.
Open: Mon–Sat 5–10pm, Sun noon–9pm.
This restaurant is a favorite in the Tampa Bay area and has won many local awards. For full description, see Chapter 6, "St. Petersburg Dining: North of Downtown."

LUCY HO'S BAMBOO GARDEN, 2740 E. Fowler Ave. Tel. 977-2783.
Cuisine: CHINESE. **Reservations:** Accepted only for parties of five or more. **Directions:** Northwest of Busch Gardens, in University Collection Shopping Center, just west of the USF campus.
$ Prices: Lunch buffet $5.50; entrées $5–$15 dinner. AE, DC, MC, V.
Open: Mon–Sat 11:30am–10pm, Sun 11:30am–9pm.
A standout in the Asian-cuisine category, this restaurant usually comes out on top in reader polls taken by local newspapers and magazines. There are two branches, but this one is the original and well worth trying. The menu features a blend of Mandarin, Cantonese, and Szechuan dishes, such as Mongolian beef, cashew chicken, pepper steak, and whole fish Hunan-style. Chinese alcohol and beer are also available.

The second branch is located in the Greenhouse Shopping Center at 3611 W. Hillsborough Ave., at Dale Mabry Highway (tel. 874-8818).

RUMPELMAYER'S RESTAURANT, 4812 E. Busch Blvd. Tel. 989-9563.
Cuisine: GERMAN/EUROPEAN. **Reservations:** Suggested, especially for parties of six or more. **Directions:** East of Busch Gardens at 48th Street, in Ambassador Square Shopping Center.
$ Prices: Entrées $7.50–$17.50. MC, V.
Open: Tues–Sun 5–10pm.
Open only for dinner, this small (60-seat) Old-World restaurant is presided over by Lou Rumpelmayer, a former chef on the *Delta Queen* steamboat and at various Hilton Hotels throughout the world. He has aptly paired his culinary experience and native background to create an authentic bit of Bavaria within walking distance of Busch Gardens.

Tasty and traditional entrées range from Haringsla (a cold plate of

North Sea herring with red beets, apples, and onions), to assorted wursts, wienerschnitzel, sauerbraten, Hungarian stuffed cabbage, Polish kolbaszi, and a house special, veal à la Schill (veal and beef tenderloin, with tomato and Swiss cheese, breaded in savory crumbs, laced with dill, and topped with a mushroom-tomato sauce). Seafood lovers take delight in the smoked mackerel from the North Sea; Garnalen (shrimp scampi with Moselle wine); and Dutch flounder sautéed in brown butter. All come with German potato salad and a choice of kraut. Live German music is usually on tap, as are more than 20 European beers and wines.

INEXPENSIVE

MEL'S HOT DOGS, 4136 E. Busch Blvd. Tel. 985-8000.
   Cuisine: AMERICAN. **Reservations:** Not accepted.
   Directions: East of Busch Gardens, at 42nd Street.
$ Prices: All items 99¢–$4.99. No credit cards.
   Open: Mon–Sat 10am–10pm, Sun 11am–9pm.

If you crave an old-fashioned Chicago-style all-beef hot dog before or after a foray into the Dark Continent, look no further. Considered the "big daddy" of hot-dog eateries, this informal establishment specializes in hot-dog dishes, from "bagel dogs" to bacon, cheddar or corn dogs. Most choices are served on a poppy-seed bun, and most come with homemade coleslaw. Even the decor is dedicated to wieners, with walls and windows lined with hot-dog memorabilia. And just in case hot-dog mania hasn't won you over, there are a few alternate choices (sausages, chicken breast, and burgers). Beer and wine available.

SHELLS, 11010 N. 30th St. Tel. 977-8456.
   Cuisine: SEAFOOD. **Reservations:** Not accepted.
   Directions: North of Busch Gardens, between Bougainvillea and Fowler avenues.
$ Prices: Entrées $4.95–$12.95. No credit cards.
   Open: Sun–Thurs 5–10pm, Fri–Sat 5–11pm.

For full description, see main branch listing under "Airport/ West Shore," above in this chapter.

7. TAMPA RESTAURANTS

BY CUISINE

AMERICAN
Bern's Steak House (page 187)   VE
Café by the Bay (page 192)   I
The Castaway (page 198)   M
Cha Cha Coconuts (page 187)   I

CK's (page 198)   E
The Colonnade (page 189)   M
Harbour View Room (page 184)   E
Hooters (page 196)   I
Mel's Hot Dogs (page 202)   I
Outback Steakhouse (page 196)   M
rg's Downtown (page 185)   E
Rough Riders (page 194)   M
Saltwaters Bar and Grille (page 185)   E
Silver Ring (page 194)   I
Tampa Bay Brewing Company (page 197)   I
Whiskey Joe's (page 200)   I
AMERICAN SOUTHWEST
Cactus Club (page 189)
AUSTRALIAN
Outback Steakhouse (page 196)   M
CAJUN/CREOLE
Café Creole and Oyster Bar (page 193)   M
Fat Jacque's Cajun Café (page 195)   M
Selena's (page 188)   E
CHINESE/JAPANESE
Arigato Japanese Steakhouse (page 201)   M
Lucy Ho's Bamboo Garden (page 201)   M
CONTINENTAL
CK's (page 198)   E
Rusty Pelican (page 200)   M
FRENCH
Le Bordeaux (page 189)   M
GERMAN
Rumpelmayer's (page 201)   M
ITALIAN
Armani's (page 197)   E
Donatello (page 194)   E
Selena's (page 188)   E
LIGHT, CASUAL, AND FAST FOOD
Cactus Club (page 189)   I
Café by the Bay (page 192)   I
Cha Cha Coconuts (page 187)   I
Mel's Hot Dogs (page 202)   I
Rough Riders (page 194)   M
Silver Ring (page 194)   I
Tampa Bay Brewing Company (page 197)   I
Whiskey Joe's (page 200)   I
MEXICAN
Cactus Club (page 189)   I
POLYNESIAN
The Castaway (page 198)   M
REGIONAL
Crawdaddy's (page 199)   M
Whiskey Joe's (page 200)   I

SEAFOOD

Café Creole and Oyster Bar (page 193)	M
The Castaway (page 198)	M
The Colonnade (page 189)	M
Crabby Tom's (page 195)	M
Crawdaddy's (page 199)	M
Oystercatchers (page 199)	M
Parker's Lighthouse (page 186)	M
Rusty Pelican (page 200)	M
Saltwaters Bar and Grille (page 185)	E
Shells (page 196 & 202)	I

SPANISH

The Columbia (pages 186 & 192)	M
Silver Ring (page 194)	I

STEAKHOUSES

Arigato Japanese Steakhouse (page 201)	M
Bern's Steak House (page 187)	VE
Outback Steakhouse (page 196)	M

SPECIALTY DINING

COOL FOR KIDS

Arigato Japanese Steakhouse (page 201)	M
CK's (page 198)	E
Crabby Tom's (page 195)	M
Hooters (page 196)	I
Mel's Hot Dogs (page 202)	I
Outback Steakhouse (page 196)	M
Parker's Lighthouse (page 186)	M
Rough Riders (page 194)	M
Shells (page 196 & 202)	I
Whiskey Joe's (page 200)	I

DINING WITH A VIEW

Armani's (page 197)	E
The Castaway (page 198)	M
Cha Cha Coconuts (page 187)	I
CK's (page 198)	E
The Columbia, Harbour Island (page 186)	M
The Colonnade (page 189)	M
Crawdaddy's (page 199)	M
Harbour View Room (page 184)	E
Oystercatchers (page 199)	M
Parker's Lighthouse (page 186)	M
rg's Downtown (page 185)	E
Rusty Pelican (page 200)	M
Whiskey Joe's (page 200)	I

HOTEL DINING

Armani's (page 197)	E
CK's (page 198)	E
Harbour View Room (page 184)	E

CHAPTER 11

WHAT TO SEE AND DO IN TAMPA

A business and recreational hub, Tampa is a city of many parts. From the sleek skyscrapers downtown and near the airport, to the historic districts of Ybor City and Hyde Park or the exotic habitats of Busch Gardens, this city offers much to see and do.

SIGHT-SEEING STRATEGIES

If you have one day: Take your pick— the Dark Continent at Busch Gardens, or downtown Tampa. It's hard to narrow the choice to one or the other, but the Dark Continent offers so many activities, shows, and sights, that it takes at least eight hours to do it justice. Since Busch Gardens is one of the top tourist attractions in Florida, it's obvious that most visitors head there as a top priority. If you prefer to see what makes Tampa tick as a city, however, explore downtown. Walk the Franklin Street Mall, visit the Tampa Bay Performing Arts Center and the Tampa Museum of Art, tour the new convention center, and then take the People Mover over to Harbour Island for some shopping, a meal overlooking the water, and perhaps a gondola ride to cap the day.

If you have two days: It's obvious—take the first day to explore downtown and Harbour Island and the next day head up to Busch Gardens. Plan to spend part of a day in Ybor City, Tampa's Latin Quarter, winding up at the landmark Columbia restaurant in time to see its famous flamenco show.

If you have three days: Assuming you've seen the best of downtown, Harbour Island, and Busch Gardens, take a drive to some of the nearby attractions, such as the H. B. Plant Museum, Bayshore Boulevard, or Old Hyde Park Village. If you want to take a stroll on a nearby beach or see the sun set over Old Tampa Bay, head to the

FROMMER'S FAVORITES—
TAMPA EXPERIENCES

A Gondola Trip Cruise by Tampa's landmarks along the Hillsborough River and Tampa Bay on board an authentic gondola.

Strolling down the Franklin Street Mall A relaxing respite in an oasis of trees, flowers, and waterfalls, amid the skyscrapers of downtown Tampa.

Taking a Ride on the People Mover Whisk your way between downtown Tampa and Harbour Island in 90 seconds.

Along Bayshore Boulevard Drive, walk, or run along the 6.3-mile scenic sidewalk overlooking Hillsborough Bay.

Skating in the Streets Follow or join the Radiant Rollers as they glide through the streets of Tampa on Friday and Saturday nights.

Meandering in Ybor City Listen to the Spanish melodies in the air, peek into artists' studios, sip a cup of strong Cuban coffee in a café, or just savor the diverse aromas—from freshly baked breads to hand-rolled cigars.

Down on the Docks Watch the shrimp boats unload a day's catch at Hooker Point, off the 22nd Street Causeway in South Tampa.

Courtney Campbell Causeway area. You might prefer to spend an afternoon at Tampa Bay Downs, the Tampa Greyhound Track, Tampa Jai-Alai, or Seminole Bingo.

If you have five or more days: There's lots more to see, from Lowry Park Zoo to the Seminole Indian Village, or the Museum of Science and Industry. Take time to browse at Alessi Farmers Market and the many area shopping malls. Check the local papers to see if there's a game or major concert on at Tampa Stadium or the USF Sun Dome, or take a drive to Plant City to watch the Tampa Bay Polo Club play at Walden Lake. If you're here on a Thursday, take a cruise along the Hillsborough River on the paddlewheeler *Starlight Princess.* From Tampa, it's just a half-hour drive westward to St. Petersburg and the Gulf Coast beaches. You can also head inland to such nearby attractions as Walt Disney World and Disney-MGM Studios, EPCOT Center, Cypress Gardens, and Universal Studios-Florida.

1. THE TOP ATTRACTIONS

BUSCH GARDENS, 3000 E. Busch Blvd., Tampa. Tel. 971-8282.

Founded 30 years ago as a hospitality garden for the local Anheuser-Busch brewery, this 300-acre family entertainment center has grown to become the most popular attraction on Florida's west coast. Designed to reflect a "Dark Continent" theme, the park conveys the atmosphere of turn-of-the-century Africa, with one of the largest collections of free-roaming wild animals in the United States, as well as dozens of rides, live entertainment, restaurants, and shops. It is divided into eight distinct sections:

Timbuktu, an ancient desert trading center, features African artisans at work, a shopping bazaar, and a theater featuring dolphin shows, plus a "sandstorm" ride, boat-swing ride, roller coaster, and electronic-games arcade. This area also contains one of the best places to eat, Das Festhaus, a 1,200-seat dining hall with German-style food, music, and dancing.

Morocco is a walled city with elaborate tilework and exotic architecture, Moroccan craft demonstrations, a sultan's tent with snake charmers, and the Moroccan Palace Theater, which presents a Broadway-style musical revue, *Kaleidoscope.*

Serengeti Plain, a serene and open area, is home to hippos, buffalo, impala, gazelles, reticulated giraffes, black rhino, elephants, and zebras, as well as antelope, crocodiles, dromedaries, flamingos, and ostriches. Visitors can observe the animals, without disturbing them, from a passing steam locomotive or via overhead skyrides and monorails.

Nairobi is home to a baby-animal nursery as well as a petting zoo, reptile displays, and Nocturnal Mountain, where a simulated environment allows visitors to observe animals that are active in the dark. **Stanleyville,** a prototype African village, features a shopping bazaar and live entertainment, as well as two water rides, the Tanganyika Tidal Wave and Stanley Falls. **The Congo** features Claw Island, a display of rare white Bengal tigers in a natural setting, plus attractions such as a 1,200-foot roller coaster, and white-water raft rides. **Bird Gardens,** the original core of Busch Gardens, offers rich foliage, lagoons, and hundreds of exotic birds including golden and American bald eagles, hawks, owls, and falcons, as well as a walk-through, free-flight aviary. And **Crown Colony,** the newest area of the park, is the home of a team of Clydesdale horses as well as a multilevel restaurant, an old-world and beer-brand gift shop, and the Anheuser-Busch hospitality center.

In total, there are more than 3,000 animals, birds, and reptiles and 10 different shows, plus multimedia presentations. All this, plus the Anheuser-Busch brewery tour (self-guided) to observe the beer-making process and an opportunity to sample the famous brews.

To get the most from your visit, arrive early and allow at least eight hours. Start the day by taking one or two of the rides that circle the park (the air-conditioned monorail, the open-air skyride, or the train) to get your bearings and acquaint you with the scope and location of things. The admission price covers all rides, shows, and attractions except arcade or video games.

Admission: $23.95 for adults and children 2 and over; parking $2.

Open: Daily 9am–6pm, with extended hours in summer and hol. periods. **Directions:** Northeast of downtown, take I-275 to Busch Boulevard (exit 33); go east 2 miles to entrance on 40th St. (McKinley Drive).

TAMPA MUSEUM OF ART, 601 Doyle Carlton Dr., Tampa. Tel. 223-8130.

Situated on the east bank of the Hillsborough River south of the Tampa Bay Performing Arts Center, this fine-arts complex offers six galleries with changing exhibits ranging from classical antiquities to contemporary art. Permanent exhibits include the Joseph Veach Noble Collection of Greek and Roman antiquities, the Otto Neumann German expressionist works, the C. Paul Jennewein sculpture collection, and contemporary American photography.

Admission: $2 donation is suggested.

Open: Tues–Thurs and Sat 10am–5pm, Wed 10am–9pm, Sun 1–5pm; tours Tues–Fri at noon and 1pm. **Directions:** Downtown, directly behind the Curtis Hixon Hall, off Ashley Drive.

HENRY B. PLANT MUSEUM, 401 W. Kennedy Blvd., Tampa. Tel. 254-1891.

A unique vision along the Tampa skyline, this landmark was modeled after the Alhambra Palace in Spain, with distinctive Moorish architecture topped by 13 silver minarets. It was built as the 511-room Tampa Bay Hotel in 1891, at an outrageous cost (for those days) of $2 million, by railroad tycoon Henry B. Plant, who filled it with priceless art and furnishings from Europe and Asia.

Although it ceased to operate as a hotel in 1927, the building was saved by the University of Tampa and was declared a National Historic Landmark in 1977. Today the ground-floor rooms have been converted into a museum, filled with elegant displays of Victoriana, Venetian mirrors, Wedgwood china, Louis XV and XVI furniture, and other original art objects and fashions that hark back to the hotel's heyday.

Admission: Suggested donation $2 for adults, 50¢ for children.

Open: Tues–Sat 10am–4pm. **Directions:** West of downtown on Route 60.

FLORIDA CENTER FOR CONTEMPORARY ART, 1722 E. 7th Ave., Ybor City. Tel. 248-1171.

This is Tampa's avant-garde showplace, a gallery for alternative visual arts and the hub of a growing creative colony in Ybor City. Members of the Artists Alliance who exhibit at this nonprofit space offer many of their works for sale. Recent exhibits have included

Adventure Island ④
Busch Gardens ⑤
Children's Museum
  of Tampa ⑦
Florida Center for
  Contemporary Art ⑮
Hall of Fame Golf Club ⑫
Harbour Island cruises ⑲
Henry B. Plant
  Museum ⑯
Lowry Amusement
  Park ⑨
Lowry Park Zoo ⑧
Museum of Science
  and Industry ②
Seminole Indian
  Village ⑩
Tampa Bay Downs ③
Tampa Convention
  Center ⑱
Tampa Greyhound
  Track ⑥
Tampa Jai-Alai Fronton ⑳
Tampa Museum of Art ⑰
Tampa Stadium ⑪
USF Art Museum ①
Villazon & Company
  Cigar Factory ⑬
Ybor City State
  Museum ⑭

Nebraska Ave.

1 University of South Florida

2 Fowler Ave.

582

4

56th St.

5

Busch Gardens

Temple Terrace

Busch Blvd.

580

41

Florida Ave.

baugh

6

Malcolm McKinley Dr.

Sligh Ave.

Sligh Ave.

301

10 →

275

92

Hillsborough Ave.

4

BUS 41

Tampa

Nebraska Ave.

22nd St.

Buffalo Ave.

East Lake

574

585

Florida Ave.

Columbus Dr.

14 **15**

50th St.

Ybor City

town

Adamo Dr.

60

60

19

Harbour Island

BUS 41

Crosstown Expwy.

McKay Bay

Davis Blvd.

Causeway Blvd.

Davis Islands

676

Peter O. Knight Airport

676A

Bayshore Rd.

41

ast t

Hillsborough Bay

DOWNTOWN

Tyler St.

Cass St.

17

Polk St.

18

Zack St.

Twiggs St.

Madison St.

Florida Ave.

Marion St.

Morgan St.

Hillsborough River

Kennedy Blvd.

Jackson St.

Washington St.

Whiting St.

Tampa St.

Franklin St.

Crosstown Expwy.

Ashley St.

Airport ✈

"Electric Pictures," an exhibit of computer imagery by artists across the state.

Admission: Free.

Open: Tues–Sat 11am–4pm. **Directions:** Northeast of downtown, between 17th and 18th streets.

USF ART MUSEUM, Building FAM 101, University of South Florida, W. Holly Drive, Tampa. Tel. 974-2849.

On the western side of the campus, this 10,630-square-foot facility spotlights artists and artworks from around the world. In particular, there are valuable collections of pre-Columbian and African artifacts, as well as contemporary prints from the southeastern United States.

Admission: Free.

Open: Tues and Thurs–Fri 10am–5pm, Wed 10am–8pm, Sat–Sun 1–4pm. **Directions:** Northeast of downtown, one block north of Busch Gardens, between Fowler and Fletcher avenues.

YBOR CITY STATE MUSEUM, 1818 9th Ave., Ybor City. Tel. 247-6323.

The focal point of Ybor City, this museum is housed in the former Ferlita Bakery (1896–1973), a century-old yellow brick building. Various exhibits within the museum depict the political, social, and cultural influences that shaped this section of Tampa. There is particular emphasis on the cigar industry and the fact that Ybor City was once known as the "cigar capital of the world."

You can take a self-guided tour around the museum, which includes a collection of cigar labels, cigar memorabilia, and works by local artisans. Adjacent to the museum is Preservation Park, the site of three renovated cigar workers' cottages, furnished as they were at the turn of the century. Other historic sights nearby include Ybor Square, formerly the largest cigar factory in the world and now converted into a shopping plaza (see "Shopping," below in this chapter); El Pasaje Hotel, a splendid example of Spanish-American architecture and now the Café Creole (see Chapter 10, "Tampa Dining,"), the Cuban Club, a social and fraternal society that dates back to 1902, and José Martí Park, a small plot of land dedicated in honor of a Cuban revolutionary hero.

Admission: 50¢ for adults and children 12 and up.

Open: Tues–Sat 9am–noon and 1–5pm. **Directions:** Northeast of downtown, between 18th and 19th streets.

SEMINOLE INDIAN VILLAGE, 5221 N. Orient Rd., Tampa. Tel. 621-7349.

Located on Tampa's Seminole Reservation, this museum is designed to trace the history of the Seminoles in the area. It is laid out in an eight-sided star configuration, representing the eight clans of the tribe. The structures include chickees (thatched huts built in the style of 150 years ago), which shelter skilled Seminole craftspeople as they practice beadwork, wood carving, basket-making, and patchwork sewing. Other more lively demonstrations include alligator wrestling and snake-handling. The grounds also serve as a natural habitat for

Florida black bears, panthers, otters, bobcats, and deer. The gift shop is a good source for turquoise jewelry, moccasins, sweetgrass baskets, and beadwork.

Admission: $4.50 for adults, $3.50 for seniors, and $3.75 for children.

Open: Mon–Sat 9am–5pm, Sun noon–5; tours every hour on the half hour, with last tour at 3:30pm. **Directions:** Northeast of downtown, off exit 5 of I-4.

VILLAZON & COMPANY CIGAR FACTORY, 3104 N. Armenia Ave., Tampa. Tel. 879-2291.

If the cigar-making history of this city intrigues you, head to this working factory on Tampa's west side. It offers a daily 20-minute guided tour, focusing on the art and science of cigar-making. See how cigars are made—hand-rolled, packaged, and readied for shipping.

Admission: Free.

Open: Tour Mon–Fri 9:30am. **Directions:** East of the airport, off Columbus Drive, between Kathleen and Aileen streets.

2. COOL FOR KIDS

MUSEUM OF SCIENCE AND INDUSTRY (MOSI), 4801 E. Fowler Ave., Tampa. Tel. 985-5531.

Located north of Busch Gardens, MOSI offers permanent and changing exhibits that focus on industry, technology, and the physicial and natural sciences. Housed in a unique three-floor open-air setting, it includes a ham radio station, communications gallery, power plant model, and weather station.

The newest attraction is the Challenger Center, a memorial to the seven Challenger astronauts who perished in 1986. It simulates a space-shuttle mission from both the space vehicle and mission-control aspects.

Admission: $4 for adults, $2 for children 5–15.

Open: Daily 10am–4:30pm. **Closed:** Major hols. **Directions:** North of downtown, across from the University of South Florida campus, and 1 mile northeast of Busch Gardens.

ADVENTURE ISLAND, 4545 Bougainvillea Ave., Tampa. Tel. 971-7978.

Adjacent to Busch Gardens and owned and operated by Busch Entertainment Corp., this is a separate 19-acre outdoor water theme park. A favorite with kids and teens, it has three swimming pools and several water-slide/play areas with names like River of No Return, Gulf Scream, Everglides, Courageous Falls, and Tampa Typhoon. There is also an outdoor café, picnic and sunbathing areas, games arcade, and dressing-room facilities. Wear a bathing suit and bring towels.

FROMMER'S COOL FOR KIDS

HOTELS

Days Inn–Busch Gardens (see p. 181). With outdoor pool, children's playground, volleyball court, badminton, tennis courts, and rentals for paddle boats.

Hyatt Regency Westshore (see p. 175). Set amid a 35-acre nature preserve, with walking trails and water sports.

Saddlebrook (see p. 182). Has a supervised children's program, a tennis school for junior players, plus swimming pool with lifeguard, bicycle rentals, and more.

RESTAURANTS

CK's (see p. 198). A revolving rooftop restaurant with views of airplanes taking off and landing.

Mels' Hot Dogs (see p. 202). For hot dogs of all styles, topped with anything a little heart desires.

Parker's Lighthouse (see p. 186). Offers great views of the passing boats and balloons for little diners.

Rough Riders (see p. 194). For burgers, steaks, and sandwiches amid pictures portraying the escapades of Teddy Roosevelt and his troops during the Spanish-American War.

Admission: $14.95 per person; free for children under 2. Lockers $1.

Open: April–Oct Mon–Sat 10am–5pm, Sat–Sun 9:30am–6pm; hours extended in summer months. **Directions:** Northeast of downtown, take I-275 to Busch Boulevard (exit 33), go east 2 miles to 40th Street (McKinley Drive), make a left and follow signs.

LOWRY PARK ZOO, 7530 North Blvd., Tampa. Tel. 935-8552.

Recently renovated and expanded with lots of greenery, bubbling brooks, and cascading waterfalls, this 24-acre zoo aims to display animals in settings that closely resemble their natural habitats. Among the major attractions are a 45-foot aviary in a subtropical forest setting; a wildlife center, showcasing Florida's native plants and animals; and a Florida at Night building, specializing in rare nocturnal animals. The zoo offers insight into breeding and rehabilitation through its aviary nursery and manatee hospital. There are also areas devoted to primates, Asian animals, and a children's petting zoo.

Prices: $4 for adults, $3 for seniors, $2 for children 4–11, free for children 3 and under.

Open: Daily, Apr–Oct 9:30am–6pm, Nov–Mar 9:30am–5pm.
Directions: Take I-275 to Sligh Avenue (exit 31), follow signs to Lowry Park.

LOWRY AMUSEMENT PARK, Sligh Avenue at North Blvd., Tampa. Tel. 935-5503.

Founded over 30 years ago and rejuvenated in 1990, this old-fashioned park offers a dozen traditional kiddie rides, from a big Ferris wheel and merry-go-round to bumper cars. It has a small-town atmosphere and is a favorite with the locals who usually combine a visit here with the adjacent zoo and other attractions.

Admission: Free, rides 50¢–$1 each; coupon books are $4.95.

Open: Mon–Thurs 10am–8pm, Fri–Sun 10am–10pm. **Directions:** Take I-275 to Sligh Avenue (exit 31), follow signs to Lowry Park.

CHILDREN'S MUSEUM OF TAMPA, 7530 North Blvd., Tampa. Tel. 935-8441.

Geared for those aged 2 through 10, this museum invites children to touch and test, explore and examine, pretend and play in exhibits that are designed to increase curiosity and imagination. Activities range from grocery shopping to blowing giant bubbles or paper-making. A visit here can also be combined with a tour of Safety Village, a satellite of the museum, that presents Tampa in miniature. Kids can have the run of this scaled-down city, and learn the rules of safety, with miniature traffic lights, buildings, and paved streets.

Price: $1 for adults and children 2 and over; 75¢ for seniors; free for children under 2.

Open: Tues–Sat 10am–5pm, Sun 1–5pm. **Directions:** Take I-275 to Sligh Avenue (exit 31), follow signs to Lowry Park.

---

3. ORGANIZED TOURS

WATER AND LAND TOURS

GONDOLA GETAWAY CRUISES, Waterwalk, Harbour Island. Tel. 888-8864.

See the skyscrapers and other downtown highlights as you float across the waters of Tampa Bay and the lower Hillsborough River in an authentic 70-year-old Venetian gondola. Local boating enthusiast Keith Ziegler, a former social worker/therapist, has restored three 30-foot gondolas, each capable of carrying up to four passengers on 35- to 45-minute trips. With Ziegler or one of his family steering the craft and providing a commentary on downtown sights, you'll drift along channels and under bridges as fish jump in the sparkling waters and Italian opera plays on a cassette player on board. Ziegler will even supply a bucket of ice and glasses if you want to bring your own champagne or wine. Close your eyes and you'll think you're in Venice, but instead it's the ideal way to get your bearings in Tampa—a unique and delightful tour.

Prices: $20 per couple, additional persons $5 each; maximum of four persons per cruise.

Schedule: Mon–Sat 6pm–midnight, Sun noon–9pm, other times by appointment; reservations accepted 9am–7pm. **Directions:** On the Waterwalk dock on Harbour Island.

TAMPA TOURS, 5805 50th St. N., Tampa. Tel. 621-6667.

This company offers two-hour escorted motor-coach tours of downtown Tampa and nearby sights, including the Henry B. Plant Museum, Old Hyde Park Village, and Ybor City. All tours depart from the Tampa Visitor Information Center and should be booked through the center at 111 Madison St., Suite 110 (tel. 223-1111 or toll free 800-44-TAMPA).

Price: $12.

Schedule: Mon–Sat 10am and 2pm. **Directions:** All departures are downtown, from the Tampa Visitor Information Center in the First Florida Tower, corner of Ashley and Madison streets.

TAMPA WATER TRANSIT CO., Waterwalk, Harbour Island. Tel. 223-4168.

This motorized 36-foot pontoon boat cruises around Harbour Island and the Hillsborough River through downtown Tampa, with an informal live commentary on the major sights. Each tour lasts 30 minutes, and departs on the hour.

Price: $3.

Open: Mon–Fri 4–9pm, Sat–Sun noon–9pm. **Directions:** On the Waterwalk dock on Harbour Island.

STARLIGHT PRINCESS, The Waterwalk, Harbour Island. Tel. 854-1212.

Once a week, this authentic 106-foot-long paddlewheeler provides a three-hour dinner-dance cruise around Hillsborough Bay, with waterside views of the Tampa skyline and neighboring sights. The price includes a four-course sit-down dinner (entrée choice of filet mignon, seafood thermidor, chicken marsala, or fresh fish catch of the day). Boarding is half an hour before departure. Reservations required.

Price: $26.45 per person including tax.

Schedule: Thurs 7:30–10:30pm. **Directions:** Departs from the Waterwalk dock at Harbour Island.

A CRUISE

HOLLAND AMERICA CRUISE LINE, Port of Tampa. Tel. toll free 800/426-0327.

From Tampa, you can embark on a seven-day cruise in the Gulf of Mexico and beyond on board the *Nieuw Amsterdam.* Accommodating up to 1,214 passengers, the 704-foot luxury vessel makes stops at Key West; Playa del Carmen and Cozumel, Mexico; Ocho Rios, Jamaica; and Georgetown, Grand Cayman. Decorated with extensive collections of art and antiques, it has nine decks, including an upper promenade that completely encircles the ship, dining rooms, outdoor swimming pools, health spa, and movie theater.

Price: $1,099 to $2,139, including air transportation from major gateways.

Schedule: Mid–Oct to mid–Apr, Sat departures. **Directions:** Departs from the cruise-ship dock at the Port of Tampa, east of downtown.

4. SPORTS AND RECREATION

SPECTATOR SPORTS

BASEBALL   For more baseball venues within a half hour's drive, see Chapter 7, "What to See and Do in St. Petersburg."

PLANT CITY STADIUM, Park Road, Plant City. Tel. 752-1878.

About a half hour's drive from downtown Tampa, this is the winter home of the Cincinnati Reds who hold their spring training here each year.

Admission: $4–$6.

Schedule: Mid-Feb to Apr. **Directions:** Take I-4 east, 25 miles to Park Road (exit 14), and follow signs.

DOG RACING

TAMPA GREYHOUND TRACK, 8300 Nebraska Ave., Tampa. Tel. 932-4313.

A modern, climate-controlled, fully enclosed facility, this track features 13 races daily, with eight dogs competing in each. Facilities include a restaurant, lounge, and closed-circuit TVs for viewing the races and playbacks.

Admission: $1 grandstand, $2.50 clubhouse. Parking 50¢–$1.

Open: Sept–Jan Mon–Sat 7:30pm, matinees Mon, Wed, and Sat noon. **Directions:** North of downtown, take I-275 to Bird Street (exit 32).

FOOTBALL, SOCCER, ETC.

TAMPA STADIUM, 4201 N. Dale Mabry Highway, Tampa. Tel. 872-7977.

Home base for the Tampa Bay Buccaneers football team and the Tampa Bay Rowdies soccer team, this 74,296-capacity stadium caters to sporting events of all sizes and calibers from the Super Bowl to horse shows, wrestling, rodeos, motorcycle races, and tractor-pulling. The stadium also hosts the Hall of Fame Bowl each New Year's Day, the Florida Classic, and a wide range of other college football games.

Prices: $5–$35 or higher, depending on the event.

Schedule: Box office for Bucs Games (tel. 879-BUCS) Mon–Fri 9am–5pm; for other events, temporary box offices are set up on-site several days or weeks in advance, with various hours and days of operation; call in advance for particulars or reserve through Ticketmaster outlets. Times of games and events vary. **Directions:** North of downtown and east of the airport, at Buffalo Avenue.

HORSE RACING

TAMPA BAY DOWNS, 12505 Racetrack Rd., Oldsmar. Tel. 855-4401.

The only Thoroughbred oval horse-race course on Florida's west coast, this is the home of the Tampa Bay Derby, a key test for Triple Crown hopefuls. The program features 10 races a day, and facilities include a restaurant, a lounge, and a gallery with big screens where replays are shown. The 1991–92 season marks the 45th consecutive year of racing here.

Admission: $1.50 grandstand, $3–$5 clubhouse and gallery. Free grandstand admission for seniors on Wed and for ladies on Thurs. Parking $1.

Open: Dec–Apr daily except Tues, post time 1pm. **Directions:** North of Tampa, off Route 580.

JAI-ALAI

TAMPA JAI-ALAI FRONTON, 5125 S. Dale Mabry Highway, Tampa. Tel. 831-1411.

Having originated in Spain, and bearing similarities to racquetball, this is considered the world's fastest ball game (the ball can travel more than 180 mph). Professional players volley the lethal *pelota* with a long, curved glove called a *cesta*. Facilities include a restaurant and parimutuel wagering.

Admission: $1–$3 per person. Parking $1 or free.

Open: Jan–Sept Mon–Sat 7pm, matinees Wed and Sat noon. **Directions:** Southwest of downtown, at the corner of Gandy Boulevard.

POLO

TAMPA BAY POLO CLUB, Walden Lake Polo and Country Club, 1602 W. Timberlane Drive, Plant City. Tel. 754-1894.

Touted as the oldest team sport, polo is played regularly at this sylvan site east of Tampa. Each week a different local charity or nonprofit fund benefits from the proceeds.

Admission: Free, but parking is $5–$7.

Open: Mid–Jan to Apr, Sun 2pm. **Directions:** Take I-4 to exit 11 and follow the signs south.

RECREATION

BINGO This low-energy activity is big business in the Tampa Bay area. There are at least three dozen local organizations (church groups, fraternal orders, ethnic groups) that sponsor bingo sessions each week. A listing of them all can be found in *The Suncoast Bingo Magazine,* a free publication available monthly at tourist offices, shops, and malls. Of all the bingo venues, however, two of the most popular are owned and operated by the Seminole Tribe of Florida, located side-by-side 7 miles east of downtown Tampa.

SEMINOLE BINGO OF TAMPA, 5223 North Orient Rd., Tampa. Tel. 621-1302.

Opened in 1982, this facility offers continuous high-stakes bingo, all week long. There are four sessions every day, with seating for 2,000 persons. Prices depend on how many games are played, which can be as few as 10 or as many as 33. Instant bingo is also available, as are smoke-free areas.

Prices: $5–$43, depending on the number of games played; discounts are offered at some Tues, Thurs, and Sun matinees.

Open: Daily 11am–midnight; matinee sessions at 11am and 2:15pm; evening sessions at 7pm and 10:30pm. **Directions:** From downtown, take I-4 to Orient Road (exit 5); go north 500 yards to entrance.

SEMINOLE BINGO PALACE, 5223 North Orient Rd., Tampa. Tel. 621-1302.

A departure from the traditional bingo setup, this smaller facility was opened in 1988, south of the main hall. Instead of playing an entire session, players can opt for as few as one game or as many as 100. In addition, there is less competition—usually there are 20 or 25 people sitting around a table. This hall originated two new forms of bingo, decision bingo and carousel bingo, both of which are spreading to other halls around the country.

Price: $1–$2 per game.

Open: Wed–Thurs and Sun 5pm–3am, Fri–Sat 5pm–4am. **Directions:** From downtown, take I-4 to Orient Road (exit 5); go north 500 yards to entrance.

FISHING Like the St. Petersburg area, Tampa offers many opportunities for casting a line. Unlike St. Pete, however, Tampa does not have a huge coast along the Gulf of Mexico, so Tampa-area fishing is confined mainly to lakes, rivers, and bays. Tampa fishing is also more informal, with no organized programs or fleets of party boats lined up along local marinas to offer day trips to visitors.

According to local experts, you'll find good freshwater fishing for trout in Lake Thonotosassa, east of the city, or for bass along the Hillsborough River. Pier fishing on Hillsborough Bay is also available from Ballast Point Park, 5300 Interbay Blvd. (tel. 831-9585).

For information on required licenses, see Chapter 7, "What to See and Do in St. Petersburg: Sports and Recreation."

GOLF

HALL OF FAME GOLF CLUB, 2222 N. Westshore Blvd., Tampa. Tel. 876-4913.

You can literally step off the plane and play a round of golf at this 18-hole par-72 course, situated adjacent to Tampa Airport. Facilities include a driving range and golf-club rentals. Lessons are also available.

Price: $10; with cart $17.

Open: Daily 7am–dusk. **Directions:** At the intersection of Spruce Avenue, at the southeast corner of the airport.

ROCKY POINT GOLF MUNICIPAL GOLF COURSE, 4151 Dana Shores Drive, Tampa. Tel. 884-5141.

Situated between the airport and Old Tampa Bay, this is an 18-hole par-71 course with pro shop, practice range, putting greens, snack bar, and lounge. Lessons and golf-club rentals are also available.

Price: $16; with cart $26.50.

Open: Daily 7am–dusk. **Directions:** 2 miles west of Tampa Airport, off Memorial Highway.

ROGERS PARK MUNICIPAL GOLF COURSE, 7910 N. 30th St., Tampa. Tel. 234-1911.

On the Hillsborough River in north Tampa, this 18-hole par-72 championship course has a lighted driving range, practice range, snack bar, and lounge. Lessons are available as are clubs for rent.

Price: $12.75; with cart $22.25.

Open: Daily 7am–dark. **Directions:** Take I-275 north to Sligh Avenue (exit 31), then east to 30th Street.

UNIVERSITY OF SOUTH FLORIDA GOLF COURSE, 4202 Fowler Ave., Tampa. Tel. 974-2071.

Located just north of the USF campus, this 18-hole par-72 course is nicknamed "the Claw" because of its challenging layout. It offers lessons, club rentals, and a snack bar.

Price: $15; with cart $25.

Open: Daily 7am–dusk. **Directions:** From downtown, take I-275 to Fletcher Avenue (exit 35); go east 2 miles.

BABE ZAHARIAS MUNICIPAL GOLF COURSE, 11412 Forest Hills Dr., Tampa. Tel. 932-8932.

Situated north of Lowry Park between the Carrollwood and Temple Terrace areas, this is an 18-hole par-70 course. It has a pro shop, putting greens, driving range, and snack bar. Golf-club rentals and lessons are available.

Price: $16; with cart $26.50.

Open: Daily 7am–dusk. **Directions:** From downtown, take I-275 north to Fowler Avenue (exit 34); go west ½ mile to Forest Hills Drive.

RUNNING Bayshore Boulevard, a 7-mile stretch along Hillsborough Bay, is famous for its 6.3-mile sidewalk. It is reputed to be the world's longest continuous sidewalk, and is a favorite for runners, joggers, walkers, and cyclists. The route goes from the western edge of downtown in a southward direction, passing stately old homes, condos, retirement communities, and houses of worship, and ending at the grounds of MacDill Air Force Base.

In addition, you might try some of the local Hillsborough County parks, such as the 240-acre Lettuce Lake, 6920 Fletcher Ave. at the Hillsborough River (tel. 985-7845), northeast of downtown. Launched in 1982, it is one of the area's newest parks and a hub for outdoor enthusiasts. There is a jogging trail, with a fitness course, plus a bicycle path and picnic areas.

For more information on recommended running areas, contact the Parks and Recreation Department, 7225 North Blvd., Tampa (tel. 223-8230).

SWIMMING The nearest public beach to downtown is the Ben T. Davis Beach on the Courtney Campbell Causeway (Fla. Rte. 60), on Old Tampa Bay. If you keep driving, the Campbell Causeway will lead you to Clearwater Beach and the many other Gulf beaches in neighboring Pinellas County (see Chapter 7, "What to See and Do in St. Petersburg: Sports and Recreation").

TENNIS

CITY OF TAMPA TENNIS COMPLEX, Hillsborough Community College, 4001 Tampa Bay Blvd., Tampa. Tel. 870-2383.

Situated across from Tampa Stadium, this is one of two tennis sites in the area recently awarded the U.S. Tennis Association's national facility award. It is the largest public complex in Tampa, with 16 hard courts and 12 clay courts. It also offers racquetball courts, plus a pro shop, locker rooms, showers, and lessons. Reservations required.

Price: $2–$4 per person per hour.

Open: Mon–Fri 8am–9pm, Sat–Sun 8am–6pm. **Directions:** East of the airport, at the intersection of Buffalo Avenue and Dale Mabry Highway.

MARJORIE PARK, 59 Columbia Dr., Davis Islands, Tampa. Tel. 253-3997.

Located on the water and overlooking Harbour Island, this complex has eight clay courts. It is one of two tennis complexes in the area that were recently awarded the U.S. Tennis Association's national facility award. Reservations are required.

Price: $2–$4 per person per hour.

Open: Mon–Fri 8am–9pm, Sat–Sun 8am–6pm. **Directions:** On Davis Islands, southwest of downtown, off Bayshore Boulevard.

RIVERFRONT PARK, 900 North Blvd., Tampa. Tel. 223-8602.

This facility is located at the north end of the University of Tampa, across the river from the Tampa Bay Performing Arts Center. There are 11 courts here, and visitors are welcome to use them on a first-come basis. The courts are lit until 10pm and there is no charge for lights. There are 10 other unstaffed facilities such as this spread throughout the city. For locations, call 223-8602.

Price: Free.

Open: Daily 7am–10pm. **Directions:** At the north end of the University of Tampa.

HARRY HOPMAN/SADDLEBROOK INTERNATIONAL TENNIS SCHOOL, 100 Saddlebrook Way, Wesley Chapel. Tel. 973-1111 or toll free 800/237-7519; in Florida 800/282-4654.

If you're serious about your tennis, this place allows you to build a whole vacation around the sport. Founded by the late Harry Hopman, one of the most successful captain-coaches in Davis Cup history, this well-equipped school, with 37 tennis courts, caters to beginners and skilled players of all ages.

The basic five-day, six-night instructional package includes 25 hours (minimum) of tennis instruction, unlimited playing time, match play with instructors, audiovisual analysis, fitness and agility exercises, use of bicycles and fishing equipment, and accommodations at the Saddlebrook resort. A similar program for juniors (aged 9 through 19) is also available, including meals. For more information on the resort, see Chapter 9, "Tampa Accommodations: East of Tampa."

Prices: $654–$864 per person, based on double occupancy for adults; $597–$636 for junior program.

Open: Year round. **Directions:** Off I-75, 25 miles north of Tampa.

WATER SPORTS

BANANA BAY SKI CO., 3075 N. Rocky Point Drive, Tampa. Tel. 281-2220 or toll free 800/329-4-FUN.

Situated next to the Residence Inn on Old Tampa Bay, this water-sports complex rents water skis, jet skis, windsurfers, and wave runners. If you have no experience, there is also a beginner's water-ski school here, offering half-day classes.

Prices: $30–$40 per half hour, $50–$60 per hour; $40 for classes.

Hours: Daily 9am–5pm or later; courses Mon–Sat at 10am. **Directions:** From airport, take Courtney Campbell Causeway (Fla. Rte. 60) 2 miles west.

TRIDENT BOAT RENTALS, Waterwalk, Harbour Island. Tel. 223-4168.

Rent a small electric paddle boat or a three-passenger electric boat and ply the waters of Garrison's Channel or the Hillsborough River around Harbour Island. All prices are based on half-hour rentals.

Prices: $3.50 for paddle boats; $7–$10 for electric boats.

Open: Mon–Thurs 1–10pm, Fri 1pm–midnight, Sat noon–midnight, Sun noon–9pm.

WALKING TOUR—DOWNTOWN TAMPA

Start: University of Tampa
Finish: Harbour Island
Time: Approximately 2 hours

Best Times: Weekends
Worst Times: Weekday morning or evening rush hours

FROM UNIVERSITY OF TAMPA TO FRANKLIN STREET
MALL Start just west of the downtown business district at the:

1. **Henry B. Plant Museum,** 401 W. Kennedy Boulevard, originally the site of the Tampa Bay Hotel built in 1891 by railroad magnate Henry B. Plant and now part of the campus of the University of Tampa. (See "The Top Attractions," above in this chapter.) Stroll around the beautifully landscaped University of Tampa campus and then cross the John F. Kennedy Boulevard Bridge (originally the Lafayette Street Bridge) to the hub of Tampa's downtown business district.

   After crossing the river, you come to Ashley Street, a prime north-south thoroughfare, lined with hotels, banks, office towers, and many of the city's attractions including the new:

2. **Tampa Convention Center.** A visit would require a detour to the most southerly tip of Ashley.

   At Ashley Street and Kennedy Boulevard, head north (left) for one block to Madison and, if you wish, stop for a visit at the new ground floor offices of the:

3. **Tampa/Hillsborough Convention and Visitors Association,** 111 Madison Street, at the corner of Ashley and Madison. You may want to ask specific questions or stock up on brochures and other travel information about the Tampa area.

   Continue north on Ashley, passing the NCNB Bank and Plaza on the left, to the Ashley Street entrance of the:

4. **Tampa Museum of Art,** 601 Doyle Carlton Drive (see "The Top Attractions," above in this chapter). Return to Ashley and stroll north for the next five blocks, passing various bank buildings and modern office towers and the:

5. **Curtis Hixon Hall,** a convention/exhibit center. The next building of interest along Ashley is the main branch of the:

6. **Tampa Public Library,** 900 N. Ashley Street, between Cass and Tyler streets, with a small fine-arts gallery featuring rotating exhibitions of local artists. Behind the library, on Ashley Drive, is a 25-foot red steel sculpture, *America, America,* by Barbara Neijna.

   At Tyler, take a left and visit the:

7. **Tampa Bay Performing Arts Center,** a modern $57 million riverfront entertainment complex. Guided tours are conducted each Wednesday and Saturday at 10am. Directly north of the arts center, off Fortune Street, is the:

8. **Holiday Inn,** one of Tampa's contemporary downtown hotels.

REFUELING STOP If you'd like some refreshment amid an artsy decor, try the **Backstage Restaurant** of the Holiday Inn, or, for lighter fare, **the Deli** of the same hotel.

Return to Ashley Street and retrace your steps two blocks to Cass Street. Go east on Cass two blocks to Franklin Street and turn right. You are now on the Franklin Street Mall, a largely pedestrianized area and the focal point of downtown Tampa. Stroll in a southward direction, and, after crossing the intersection of Polk Street, look to the east side for the:

9. Tampa Theatre, 711 N. Franklin Street, a restored 1926 building that is listed on the National Register of Historic Places. The interior is noted for its ornate colonnades, balconies, and replicas of Greek and Roman statuary. Across the street, to the west, is:

10. TECO (Tampa Electric Company) Plaza, 702 N. Franklin St., with a public gallery used to showcase the works of Tampa Bay area artists. On the northwest corner of Franklin and Zack streets, be sure to note *Solaris,* a solar-powered hanging sculpture by William Severson.

The next cross street, Zack, offers a slight detour. Make a left and walk one block east to Florida Avenue. Here you will see the:

11. YMCA building, dating back to 1908, and currently earmarked for restoration and transformation into a new upscale 89-unit hotel, to be known as the Zack Street Inn. Return to Franklin Street where several other structures are slated for restoration, including the:

12. Maas Brothers building between Zack and Twiggs streets. As you continue between Twiggs and Madison, notice a mural on the east side of Franklin Street, *Franklin Street 1925,* by Carl Cowden III and Randall Williams. Across the street, at the corner of Franklin and Madison streets, is a striking aluminum sculpture, *Family of Man,* by Geoffrey Naylor.

Continue southward along Franklin, crossing over Kennedy Boulevard and Jackson Street. The latter is considered the "Wall Street of Tampa" and the site of the:

13. Tampa Financial Center. Between Jackson and Washington Streets on Franklin, you will see a number of the city's new developments including:

14. Tampa City Center, to the east of Franklin, and the:

15. Hyatt Regency Hotel, to the west of Franklin. Beside the Tampa City Center on Franklin, there is also an open-air:

16. Esplanade area, with waterfalls, fountains, trees, and flowers. This site was once part of Fort Brooke (1835–1842), the original U.S. army settlement around which Tampa grew up.

REFUELING STOP If you'd like to take a break, the **Esplanade** offers a number of cafés, coffee shops, and fast-food outlets, most of which have outdoor seating under the trees. For an extra-special lunch or dinner, try **17. rg's Downtown,** 110 N. Franklin Street (see Chapter 10, "Tampa Dining: Downtown.")

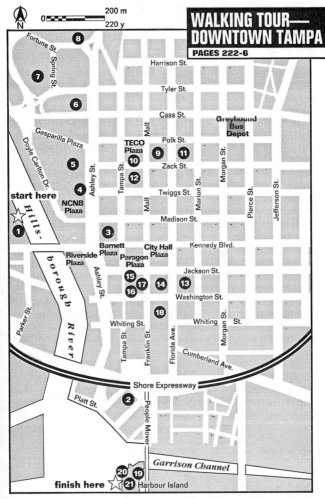

200 m
0 ———
220 y

N

Fortune St.
Spring St.
Harrison St.
Tyler St.
Cass St.
Gasparilla Plaza
Doyle Carlton Dr.
Greyhound Bus Depot
Polk St.
TECO Plaza
Zack St.
Ashley St.
Tampa St.
Twiggs St.
Marion St.
Morgan St.
Pierce St.
Jefferson St.
start here
NCNB Plaza
Madison St.
Mall
Barnett Plaza
Riverside Plaza
City Hall Plaza
Paragon Plaza
Kennedy Blvd.
Jackson St.
Ashley St.
Washington St.
Whiting St.
Whiting St.
Florida Ave.
Morgan St.
Tampa St.
Franklin St.
Cumberland Ave.
Shore Expressway
Platt St.
People Mover
Garrison Channel
finish here
Harbour Island

Parker St.
Hills-borough River

- ❶ Henry B. Plant Museum
- ❷ Tampa Convention Center
- ❸ Tampa/Hillsborough Convention and Visitors Association
- ❹ Tampa Museum of Art
- ❺ Curtis Hixon Hall
- ❻ Tampa Public Library
- ❼ Tampa Bay Performing Arts Center
- ❽ Holiday Inn, Backstage Restaurant
- ❾ Tampa Theatre
- ❿ TECO Plaza
- ⓫ YMCA Building
- ⓬ Maas Brothers building
- ⓭ Tampa Financial Center
- ⓮ Tampa City Center
- ⓯ Hyatt Regency Hotel
- ⓰ Esplanade area, Tampa City Center
- ⓱ rg's Downtown
- ⓲ Old Fort Brooke Parking Garage
- ⓳ Harbour Island Food Court
- ⓴ Waterwalk
- ㉑ Wyndham Harbour Island Hotel

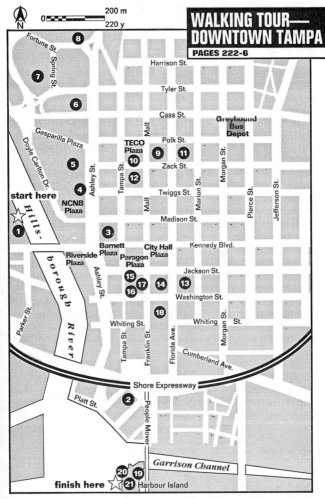

FRANKLIN STREET MALL TO HARBOUR ISLAND   After a refreshing stroll through the Esplanade area, you are now at the entrance to the:

18. **Old Fort Brooke Parking Garage** and the downtown terminal for the People Mover (on the third floor). It takes 25¢ in exact change, and 90 seconds, for the People Mover to whisk you over to:

19. **Harbour Island.** Once on Harbour Island, you can browse among the interesting shops, offering everything from fashions and resort wear to arts and crafts and jewelry. Along the:

20. **Waterwalk** outside, you can also arrange to take a gondola ride or rent a paddle boat, among other water-sports activities. Harbour Island is a destination in itself and a perfect finale for your walking tour of Tampa.

REFUELING STOP   If you have waited till now for a bit of refreshment, then you have lots of choices. The **Harbour Island Food Court** offers burgers, pizza, and ethnic fast foods. Restaurants in the complex include a branch of the famous Spanish restaurant the Columbia, as well as Parker's Lighthouse for seafood, and Blueberry Hill and Cha Cha Coconuts for lighter fare. For an elegant setting overlooking the water, try the restaurant or lounge of the adjacent **21. Wyndham Harbour Island Hotel.**

---

5. SHOPPING

MALLS, MARKETS, AND SHOPPING CLUSTERS

ALESSI FARMERS MARKET, 4802 Gunn Highway, Tampa. Tel. 968-6663.

Housed in a large warehouse-style building with a Mexican tile roof, this unique shopping emporium offers a wide selection of fresh produce and vegetables, as well as gourmet foods including cheeses, pastas, breads, herbs, spices, dressings, pastries, and ice cream. There are also areas devoted to boutique wines and imported beers, as well as cooking utensils, plants, and flowers. Locally known as "the funnest fresh food market anywhere," this is a sight-seeing attraction as well—with 60,000 live honey bees in observation hives, a candy factory, and a canning kitchen.

Open: Mon–Sat 9am–9pm, Sun 9am–7pm. **Directions:** Take I-275 north to Busch Boulevard (exit 33); proceed west to Gunn Highway.

BELZ FACTORY OUTLET, 6302 E. Buffalo Ave., Tampa. Tel. 621-6047.
Buy direct from the manufacturer at this complex of 50 outlets. You'll find everything from fashions and footwear to ribbons and raingear selling for up to 75% off the normal price. Brand names represented include Bass, Totes, Aileen's, Fieldcrest, and Monet. There is even a bookstore called Bookland Outlet.
Open: Mon–Sat 10am–9pm, Sun noon–6pm. **Directions:** Northeast of downtown, at the intersection of I-4 and Buffalo Avenue, across from the fairgrounds.

OLD HYDE PARK VILLAGE, 712 S. Oregon Ave., Hyde Park. Tel. 251-3500.
Located in one of the city's oldest and most historic neighborhoods, this is the Rodeo Drive of Tampa, a cluster of 50 upscale shops and boutiques arranged in a village atmosphere. The selection includes Brooks Brothers, Crabtree & Evelyn, Godiva Chocolatier, Jaeger, Laura Ashley, Polo-Ralph Lauren, Victoria's Secret, Williams-Sonoma, and a Doubleday bookshop. In addition to the shops, there are a half dozen restaurants, a multiscreen movie theater, and three free parking garages (on Oregon, Swann, and Rome avenues).
Open: Mon–Wed 10am–6pm, Thurs–Fri 10am–9pm, Sat 10am–6pm; Sun hours vary. **Directions:** West of downtown, off Swann Avenue.

THE SHOPS ON HARBOUR ISLAND, 601 S. Harbour Island Blvd., Harbour Island. Tel. 228-7807.
This is Tampa's waterfront marketplace, on an island directly south of downtown and well worth a day's outing. The 20 different shops include art galleries and fashion boutiques, as well as outlets for swimwear, sportswear, sunglasses, candies, collectables, and Asian treasures. The complex also includes a food court, restaurants, hotel, water-sports activities, gondola rides, and more.
Open: Mon–Sat 10am–9pm, Sun 11am–6pm. **Directions:** Accessible from downtown via Franklin Street Bridge or the elevated tram-style People Mover.

TAMPA BAY CENTER, 3302 W. Buffalo Ave., Tampa. Tel. 870-0876.
Skylights, palm trees, and fountains dominate the decor of this massive 160-store mall. The complex includes three department stores—Sears, Burdines, and Montgomery Ward—and an assortment of boutiques, known for selling trendy new fashions, jewelry, and accessories. There are also stores for gifts, stationery, arts and crafts, and two booksellers, B. Dalton and Waldenbooks.
Open: Mon–Sat 10am–9:30pm, Sun noon–6pm. **Directions:** East of the airport, at intersection of Buffalo and Himes avenues.

UNIVERSITY SQUARE MALL, 2200 E. Fowler Ave., Tampa. Tel. 971-3465.

Ideally situated next to the USF campus and a mile north of Busch Gardens, this is Tampa's largest shopping center, with five department stores—Burdines, J. C. Penney, Maas Brothers, Maison Blanche, and Sears—and 130 others selling everything from gifts and souvenirs to jewelry and high fashion.

Open: Mon–Sat 10am–9pm, Sun noon–5:30pm. **Directions:** Take I-275 north to Fowler Avenue (exit 34); travel east 1 mile to 22nd Street.

WEST SHORE PLAZA, 253 Westshore Blvd., Tampa. Tel. 286-0790.

Opened in 1967 and one of the first large regional shopping centers on Florida's west coast, this mall is within walking distance of many of the major hotels in the West Shore business and banking district. It comprises of 100 specialty stores, an international food court, and three department stores—Maas Brothers, J. C. Penney, and Maison Blanche.

Open: Mon–Sat 10am–9pm, Sun noon–5:30pm. **Directions:** At the intersection of Westshore and Kennedy boulevards.

YBOR SQUARE, 1901 13th St., Ybor City. Tel. 247-4497.

Listed on the National Register of Historic Places, this complex consists of three brick buildings (dating to 1886) that once comprised the largest cigar factory in the world, employing over 4,000 workers. Today it is a specialty mall, with over three dozen shops and eateries, all housed in a setting of original wooden interiors, hand-blown glass windows, classic brick masonry, and wall-size murals that depict earlier days. The highlights include the Nostalgia Market, a collection of individual antique shops selling everything from rare magazines to clothing, linens, handcrafts, jewelry, quilts, and furniture; and Tampa Rico, an old-world cigar shop where you can purchase hand-rolled cigars and watch them being made. If you're a smoker, it's one place where you're sure to feel welcome—a sign on the wall says THANK YOU FOR SMOKING.

Open: Mon–Sat 9:30am–5:30pm, Sun noon–5:30pm; cigar-rolling demonstrations Tues–Sun noon–5:30pm. **Directions:** Take I-4 to Ybor City (exit 1); follow signs to 8th Avenue and 13th Street.

6. EVENING ENTERTAIMENT

Whether you're a fan of drama or dance, rock or reggae, comedy or the classics, chances are you'll find it in Tampa. To assist visitors, the Tampa/Hillsborough Arts Council maintains an Artsline (tel. 229-ARTS), a 24-hour information service providing the latest on current and upcoming cultural events.

The best way to keep abreast of what's on is to read the *Tampa Tribune,* the city's daily newspaper. In particular, don't miss the Friday edition, which includes "Friday Extra/The Tampa Bay

Times," a supplement packed with information on theaters, shows, nightclubs, festivals, and all sorts of local activities. Another excellent publication is *Tampa Bay Life,* a monthly magazine that covers all facets of the lively arts in the area. It is on sale at all local newsstands.

Like St. Petersburg, Tampa does not have a central reduced-rate same-day ticket booth, although some venues do offer "rush" tickets, discounted rates for students and seniors at the last minute. If you can't get to an individual box office, Ticketmaster (tel. 287-8844) will reserve tickets by phone or at one of its outlets (downtown at Curtis Hixon Hall and the Tampa Theatre, or throughout the city at Maison Blanche department stores).

THE PERFORMING ARTS
MAJOR CONCERT/PERFORMANCE HALLS

TAMPA BAY PERFORMING ARTS CENTER, 1010 N. MacInnes Place, Tampa. Tel. 221-1045 or toll free 800/ 955-1045.

Opened in 1987, this $57 million three-theater complex is the focal point of Tampa's performing-arts scene, and the home of the Tampa Ballet, the Tampa Players, and the Tampa Bay Chamber Orchestra. With an enviable downtown location on a 9-acre site along the east bank of the Hillsborough River, it presents a wide range of classical, orchestral, and pop concerts, operas, Broadway plays, cabarets, and special events, in a choice of three venues, the 2,400-seat Festival Hall, 900-seat Playhouse, or 300-seat Jaeb Theater.

An attraction in itself, this huge (290,000-square-foot) building sits back from the city's main thoroughfares in a well-landscaped setting, and is connected to a 1,000-car parking garage by a glass-enclosed pedestrian bridge. In conjunction with some performances, especially Broadway shows, you can book pre-theater dinner ($12.50) Tuesday through Friday, or champagne brunch ($14.50) on Sunday. **Open:** Box office Mon–Sat 10am–6pm, Sun noon–6pm; matinees at 3 or 3:30pm, evening curtain at 7:30 or 8pm. Tours Wed and Sat 10am. **Directions:** Downtown, off Tyler Street, one block west of Ashley.

Prices: Evening $12.50–$42.50; afternoon $4–$20.50; half-price rush tickets available at some events for seniors and students, two hours prior to performance. Valet parking, $6; self-parking $2–$3.

TAMPA STADIUM, 4201 N. Dale Mabry Highway, Tampa. Tel. 872-7977.

Home of Super Bowl XV and many other sporting events, this giant 74,296-capacity stadium is the largest venue for public events in the Tampa Bay area. It is frequently the site of world-class concerts, and has recently been the stage for such stars as Paul McCartney, the Rolling Stones, and U2. Box-office hours and days of operation vary; call in advance for information on a particular event, or reserve through Ticketmaster outlets. **Directions:** North of downtown and east of the airport, at the intersection of Buffalo Avenue.

Prices: $10–$35 or higher, depending on the event.

USF SUN DOME, 4202 S. Fowler Ave., Tampa. Tel. 974-3002 or 974-3001 (recorded information).

On the University of South Florida (USF) campus, this huge arena is the site of major concerts, averaging 5,000 to 10,000 in capacity. It is a frequent venue for touring pop stars, rock bands, jazz groups, and other contemporary artists. **Open:** Box office Mon–Fri 10am–5pm; performances usually Fri–Sat, curtain 7:30 or 8pm. **Directions:** Take I-275 north to Fowler Avenue (exit 34); go east 2 miles to USF campus.

Prices: $12–$25, depending on event.

THEATERS

TAMPA THEATRE, 711 N. Franklin St., Tampa. Tel. 223-8981.

On the National Register of Historic Places, this restored 1926 theater is a showcase of ornate colonnades, balconies, and replicas of Greek and Roman sculpture. There is seating for up to 1,500, with a varied program of classic, foreign, and alternative films, as well as concerts and special events.

Open: Box office Mon–Fri 11:30am–5:30pm; showtimes vary but are usually 5, 7, or 7:30pm, and 9:30 or 10pm. **Directions:** Downtown, between Polk and Zack streets.

Prices: $3.50 for adults, $3 for seniors, $1.25 for children 10 and under; 10 tickets for $20. Some special events $5–$10 or more.

RITZ THEATRE, 1503 E. 7th Ave., Ybor City. Tel. 247-PLAY

Dating back to 1917, this art deco theater is the home of the Playmakers, a professional company in residence. There are two stages, the 271-seat Mainstage, a classic proscenium stage offering contemporary drama and comedy, and the 90-seat Wild Side Cafe, presenting cabaret-style and experimental works. **Open:** Box office Mon–Fri 9:15am–5pm or later, Sat 12:30–7pm; curtain Thurs–Sun 8pm, matinees Sat 2pm. **Directions:** Take I-4 to Ybor City (exit 1); theater is at 15th Street and 7th Avenue.

Prices: $10–$15.

THE CLUB AND MUSIC SCENE
NIGHTCLUBS/CABARET

BAJA BEACH CLUB, 901 N. Franklin St., Tampa. Tel. 225-1556.

One of the hottest nightspots downtown, this club has a beach theme, with DJ or live music from the fifties to the eighties. Some nights feature special shows, such as a Sunday male revue. Dress code requires fashionably casual attire. **Open:** Wed–Fri 4:30pm–3am, Sat

9pm–3am, Sun 8pm–3am. **Directions:** Downtown, between Cass and Tyler streets.

Prices: Drinks $2.50–$4.50; varying cover charges for special events.

MASQUERADE, 1902 E. 7th Ave., Ybor City. Tel. 248-2877.

In the heart of the city's Latin Quarter, this club offers a mix of music—from European progressive dance to old wave, domestic progressive, aggressive, and other alternative styles.

Open: Nightly 9pm–3am. **Directions:** Take I-4 to Ybor City (exit 1); between 19th and 20th streets, one block west of the Columbia.

Prices: $2–$4 cover.

STINGERS, 11921 N. Dale Mabry Highway, Tampa. Tel. 968-1515.

One of the most dazzling nighttime venues in the city, this club features 15 video screens, seven bars, and two dance floors. Music is mostly Top 40 hits and some oldies, played by a DJ. Dress code requires neat attire (no jeans, no T-shirts, sneakers, etc.). **Open:** Nightly 5pm–3am. **Directions:** Northwest of downtown, in the Carrollwood section of the city.

Prices: Drinks $2–$5; no cover charge.

CLUB SYDNEY'S, 2701 E. Fowler Ave., Tampa. Tel. 972-3079.

This is a huge multilevel club with an elevated stage and a sunken dance floor. The high-energy music is mostly Top 40, although progressive music is featured on Mondays. **Open:** Mon–Thurs 4:30pm–2am, Fri–Sat 4:30pm–3am. **Directions:** Take I-275 north to Fowler Avenue (exit 34); go east 1 mile to the Holiday Inn, across from the USF campus.

Prices: $2–$4 cover.

CRAWDADDY'S CABARET, 2500 Rocky Point Rd., Tampa. Tel. 281-0407.

Overlooking Old Tampa Bay, this club has two bars, a dance floor, and indoor/outdoor seating. A DJ plays Top 40 music, or oldies on Thursday and Sunday. **Open:** Tues–Sat 4:30pm–2am, Sun 4–8pm. **Directions:** Take Route 60, 2 miles west of the airport.

Prices: $1–$3 cover.

COMEDY CLUBS

COMEDY CORNER, 3447 W. Kennedy Blvd., Tampa. Tel. 875-9129.

An ever-changing program of live comedy is on tap at this club, situated west of downtown. Shows Tues–Sun 8:30pm, Fri–Sat 8:30 and 10:45pm. **Directions:** On Route 60, between Dale Mabry Highway and MacDill Avenue, at the corner of Himes Avenue.

Prices: $3–$10 cover.

CRACKERS COMEDY CLUB, 12938 N. Dale Mabry Hwy., Tampa. Tel. 963-2500.

Located in the Carrollwood section of the city, this club presents live comedy by professional stand-up comedians on most nights, with amateur night on Tuesday. Shows Tues–Thurs 8pm, Fri–Sat 8 and 10:30pm. **Directions:** Northwest of downtown, at the corner of Fletcher Avenue.

Prices: $3–$7 cover.

ROCK AND TOP 40

BLUEBERRY HILL, 601 S. Harbour Island Blvd., Harbour Island. Tel. 221-1957.

Rock music and a decor reflecting the themes and personalities of the 1950s and 1960s are on tap at this waterside café. **Open:** Sun–Thurs 8:30pm–2am, Fri–Sat 5:30pm–2:30am. **Directions:** South of downtown, via the Franklin Street Bridge or People Mover.

Prices: $4 cover on weekends.

CHA CHA COCONUTS, 601 S. Harbour Island Blvd., Harbour Island. Tel. 223-3101.

This indoor/outdoor setting offers live rock music, harbor views, and tropical drinks. **Open:** Wed 7–11pm, Fri 8pm–midnight, Sat 2pm–midnight; Sun 2pm–10pm. **Directions:** South of downtown, via the Franklin Street Bridge or People Mover.

Prices: Drinks $1.75–$4; no cover.

MacDINTON'S TAVERN, 405 S. Howard Ave., Tampa. Tel. 254-1661.

Known locally as "Mac's," this place features live high-energy rock entertainment, as well as blues, in the Hyde Park area. **Open:** Sun–Wed 9pm–midnight, Thurs–Sat 9pm–2am. **Directions:** West of downtown, three blocks south of Kennedy Boulevard (Rte. 60), between Azeele and Horatio streets.

Prices: $2 cover on weekends.

ROCK-IT CLUB, 5016 N. Dale Mabry Hwy., Tampa. Tel. 879-3699.

This rock and roll club presents live bands including big-name recording artists. **Open:** Mon–Sat 9pm–3am, Sun 9pm–3am. **Directions:** North of Tampa Stadium, south of the intersection of Hillsborough Avenue.

Prices: $4–$12 cover.

JAZZ/BLUES/REGGAE

BROTHERS LOUNGE, 5401 W. Kennedy Blvd., Tampa. Tel. 286-8882.

A jazz haven for over 15 years and recently named one of the top two jazz spots in Tampa, this lounge concentrates solely on jazz, seven nights a week. **Open:** Mon 8:30pm–12:30am, Tues–Thurs 9:30pm–1:30am, Fri–Sat 9:30pm–2:30am, Sun 8pm–midnight. **Di-**

rections: West of downtown, in the Lincoln Center building, corner of Hoover Boulevard.
Prices: $1–$3 cover.

CAFE CREOLE, 1300 9th Ave., Ybor City. Tel. 247-6283.
Housed in a historic building in the heart of Tampa's Latin Quarter, this place presents live New Orleans–style jazz. **Open:** Wed 6–10pm, Thurs 7–11pm, Fri–Sat 8pm–midnight. **Directions:** Take I-4 to Ybor City (exit 1); go one block north of Ybor Square, at the corner of 9th Avenue and 13th Street.
Prices: Drinks $2–5; no cover.

FAT JACQUE'S CAJUN CAFE, 3605 W. Hillsborough Ave., Tampa. Tel. 874-8657.
At week's end, this place is alive with spirited New Orleans–style jazz. **Open:** Fri–Sat 8pm–midnight. **Directions:** North of downtown and east of the airport, at the intersection of Dale Mabry Highway in the Greenhouse Shopping Center.
Prices: Drinks $2–$5; no cover.

SELENA'S, 1623 Snow Ave., Tampa. Tel. 251-2116.
In the heart of Old Hyde Park Village, this trendy spot is ranked as one of the top two jazz meccas in Tampa. **Open:** Wed 8–midnight; Fri–Sat 9pm–1am. **Directions:** West of downtown, between Swan and Morrison avenues.
Prices: Drinks $2–$5; no cover.

SKIPPER'S SMOKEHOUSE, 910 Skipper Rd., Tampa. Tel. 971-0666.
This is a prime spot for live reggae and blues, and zydeco, a new sound from southwest Louisiana that combines Creole music, blues, soul, and more. **Open:** Tues–Wed and Sat–Sun 6:30–11pm, Fri 8–11pm. **Directions:** North of downtown, at Nebraska Avenue.
Prices: $2–$6 cover; special events $10 or more.

MORE ENTERTAINMENT

CHAMPIONS, 1001 N. West Shore Blvd. Tel. 287-2555.
One of a group of a dozen Champions bars scattered primarily in the south and west, this sports-themed lounge is unique in the Tampa Bay area, with dozens of TV monitors and walls lined with pennants, trophies, uniforms, magazine covers, and memorabilia. It's an ideal spot to catch a sporting event or just to mix with other sports-minded local fans and players. A resident DJ spins Top 40 dance music as well. **Open:** Sun–Thurs 6pm–2am, Fri–Sat 6pm–3am. **Directions:** South of the airport, between Spruce and Cypress streets, in the Tampa Marriott Westshore Hotel.
Prices: $2–$5 drinks; no cover.

RADIANT ROLLERS, 919 Rome Avenue S., Tampa. Tel. 251-0003.
Whether you watch or participate, this is a unique Tampa tradition. On an average night, 50 to 80 people fasten on their roller

skates and travel as a group through the streets of Hyde Park, Harbour Island, and downtown, for a total skating course of seven miles. The route takes in various nightclubs, where participants usually step inside and dance, with or without their skates. Rates include skate rental; registration is one hour before departure. **Schedule:** Fri–Sat 9pm–2am. **Directions:** Skaters assemble west of downtown at the corner of Rome and Watrous avenues in the Hyde Park area.

Prices: $8 per person.

THREE BIRDS, 1618 7th Ave., Ybor City. Tel. 247-7041.

Although open all day, this bookstore/coffee room comes alive in the evening, as a popular gathering spot for the literati of Tampa, particularly on Saturday and Thursday when poetry readings are given.

Anyone can sign up to do a 10-minute reading, although original works are preferred. It's a bright airy place, with surrealist paintings and drawings on the walls, jazz or blues music in the background, and lots and lots of books—from volumes on poetry and music to world affairs, sociology, gay and lesbian studies, and beat-generation literature. The coffee bar serves imported coffees and teas, home-made muffins, and cheesecakes. No alcohol. **Open:** Mon–Wed 10am–7pm, Thurs–Fri 10am–10pm, Sat 11am–10pm. **Directions:** Take I-4 to Ybor City (exit 1); situated between 16th and 17th streets.

Prices: 50¢–$1.50 for coffee, tea, or baked goods.

CHAPTER 12

DAY TRIPS FROM TAMPA AND ST. PETERSBURG

Conveniently located in the heart of central Florida's west coast, the St. Petersburg/Tampa area makes an ideal base for travel to other nearby destinations. Below are a few of our favorite side trips.

Note: Sight-seeing bus tours from the St. Petersburg/Tampa area to some of the areas described, such as Sarasota, Sea World, Walt Disney World, and Cypress Gardens, are operated by Gray Line, 921 3rd St. S., St. Petersburg, FL 33701 (tel. 813/822-3577 or 813/273-3577).

1. DUNEDIN AND CALADESI ISLAND

Founded by Scottish settlers in 1870, Dunedin (pronounced "Dunn-*eee*-din") is a quiet little town just 3 miles north of Clearwater. In many ways it is a pocket of old-world charm, with street names such as Brae-Moor, Dundee, Highland, Inverness, McLean, and Scotland. Every April the town celebrates its heritage with a series of traditional **highland games** including bagpipe and drum performances, dancing, and athletic competitions.

For natural beauty, Dunedin's biggest attractions are its offshore islands—Honeymoon and Caladesi. You can drive to Honeymoon Island, a combination of condominium strip and state park, via the Dunedin Causeway (Fla. Rte. 586), but Caladesi is more remote, accessible only by passenger ferry from Honeymoon Island.

The ferries are operated by Caladesi Island Ferry Service, at the west end of Route 586, Dunedin (tel. 813/734-5263). Reservations are accepted (but not required) for the 15-minute ride. The ferry runs

March through November weekdays hourly 10am to 5pm, weekends every half hour from 10am to 6pm; reduced service December through February. Round-trip fare: $3.75 for adults and $2.10 for children 12 and under.

The 640-acre Caladesi Island State Park, 3 miles long and ½ mile wide, is one of Florida's few remaining undisturbed barrier islands. No cars are allowed.

Ideal for swimming, shelling, and scuba diving, the island's beaches front the Gulf of Mexico; there is a mangrove swamp on the bay side, and much of the interior is dominated by virgin pine forest. Sea turtles nest on the beaches during summer nights, and many wading birds and shorebirds seek refuge here. Because Caladesi is surrounded by water, it is always several degrees cooler than the mainland. Facilities include palm-shaded picnic pavilions, snack bar, boardwalks, shower houses and rest rooms, playground, and a 3-mile nature trail. Hours are 8am to sunset.

For more information about the Dunedin area, which also serves as spring training ground for the **Toronto Blue Jays,** contact the **Dunedin Chamber of Commerce,** 434 Main St., Dunedin, FL 34698 (tel. 813/736-5066 or 733-3197).

2. TARPON SPRINGS

Stroll down Dodecanese Boulevard in Tarpon Springs, listen to the Greek music and smell the freshly baked pastries. It seems like an exotic Greek isle, but it's only 10 miles north of Clearwater and 35 miles from St. Petersburg or Tampa.

First settled in 1876 by Greek immigrants, this town is an enclave of Hellenic traditions, foods, and crafts. It is also the home of a native sponge industry, earning Tarpon Springs the title of "America's Sponge Capital." Here you not only can purchase a wide array of locally harvested sponges, but you can board one of the many excursion boats and watch divers plunge into nearby waters to pull up sponges straight from the sea.

St. Nicholas Greek Orthodox Cathedral, 30 N. Pinellas Ave., Tarpon Springs (tel. 813/937-3540), is a replica of St. Sophia's in Istanbul, and an excellent example of New Byzantine architecture, with an interior of sculptured Grecian marble, elaborate icons, and stained glass. It was built in 1943, replacing a smaller structure erected in 1907 by the community's early settlers. Admission is by donation; the cathedral is open daily 9am to 5pm.

Spongeorama, 510 Dodecanese Blvd., Tarpon Springs (tel. 813/942-3771), is located on the site of the town's original sponge exchange. This is a museum/theater with exhibits tracing the history of the city's sponge industry and its Greek settlers, and a film demonstrating sponge-diving. Admission is $1 for adults, 75¢ for children; Spongeorama is open daily 10am to 6pm.

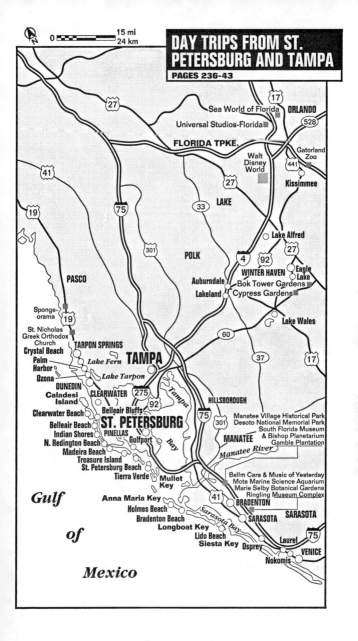

0 ⌷ 15 mi
24 km

Sea World of Florida

Universal Studios-Florida

ORLANDO

FLORIDA TPKE.

Gatorland
Zoo

Walt
Disney
World

Kissimmee

LAKE

Lake Alfred

POLK

WINTER HAVEN Eagle
Lake
Auburndale Bok Tower Gardens
Lakeland Cypress Gardens

Lake Wales

Sponge-
orama

St. Nicholas
Greek Orthodox
Church
Crystal Beach **TARPON SPRINGS**
Palm *Lake Fern* **TAMPA**
Harbor
Ozona *Lake Tarpon*
DUNEDIN
Caladesi **CLEARWATER**
Island
Clearwater Beach Belleair Bluffs
Belleair Beach
Indian Shores **ST. PETERSBURG**
N. Redington Beach **PINELLAS**
Madeira Beach Gulfport
Treasure Island
St. Petersburg Beach
Tierra Verde **Mullet
Key**

HILLSBOROUGH

Tampa

Manatee Village Historical Park
Desoto National Memorial Park
South Florida Museum
& Bishop Planetarium
Gamble Plantation

MANATEE

Manatee River

Bay

Gulf

Anna Maria Key

Holmes Beach
Bradenton Beach
Longboat Key
Lido Beach
Siesta Key

Sarasota Bay

BRADENTON

SARASOTA

Osprey

Bellm Cars & Music of Yesterday
Mote Marine Science Aquarium
Marie Selby Botanical Gardens
Ringling Museum Complex

SARASOTA

Laurel

VENICE

Nokomis

of

Mexico

3. BRADENTON

Heading about an hour south of St. Petersburg or an hour and a half from the Tampa area, you'll know you have reached Bradenton when the sweet aroma of fresh oranges fills the air. As the home of Tropicana, this city of 40,000 people is a major producer of orange juice, as well as of other agricultural products such as tomatoes.

Set on the Manatee River, Bradenton is also famous as the home of the **Nick Bollettieri Tennis Academy** and as the spring training ground for the **Pittsburgh Pirates.** Its historic **"Old Main Street"** (12th Street in today's city layout), and many Spanish-style buildings are also well-known. Bradenton's star attraction, however, is **Anna Maria Island,** a 7.5-mile stretch of quiet, tree-shaded beaches that rim the Gulf of Mexico.

Situated west of downtown Bradenton, the island is accessible by two causeways (Rte. 64 and Rte. 684). On the northern end is Anna Maria Bayfront Park, a favorite local haunt for finding unbroken sand dollars and scalloped cockle shells. To the south are Holmes Beach, Manatee County Beach, Cortez Beach (also known as Bradenton Beach), and Coquina Beach, a secluded area at the southern tip of the island lined with sand dunes, pines, and extensive picnic facilities. The Bradenton city line also extends to the top half of neighboring Longboat Key.

Other area attractions include:

DeSOTO NATIONAL MEMORIAL PARK, 75th St., off Rte. 64, Bradenton. Tel. 813/972-0458.

Commemorating the Spanish explorer Hernando de Soto's 1539 landing in Florida, this park reflects the look and atmosphere of 400 years ago. Highlights include a restoration of de Soto's original camp site, and a scenic half-mile nature trail that circles a mangrove jungle and leads to the ruins of one of the first settlements of the area. From December through April, park employees also dress in 16th-century costumes and portray the way the early settlers lived, including demonstrations of cooking and musket-firing.

Admission: $1 per person.
Open: Daily 8am–5:30pm.

GAMBLE PLANTATION, 3708 Patten Ave., Ellenton. Tel. 813/722-1017.

Situated northeast of downtown Bradenton, this is one of the south's few remaining Confederate museums, and a fine example of an antebellum plantation home. Built over a six-year period in the late 1840s by Major Robert Gamble, it is constructed primarily of a primitive material known as "tabby" (a mixture of oyster shells, sand, molasses, and water), with 10 rooms, verandas on three sides, 18 exterior columns, and eight fireplaces. It is maintained as a state historic site, and includes a fine collection of 19th-century furnishings. Entrance into the house is by tour only, although the grounds may be explored independently.

    Admission (including tour): $1 for adults, 50¢ for children under 13.

    Open: Thurs–Mon 9am–5pm. Guided tours of the house on the hour 9–11am and 1–4pm.

MANATEE VILLAGE HISTORICAL PARK, 6th Ave. E. and 15th Street E., Bradenton. Tel. 813/749-7165.

    A tree-shaded park with a courtyard of hand-laid bricks, this national historic site features restored buildings from the city of Bradenton and the surrounding county. It contains the Manatee County Court House, dating back to 1860 and the oldest structure of its kind still standing on the south Florida mainland; a Methodist church built in 1887; a typical "Cracker Gothic" house built in 1912; and the Wiggins General Store, dating to 1903 and full of local memorabilia from swamp root and grub dust to louse powder, as well as antique furnishings and an art gallery.

    Admission: Free; donations welcome.

    Open: Mon–Fri 9am–5pm, Sun 2–5pm. Closed: Sun in July–Aug.

SOUTH FLORIDA MUSEUM AND BISHOP PLANETARIUM, 201 10th St. W., Bradenton. Tel. 813/746-4131.

    The story of Florida's history, from prehistoric times to the present, is told in exhibits including a Native American collection with life-size dioramas; a Spanish courtyard containing replicas of 16th-century buildings; and an indoor aquarium, the home of Snooty, the oldest manatee (or sea cow) born in captivity (1948). The adjacent Bishop Planetarium features a 50-foot hemispherical dome for laser light shows and star-gazing activities.

    Admission: $4 for adults, $2 for children 5–12.

    Open: Tues–Sat 10am–5pm, Sun 1–5pm.

    For more information, contact the **Manatee County Convention & Visitors Bureau,** 1111 3rd Ave. W., P.O. Box 788, Bradenton, FL 34206-0788 (tel. 813/746-5989). The county also maintains a walk-in **Visitor Center** at 1323 U.S. 301, at the I-75 and U.S. 301 interchange, Ellenton (tel. 813/729-7040), open daily from 8:30am to 5:30pm.

4. SARASOTA

Often referred to as "the circus town," Sarasota is closely associated with circus legend John Ringling, who has left his imprint in many ways. A bright and thriving city of 50,000 people, Sarasota is about a 1½- to 2-hour drive south of the St. Petersburg/Tampa area.

    Sarasota's main attractions, like Bradenton's, are its pristine beaches, spread over 20 miles along four keys between Sarasota Bay and the Gulf of Mexico—Siesta Key, a quiet and mostly residential island; Lido Key, a lively and well-developed island with a string of motels, restaurants, and nightclubs; St. Armand's Key, a tiny enclave of lush landscaping, statuary, courtyards, and an exclusive circle of international shopping/dining establishments; and Longboat Key, dubbed "the Park Avenue of Sarasota," a narrow stretch of posh resorts and residences. The beaches are connected to the mainland via three causeways, two of which lead to Siesta Key and one to St. Armand's, which connects to Lido and Longboat keys.

Sarasota is also home to a respected performing-arts center, **Van Wezel Hall,** and serves as the winter training ground for the **Chicago White Sox.** South of Sarasota is the little town of Venice, winter headquarters of the **Ringling Brothers Barnum and Bailey Circus** and the site of the **Ringling Clown College.**

Here are some of the other main attractions:

BELLM CARS & MUSIC OF YESTERDAY, 5500 N. Tamiami Trail (U.S. 41), Sarasota. Tel. 813/355-6228.

This museum displays over 200 classic and antique autos, from Rolls-Royces and Pierce Arrows to the five cars used personally by circus czar John Ringling. In addition, there are over 1,200 antique music machines, from tiny music boxes to a huge 30-foot Belgian organ.

Admission: $5.50 for adults and $3 for children 6–16.
Open: Mon–Sat 8:30am–6pm, Sun 9:30am–6pm.

MARIE SELBY BOTANICAL GARDENS, S. Palm Ave., off U.S. 41, Sarasota. Tel. 813/366-5730.

A 7-acre museum of living plants, this facility is said to be the only botanical garden in the world to specialize in the preservation, study, and research of epiphytic plants ("air plants") such as orchids, pineapples, and ferns. It is home to more than 20,000 exotic plants, including over 6,000 orchids, and features a bamboo pavilion, a waterfall garden, a cactus and succulent garden, a fernery, a hibiscus garden, a palm grove, a tropical food garden, and a native shore plant community, plus a museum of botany and the arts.

Admission: $4 for adults; children under 12 free with an adult.
Open: Daily 10am–5pm.

MOTE MARINE SCIENCE AQUARIUM, 1600 City Island Park, Sarasota. Tel. 813/388-2451.

Part of the noted Mote Marine Laboratory complex, this facility focuses on the marine life of the Sarasota area. Displays include a living mangrove swamp and seagrass environment, a 135,000-gallon shark tank, loggerhead turtles and their eggs, dolphins, manatees, and an extensive shell collection. In addition, there are many "research-in-progress" exhibits on such topics as the red tide, aquaculture enhancement, cancer in sharks, and the effects of pesticide and petroleum pollution on the coast. The aquarium is located on City Island, just south of Longboat Key.

Admission: $5 for adults, $3 for children 6–17.
Open: Daily 10am–5pm.

RINGLING MUSEUM COMPLEX, 5401 Bayshore Rd., Sarasota. Tel. 813/355-5101 or 813/351-1660 (recorded information).

The former estate of circus entrepreneur John Ringling, this 38-acre site overlooking Sarasota Bay offers four attractions. Foremost is the John and Mable Ringling Museum of Art, Florida's official state art museum, which houses a major exhibit of baroque art as well as collections of decorative arts and traveling exhibits. Next is the 30-room "Ca'd'Zan" (House of John), the Ringling winter residence, built in 1925 and modeled after a Venetian palace, and the Gallery of the Circus, a building devoted to circus memorabilia including parade wagons, calliopes, costumes, and colorful posters. The grounds also include the Asolo Center for the Performing Arts, a professional theater company, plus restaurants and shops.

Admission: $6 for adults, $1.75 for children 6–12.

Open: Fri–Wed 10am–6pm, Thurs 10am–10pm.

For more information, contact the **Sarasota Convention & Visitors Bureau,** 655 N. Tamiami Trail (U.S. 41), Sarasota, FL 34236 (tel. 813/957-1877 or toll free 800/522-9799).

5. ORLANDO

Situated about two hours' driving time from the St. Petersburg/ Tampa area, Orlando is one of Florida's fastest-growing destinations, although it is far from the coastal lures of surf and sand. Instead it is a city built on the success of its artificial attractions, especially the following theme parks:

GATORLAND ZOO, 14501 S. Orange Blossom Trail, Orlando, FL 32821. Tel. 407/855-5496.

For a close-up look at alligators and crocodiles of every size and species frolicking in a 7-acre lake, spend a couple of hours at this unusual zoo and commercial alligator farm. Visitors are given a 10-minute orientation tour and then permitted to feed the alligators from covered walkways beside the lake. In addition, there are scores of snakes, other reptiles, birds, and animals in 35 acres of natural-habitat settings. It's located south of Orlando, on U.S. 17, 19, and 441.

Admission: $6.95 for adults and children 12 or over; $4.95 for children 3–11.

Open: Daily, summer 8am–8pm, winter 8am–6pm.

SEA WORLD OF FLORIDA, 7007 Sea World Dr., Orlando, FL 32821. Tel. 407/351-3600 or toll free 800/327-2424.

As its name implies, this 150-acre facility focuses on marine life, and is home to hundreds of penguins, seals, dolphins, sea lions, and sharks, not to mention killer whales that perform in special aquatic shows. There are also water-ski shows, a 400-foot observation tower, and a variety of exhibits, plus various marine-themed rides, shops, and restaurants.

Admission: $25.40 for adults, $21.15 for children 3–9.
Open: Daily 9am–6pm or later.

UNIVERSAL STUDIOS–FLORIDA, 1000 Universal Studios Plaza, Orlando, FL 32819. Tel. 407/363-8000 or toll free 800/232-7827.

Opened in May 1990, this $600 million, 444-acre attraction includes a full-scale movie and TV production studio, with more than 50 sets, from a New England Village to New York City's Upper East Side. In addition to viewing behind-the-scenes production work, you can learn about set design, costuming, makeup, filming, editing, mixing, dubbing, animation, sound effects, and special effects. To enhance the ambience, celebrity lookalikes—the likes of Mae West, Charlie Chaplin, Marilyn Monroe, and W. C. Fields—as well as Hanna-Barbera cartoon figures, roam the grounds and interact with visitors. The park also includes rides, live shows, and over 40 restaurants and shops.

Admission: $30.74 for adults, $23 for children.
Open: Daily summer 9am–11pm; rest of year hours vary.

WALT DISNEY WORLD, P.O. Box 10040, Lake Buena Vista, FL 32830-0040. Tel. 407/824-4321.

Located 20 miles southwest of Orlando, this granddaddy of Florida's artificial wonders currently has three theme parks (with plans for another one) spread over 6,600 acres.

The Magic Kingdom, home of Mickey Mouse and Donald Duck, is the 100-acre centerpiece of the Disney domain in central Florida. Opened in 1971, it offers 45 major attractions, restaurants, and shops, all based on favorite Disney themes, from Frontierland and Fantasyland to Adventureland, Tomorrowland, and Mickey's Birthdayland.

EPCOT Center (Experimental Prototype Community of To-morrow), covering 260 acres, is a permanent scientific and cultural showplace. It consists of Future World, with such areas as Living Seas, Wonders of Life, Universe of Energy, World of Motion, and Spaceship Earth. The second division is the World Showcase, composed of pavilions reflecting the cultures of many countries including the United States, Canada, the United Kingdom, France, Germany, Italy, Norway, Mexico, Japan, China, and Morocco.

Disney-MGM Studios, opened in 1988, is a 135-acre working movie production facility. Visitors can take a "behind-the-scenes" tour to see feature films, television shows, and Disney animation in production. Other attractions include a ride-through movie adventure, opportunities to participate in TV shows and music videos; a sound-effects monster show; a stunt theater; a full-scale re-creation of the famous Chinese Theater of Hollywood; and a variety of movie-related shops and restaurants.

Other on-site Disney World attractions range from Pleasure Island, a complex of seven nightclubs, restaurants, and movie theaters, to Typhoon Lagoon, a 56-acre water-theme park, as well as hotels, campgrounds, a zoological park, three championship golf courses, scores of other sporting facilities, child-care center, pet-care kennels, shops, and an elaborate internal transport system of monorails, ferries, motor launches, and minibuses.

Admission: One-day, one-park ticket, $32.75 for adults, $26.40 for children aged 3–9; a four-day pass allowing admission to all three parks is $109.85 and $87.65, respectively. Parking is $3 extra.

Open: Daily 9am–7pm, with some sections open later at various times of the year.

6. WINTER HAVEN/LAKE WALES

South of Orlando and directly east of Tampa, the attractions in this area are a little over an hour's drive from Tampa and at least an hour and a half from St. Petersburg.

BOK TOWER GARDENS, Tower Boulevard and Burns Avenue, Lake Wales, FL 33853. Tel. 813/676-1408.

The serene combination of beautiful flowers and carillon bells draws many people to this inland attraction. The layout includes a historic pink-and-gray bell tower with 57 bronze bells that ring on the half hour, and a 128-acre garden, with thousands of azaleas, camellias, magnolias, and other flowering plants, set amid ferns, palms, oaks, and pines. Named for Dutch immigrant Edward W. Bok, who donated the gardens for public viewing in 1929, the site is listed on the National Register of Historic Places and sits on one of Florida's highest points of elevation, at 295 feet.

Admission: $3 for adults and children over 12.
Open: Daily 8am–5pm.

CYPRESS GARDENS, 2641 S. Lake Summit Dr., P.O. Box 1, Cypress Gardens, FL 33884. Tel. 813/324-2111 or toll free 800/237-4826.

Situated off U.S. 27 near Winter Haven, this is a 223-acre botanical garden theme park, with over 8,000 varieties of plants from 75 different countries, ranging from traditional Southern gardenias to bougainvillea, hibiscus, and chrysanthemums, as well as an all-American rose garden, with 500 varieties. Other features include a water-ski extravaganza and an ice-skating revue choreographed to classical music, lasers, and dancing fountains. In addition, there is a nationally accredited zoological park, an elaborate model railroad, a 153-foot revolving observation tower, and boat rides through a maze of landscaped canals.

Admission: $17.50 for adults, $11.50 for children 3–11.
Open: Daily 9am–6pm.

A. METRIC CONVERSIONS

LENGTH

1 millimeter	=	0.04 inches (*or* less than 1/16 inch)
1 centimeter	=	0.39 inches (*or* just under 1/2 inch)
1 meter	=	1.09 yards (*or* about 39 inches)
1 kilometer	=	0.62 mile (*or* about 2/3 mile)

To convert **kilometers to miles,** take the number of kilometers and multiply by .62 (for example, 25km × .62 = 15.5 miles). To convert **miles to kilometers,** take the number of miles and multiply by 1.61 (for example, 50 miles × 1.61 = 80.5 km).

CAPACITY

1 liter	=	33.92 ounces
	=	1.06 quarts
	=	0.26 gallons

To convert **liters to gallons,** take the number of liters and multiply by .26 (for example, 50 l × .26 = 13 gal). To convert **gallons to liters,** take the number of gallons and multiply by 3.79 (for example, 10 gal × 3.79 = 37.9 l).

WEIGHT

1 gram	=	0.04 ounce (*or* about a paperclip's weight)
1 kilogram	=	2.2 pounds

To convert **kilograms to pounds,** take the number of kilos and multiply by 2.2 (for example, 75kg × 2.2 = 165 lbs). To convert **pounds to kilograms,** take the number of pounds and multiply by .45 (for example, 90 lb × .45 = 40.5kg).

TEMPERATURE

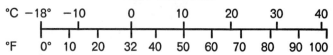

To convert **degrees C to degrees F,** multiply degrees C by 9, divide by 5, then add 32 (for example 9/5 × 20°C + 32 = 68°F). To convert **degrees F to degrees C,** subtract 32 from degrees F, then multiply by 5, and divide by 9 (for example, 85°F − 32 × 5/9 = 29°C).

B. SIZE CONVERSIONS

The following charts should help foreign visitors choose the correct clothing sizes in the U.S. However, sizes can vary, so the best guide is simply to try things on.

WOMEN'S DRESSES, COATS, AND SKIRTS

American	3	5	7	9	11	12	13	14	15	16	18
Continental	36	38	38	40	40	42	42	44	44	46	48
British	8	10	11	12	13	14	15	16	17	18	20

WOMEN'S BLOUSES AND SWEATERS

American	10	12	14	16	18	20
Continental	38	40	42	44	46	48
British	32	34	36	38	40	42

WOMEN'S STOCKINGS

American	8	8½	9	9½	10	10½
Continental	1	2	3	4	5	6
British	8	8½	9	9½	10	10½

WOMEN'S SHOES

American	5	6	7	8	9	10
Continental	36	37	38	39	40	41
British	3½	4½	5½	6½	7½	8½

MEN'S SUITS

American	34	36	38	40	42	44	46	48
Continental	44	46	48	50	52	54	56	58
British	34	36	38	40	42	44	46	48

MEN'S SHIRTS

American	14½	15	15½	16	16½	17	17½	18
Continental	37	38	39	41	42	43	44	45
British	14½	15	15½	16	16½	17	17½	18

MEN'S SHOES

American	7	8	9	10	11	12	13
Continental	39½	41	42	43	44½	46	47
British	6	7	8	9	10	11	12

MEN'S HATS

American	6⅞	7⅛	7¼	7⅜	7½	7⅝
Continental	55	56	58	59	60	61
British	6¼	6⅞	7⅛	7¼	7⅜	7½

CHILDREN'S CLOTHING

American	3	4	5	6	6X
Continental	98	104	110	116	122
British	18	20	22	24	26

CHILDREN'S SHOES

American	8	9	10	11	12	13	1	2	3
Continental	24	25	27	28	29	30	32	33	34
British	7	8	9	10	11	12	13	1	2

INDEX

GENERAL INFORMATION

SIGHTS AND ATTRACTIONS

ST. PETERSBURG

Boyd Hill Nature Park, 116
Clearwater Marine Science Center, 116
Dalí (Salvador) Museum, 109, 112
Fine Arts, Museum of, 112
Florida Suncoast Dome, 108–9
Fort DeSoto Park, 112–13
Great Explorations, 116
Haas Museum Complex, 115
Heritage Park, 115–16
John's Pass Village and Board-
walk, 113–14
Moccasin Lake Nature Park, 116–17
The Pier, 108
St. Petersburg Waterfront Historical Society Museum, 114
Suncoast Seabird Sanctuary, 113
Sunken Gardens, 114–15
Sunshine Skyway Bridge, 114
Yesterday's Air Force Museum, 115

TAMPA

Adventure Island, 213–14
Busch Gardens, 208–9
Children's Museum of Tampa, 215
Florida Center for Contemporary Art, 209, 212
Lowry Amusement Park, 215
Lowry Park Zoo, 214–15
Museum of Science and Industry (MOSI), 213
Plant (Henry B.) Museum, 209
Seminole Indian Village, 212–13
Tampa Museum of Art, 209
USF Art Museum, 212
Villazon & Company Cigar Factory, 213
Ybor City State Museum, 212

DAY-TRIP AREAS

BRADENTON
DeSoto National Memorial Park, 238
Gamble Plantation, 238–9
Manatee Village Historical Park,
239
South Florida Museum and Bishop Planetarium, 239

ACCOMMODATIONS

ST. PETERSBURG

KEY TO ABBREVIATIONS: B&B = Bed & Breakfast; B = Budget; E = Expensive; Hs = Hostel; I = Inexpensive; M = Moderately priced; VE = Very Expensive; * = author's personal favorites

TAMPA

RESTAURANTS

ST. PETERSBURG

KEY TO ABBREVIATIONS: *B&B* = Bed & Breakfast; *B* = Budget; *E* = Expensive; *Hs* = Hostel; *I* = Inexpensive; *M* = Moderately priced; *VE* = Very Expensive; * = author's personal favorites

TAMPA

NOW, SAVE MONEY ON ALL YOUR TRAVELS!
Join Frommer's™ Dollarwise® Travel Club

Saving money while traveling is never a simple matter, which is why the **Dollarwise Travel Club** was formed 31 years ago. Developed in response to requests from Frommer's Travel Guide readers, the Club provides cost-cutting travel strategies, up-to-date travel information, and a sense of community for value-conscious travelers from all over the world.

In keeping with the money-saving concept, the annual membership fee is low—$18 for U.S. residents or $20 for residents of Canada, Mexico, and other countries—and is immediately exceeded by the value of your benefits, which include:

1. Any TWO books listed on the following pages.
2. Plus any ONE Frommer's City Guide.
3. A subscription to our quarterly newspaper, *The Dollarwise Traveler*.
4. A membership card that entitles you to purchase through the Club all Frommer's publications for 33% to 50% off their retail price.

The eight-page **Dollarwise Traveler** tells you about the latest developments in good-value travel worldwide and includes the following columns: **Hospitality Exchange** (for those offering and seeking hospitality in cities all over the world); **Share-a-Trip** (for those looking for travel companions to share costs); and **Readers Ask . . . Readers Reply** (for those with travel questions that other members can answer).

Aside from the Frommer's Guides and the Gault Millau Guides, you can also choose from our Special Editions. These include such titles as *California with Kids* (a compendium of the best of California's accommodations, restaurants, and sightseeing attractions appropriate for those traveling with toddlers through teens); *Candy Apple: New York with Kids* (a spirited guide to the Big Apple by a savvy New York grandmother that's perfect for both visitors and residents); *Caribbean Hideaways* (the 100 most romantic places to stay in the Islands, all rated on ambience, food, sports opportunities, and price); *Honeymoon Destinations* (a guide to planning and choosing just the right destination from hundreds of possibilities in the U.S., Mexico, and the Caribbean); *Marilyn Wood's Wonderful Weekends* (a selection of the best mini-vacations within a 200-mile radius of New York City, including descriptions of country inns and other accommodations, restaurants, picnic spots, sights, and activities); and *Paris Rendez-Vous* (a delightful guide to the best places to meet in Paris whether for power breakfasts or dancing till dawn).

To join this Club, simply send the appropriate membership fee with your name and address to: Frommer's Dollarwise Travel Club, 15 Columbus Circle, New York, NY 10023. Remember to specify which single city guide and which two other guides you wish to receive in your initial package of member's benefits. Or tear out the next page, check off your choices, and send the page to us with your membership fee.

FROMMER BOOKS
PRENTICE HALL PRESS
15 COLUMBUS CIRCLE
NEW YORK, NY 10023
212/373-8125

Date_____

Friends:

Please send me the books checked below.

FROMMER'S™ GUIDES

(Guides to sightseeing and tourist accommodations and facilities from budget to deluxe, with emphasis on the medium-priced.)

☐ Alaska	$14.95	☐ Germany	$14.95
☐ Australia	$14.95	☐ Italy	$14.95
☐ Austria & Hungary	$14.95	☐ Japan & Hong Kong	$14.95
☐ Belgium, Holland & Lux-embourg	$14.95	☐ Mid-Atlantic States	$14.95
		☐ New England	$14.95
☐ Bermuda & The Bahamas	$14.95	☐ New York State	$14.95
☐ Brazil	$14.95	☐ Northwest	$14.95
☐ Canada	$14.95	☐ Portugal, Madeira & the Azores	$14.95
☐ Caribbean	$14.95	☐ Skiing Europe	$14.95
☐ Cruises (incl. Alaska, Carib, Mex, Hawaii, Panama, Canada & US)	$14.95	☐ South Pacific	$14.95
		☐ Southeast Asia	$14.95
☐ California & Las Vegas	$14.95	☐ Southern Atlantic States	$14.95
☐ Egypt	$14.95	☐ Southwest	$14.95
☐ England & Scotland	$14.95	☐ Switzerland & Liechtenstein	$14.95
☐ Florida	$14.95	☐ USA	$15.95
☐ France	$14.95		

FROMMER'S $-A-DAY® GUIDES

(In-depth guides to sightseeing and low-cost tourist accommodations and facilities.)

☐ Europe on $40 a Day	$15.95	☐ New York on $60 a Day	$13.95
☐ Australia on $40 a Day	$13.95	☐ New Zealand on $45 a Day	$13.95
☐ Eastern Europe on $25 a Day	$13.95	☐ Scandinavia on $60 a Day	$13.95
☐ England on $50 a Day	$13.95	☐ Scotland & Wales on $40 a Day	$13.95
☐ Greece on $35 a Day	$13.95	☐ South America on $35 a Day	$13.95
☐ Hawaii on $60 a Day	$13.95	☐ Spain & Morocco on $40 a Day	$13.95
☐ India on $25 a Day	$12.95	☐ Turkey on $30 a Day	$13.95
☐ Ireland on $35 a Day	$13.95	☐ Washington, D.C. & Historic Va. on $40 a Day	$13.95
☐ Israel on $40 a Day	$13.95		
☐ Mexico on $35 a Day	$13.95		

FROMMER'S TOURING GUIDES

(Color illustrated guides that include walking tours, cultural and historic sites, and other vital travel information.)

☐ Amsterdam	$10.95	☐ New York	$10.95
☐ Australia	$9.95	☐ Paris	$8.95
☐ Brazil	$10.95	☐ Rome	$10.95
☐ Egypt	$8.95	☐ Scotland	$9.95
☐ Florence	$8.95	☐ Thailand	$9.95
☐ Hong Kong	$10.95	☐ Turkey	$10.95
☐ London	$8.95	☐ Venice	$8.95

TURN PAGE FOR ADDITONAL BOOKS AND ORDER FORM

0690

FROMMER'S CITY GUIDES

(Pocket-size guides to sightseeing and tourist accommodations and facilities in all price ranges.)

☐ Amsterdam/Holland........$8.95	☐ Montréal/Québec City $8.95
☐ Athens $8.95	☐ New Orleans $8.95
☐ Atlanta.................$8.95	☐ New York...................$8.95
☐ Atlantic City/Cape May $8.95	☐ Orlando.....................$8.95
☐ Barcelona $7.95	☐ Paris.......................$8.95
☐ Belgium $7.95	☐ Philadelphia.................$8.95
☐ Boston $8.95	☐ Rio........................$8.95
☐ Cancún/Cozumel/Yucatán ...$8.95	☐ Rome $8.95
☐ Chicago $8.95	☐ Salt Lake City $8.95
☐ Denver/Boulder/Colorado	☐ San Diego $8.95
Springs..............$7.95	☐ San Francisco................$8.95
☐ Dublin/Ireland...........$8.95	☐ Santa Fe/Taos/Albuquerque $8.95
☐ Hawaii $8.95	☐ Seattle/Portland.............$7.95
☐ Hong Kong $7.95	☐ Sydney $8.95
☐ Las Vegas $8.95	☐ Tampa/St. Petersburg $8.95
☐ Lisbon/Madrid/Costa del Sol. .$8.95	☐ Tokyo $7.95
☐ London.................$8.95	☐ Toronto....................$8.95
☐ Los Angeles.............$8.95	☐ Vancouver/Victoria.............$7.95
☐ Mexico City/Acapulco $8.95	☐ Washington, D.C................$8.95
☐ Minneapolis/St. Paul........$8.95	

SPECIAL EDITIONS

☐ Beat the High Cost of Travel...$6.95	☐ Motorist's Phrase Book (Fr/Ger/Sp)....$4.95
☐ Bed & Breakfast—N. America $11.95	☐ Paris Rendez-Vous................$10.95
☐ California with Kids $14.95	☐ Swap and Go (Home Exchanging) $10.95
☐ Caribbean Hideaways $14.95	☐ The Candy Apple (NY with Kids) $12.95
☐ Manhattan's Outdoor	☐ Travel Diary and Record Book $5.95
Sculpture.............$15.95	

☐ Honeymoon Destinations (US, Mex & Carib) $14.95

☐ Where to Stay USA (From $3 to $30 a night) $10.95

☐ Marilyn Wood's Wonderful Weekends (CT, DE, MA, NH, NJ, NY, PA, RI, VT) $11.95

☐ The New World of Travel (Annual sourcebook by Arthur Frommer for savvy travelers) . .$16.95

GAULT MILLAU

(The only guides that distinguish the truly superlative from the merely overrated.)

☐ The Best of Chicago $15.95	☐ The Best of Los Angeles............$16.95
☐ The Best of France.........$16.95	☐ The Best of New England $15.95
☐ The Best of Hong Kong $16.95	☐ The Best of New York..............$16.95
☐ The Best of Italy..........$16.95	☐ The Best of Paris $16.95
☐ The Best of London........$16.95	☐ The Best of San Francisco $16.95

☐ The Best of Washington, D.C. $16.95

ORDER NOW!

In U.S. include $2 shipping UPS for 1st book; $1 ea. add'l book. Outside U.S. $3 and $1, respectively.

Allow four to six weeks for delivery in U.S., longer outside U.S.

Enclosed is my check or money order for $_____

NAME_____

ADDRESS_____

CITY_____ STATE_____ ZIP____

0690